FEUD

The Fred W. Morrison Series

in Southern Studies

FEUD

Hatfields, McCoys, and Social Change in Appalachia, 1860–1900

. . . .

ALTINA L. WALLER

/ ।।

THE UNIVERSITY OF NORTH CAROLINA PRESS

Chapel Hill & London

© 1988 The University of North Carolina Press
All rights reserved
Manufactured in the United States of America

The paper in this book meets the
guidelines for permanence and durability
of the Committee on Production Guidelines
for Book Longevity of the Council on
Library Resources.

92 91 90 89 88   5 4 3 2 1

Library of Congress Cataloging-in-Publication Data
Waller, Altina L. (Altina Laura), 1940–
Feud: Hatfields, McCoys, and social change in Appalachia,
1860–1900 / by Altina L. Waller.
p. cm.—(The Fred W. Morrison series in Southern studies)
Bibliography: p.
Includes index.
ISBN 0-8078-1770-8 (alk. paper)
ISBN 0-8078-4216-8 (pbk.: alk. paper)
1. Hatfield-McCoy feud. 2. Appalachian Region, Southern—Social
conditions. I. Title. II. Series.
HV6452.A128W35 1988   87-26567
975.4'404—dc 19   CIP

For

Andrew, Laura, and Miles

The Three Most Dear

Contents

Maps & Tables

Acknowledgments

The Hatfields and the McCoys have been part of my life for almost ten years now, and I have come to think of them as friends and neighbors whose defeats and triumphs have some meaning for my life as well as theirs. Although most of my knowledge of them comes from the faded and impersonal documents in county courthouses, I have also driven the mountain roads that they so often traversed on their way to those courthouses, climbed the steep mountain slopes where they buried their dead, and walked along Grapevine Creek where they fought their final battle. In the process of trying to understand what they were like and what the feud was about I have come to admire some and dislike others, but mostly I am grateful to them for teaching me something about a culture so different from my own.

The Hatfields and McCoys first came into my life when I left graduate study in Massachusetts to take my first job at West Virginia University in Morgantown. Although I did not yet know much about Appalachian history, I owe my preparation for taking on that new subject to my training in social history at the University of Massachusetts at Amherst. It was my advisor, Professor Stephen Nissenbaum, who taught me how to think about history, and even though he was never directly involved in this project it nevertheless owes much to him.

My research on the feud was originally undertaken in preparation for teaching a course at West Virginia University. It was during those first explorations in the Pike and Logan county courthouses that I began to realize what a wealth of untapped sources existed, not only for the feud itself, but for the feudists' community in the Tug River Valley. It was quickly apparent that not only was there more than enough material for a book, but that book would provide a whole new interpretation of the feud and its relationship to the social and economic transformation of the region.

As I began to delve into Appalachian history, my thinking was guided by experienced scholars in the field, some of whom I came to know personally and others whose works I read and savored. First among them was John Alexander Williams, whose chapter, "Tug Fork," in *West Virginia* sent me off in what turned out to be the correct intellectual direction. More recently he read the final manuscript, offering invaluable suggestions and saving me from embarrassing errors. Others who have influenced my thinking in the direction of Appalachian revisionism are Ron Eller, Gordon McKinney, and John Gaventa. David Whisnant, whose own work has given me considerable insight, read an earlier paper as well as the final manuscript and provided much-needed encouragement.

The research phase of my work was enhanced by the hospitality I encountered at the Logan County Courthouse, the state archives in Charleston, West Virginia, the University of Kentucky Library in Lexington, and the archives at West Virginia University. Since the bulk of my time was spent in the Logan County Courthouse, I wish to thank especially Victoria Bayliss of the county clerk's office and all those who helped me find obscure items, make copies, and gain access to the basement storeroom. Even so, the research could not have gone so smoothly without the assistance of Bradley Pyles, a Logan lawyer and a dear friend, who not only helped me find materials but also spent many hours translating the nineteenth-century legalese that threatened to confound me completely. Most of all he, more than anyone else, provided insights into the Appalachia of today and the working people he serves with so much energy and dedication. Brad's name appears nowhere in the footnotes, but to him is owed one of this book's greatest debts. In the final stages of my research, several people in both Pike and Logan counties gave more than generously of their time and wisdom in the often frustrating process of locating illustrations and old photographs. My deepest appreciation goes to Sadie McCoy of Phelps, Kentucky, Dorcas Hobbs of Pikeville, Kentucky, and Robert Y. Spence of Logan, West Virginia.

Valuable assistance has always been forthcoming from members of my family. In the early stages of the research, I was accompanied to Logan and Pikeville by my son, Andrew, who shared the search for documents and cheerfully copied endless pages of tax and deed records when there was no copying machine available or affordable.

. . . .
Acknowledgments

More recently he has contributed his superb skills as an editor of the manuscript—an effort I consider quite an honor coming from a very fine (and published) poet. My daughter, Laura, though less involved with this book than with my previous one, has read and edited parts of the manuscript with sensitivity and intelligence. But the most important contribution of both my children is their consistent love, support, and encouragement in whatever I choose to undertake.

With the documents collected in Pike and Logan counties, I have taught courses on the feud on four occasions: twice at West Virginia University; once at Southwestern at Memphis (now Rhodes College); and once at the State University of New York at Plattsburgh. With all those students I shared the excitement of discovery as together we extracted the story of the feud community from a difficult and complex set of sources. I only hope the experience has benefited them as much as it has me.

The most difficult part of finishing this project was finding an extended block of time for the actual writing of the book. Just at the point when I began to despair of ever having such time, I received a fellowship from the National Endowment for the Humanities for an entire year in 1984–85. Because of that fellowship, this book was finally brought to fruition.

Finally, I wish to thank my best friend and life's partner, Miles Martin. But that really has nothing to do with the book. Even if he had never put in hours of research at the West Virginia State Archives, the Kentucky State Archives, the Mormon Library in Albany, and the Logan Circuit Court's office; or spent hours talking out possible interpretations of the evidence; or read and reread the manuscript; or given a week of his life to transferring the manuscript from one computer system to another; or cooked meals and cleaned house when I was too preoccupied to bother with such things, I would still be grateful for the deep and abiding joy that our life together has become.

Plattsburgh, New York
March 1987

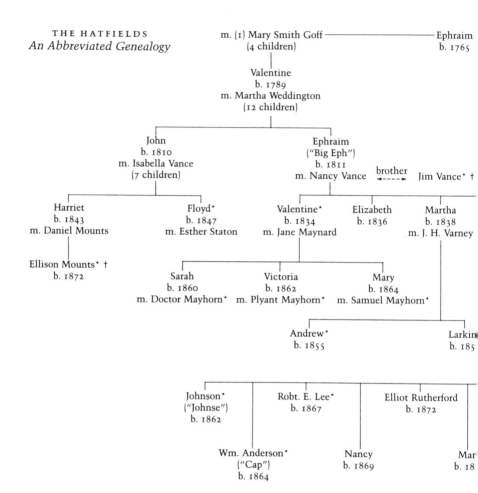

THE HATFIELDS
An Abbreviated Genealogy

Ephraim
b. 1765
m. (1) Mary Smith Goff
(4 children)

Valentine
b. 1789
m. Martha Weddington
(12 children)

John
b. 1810
m. Isabella Vance
(7 children)

Ephraim
("Big Eph")
b. 1811
m. Nancy Vance ——brother—— Jim Vance* †

Harriet
b. 1843
m. Daniel Mounts

Floyd*
b. 1847
m. Esther Staton

Valentine*
b. 1834
m. Jane Maynard

Elizabeth
b. 1836

Martha
b. 1838
m. J. H. Varney

Ellison Mounts* †
b. 1872

Sarah
b. 1860
m. Doctor Mayhorn*

Victoria
b. 1862
m. Plyant Mayhorn*

Mary
b. 1864
m. Samuel Mayhorn*

Andrew*
b. 1855

Larkin
b. 185

Johnson*
("Johnse")
b. 1862

Robt. E. Lee*
b. 1867

Elliot Rutherford
b. 1872

Wm. Anderson*
("Cap")
b. 1864

Nancy
b. 1869

Mar
b. 18

* Feudist
† Killed in feud

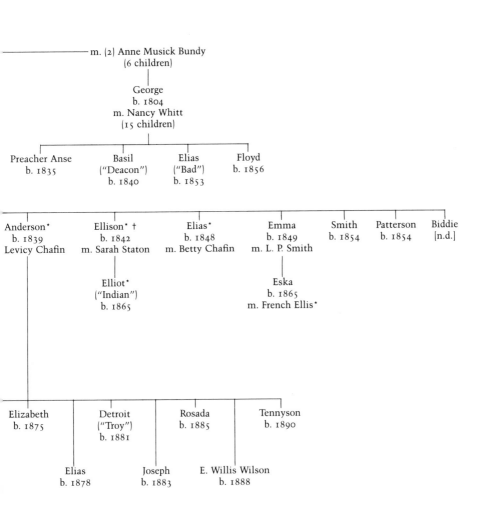

———————————— m. (2) Anne Musick Bundy
                 (6 children)

George
b. 1804
m. Nancy Whitt
(15 children)

Preacher Anse	Basil	Elias	Floyd
b. 1835	("Deacon")	("Bad")	b. 1856
	b. 1840	b. 1853	

Anderson*	Ellison* †	Elias*	Emma	Smith	Patterson	Biddie
b. 1839	b. 1842	b. 1848	b. 1849	b. 1854	b. 1854	[n.d.]
Levicy Chafin	m. Sarah Staton	m. Betty Chafin	m. L. P. Smith			

Elliot*
("Indian")
b. 1865

Eska
b. 1865
m. French Ellis*

Elizabeth	Detroit	Rosada	Tennyson
b. 1875	("Troy")	b. 1885	b. 1890
	b. 1881		

Elias
b. 1878

Joseph
b. 1883

E. Willis Wilson
b. 1888

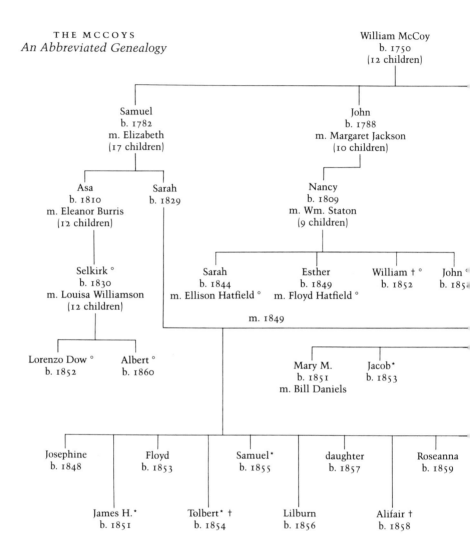

THE MCCOYS
An Abbreviated Genealogy

William McCoy
b. 1750
(12 children)

Samuel
b. 1782
m. Elizabeth
(17 children)

John
b. 1788
m. Margaret Jackson
(10 children)

Asa
b. 1810
m. Eleanor Burris
(12 children)

Sarah
b. 1829

Nancy
b. 1809
m. Wm. Staton
(9 children)

Selkirk °
b. 1830
m. Louisa Williamson
(12 children)

Sarah
b. 1844
m. Ellison Hatfield °

Esther
b. 1849
m. Floyd Hatfield °

William † °
b. 1852

John °
b. 185

m. 1849

Lorenzo Dow °
b. 1852

Albert °
b. 1860

Mary M.
b. 1851
m. Bill Daniels

Jacob *
b. 1853

Josephine
b. 1848

Floyd
b. 1853

Samuel *
b. 1855

daughter
b. 1857

Roseanna
b. 1859

James H. *
b. 1851

Tolbert * †
b. 1854

Lilburn
b. 1856

Alifair †
b. 1858

* Feudist
† Killed in feud
° Hatfield feudist

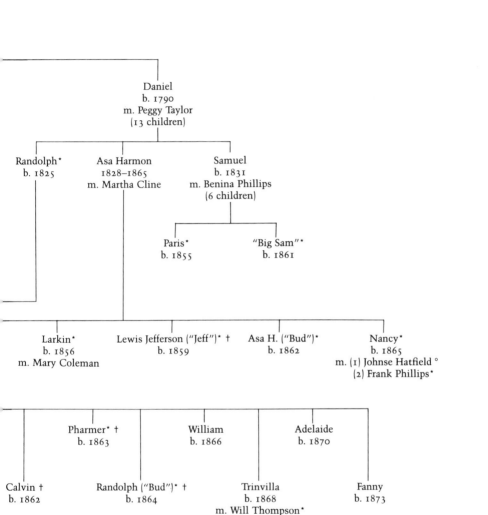

Daniel
b. 1790
m. Peggy Taylor
(13 children)

Randolph*
b. 1825

Asa Harmon
1828–1865
m. Martha Cline

Samuel
b. 1831
m. Benina Phillips
(6 children)

Paris*
b. 1855

"Big Sam"*
b. 1861

Larkin*
b. 1856
m. Mary Coleman

Lewis Jefferson ("Jeff")* †
b. 1859

Asa H. ("Bud")*
b. 1862

Nancy*
b. 1865
m. (1) Johnse Hatfield °
(2) Frank Phillips*

Pharmer* †
b. 1863

William
b. 1866

Adelaide
b. 1870

Calvin †
b. 1862

Randolph ("Bud")* †
b. 1864

Trinvilla
b. 1868
m. Will Thompson*

Fanny
b. 1873

FEUD

Introduction

THE FEUD

• •

Hatfields and McCoys—for most Americans these names conjure up images of bearded mountaineers brandishing rifles and jugs of moonshine as they defend illegal stills from federal "revenuers," enforce "shotgun" weddings, and lawlessly perpetuate inherited family grudges. We all know of the Hatfields and McCoys, for we have encountered them in comic strips, popular song, movies, and television. Indeed, they have become such an entrenched part of mythology and folklore that many Americans are surprised to discover that the feud actually happened and that the feudists were real people. Ironically, the extraordinary endurance of the folkloric legend that has grown up around the Hatfields and McCoys has obscured consideration of the feud as a serious historical event. Even historians have treated the feud, if not as myth, as an exaggerated legend instead of approaching it with the same methods of rigorous research and analysis they apply to other instances of social conflict. But the feud was a real event and can be productively analyzed within the framework of recent literature on social and cultural history. Such is my purpose. As a prologue to that endeavor, and for the benefit of those who have assumed that the Hatfields and McCoys were mythical, let us briefly summarize their story.[1]

The Hatfields and the McCoys lived on the banks of a river that forms the boundary between Kentucky and West Virginia—a river known as the Tug Fork of the Big Sandy River. In the last half of the nineteenth century it was a region almost untouched by the forces of market capitalism which, since before the American Revolution, had been transforming the rest of the country. Both of the legendary feud leaders, William Anderson or "Devil Anse" Hatfield and Randolph or "Old Ranel" McCoy, like their fathers and grandfathers before them, lived in log houses and made their living by subsistence farming supplemented with hunting. There is no evidence of animosity between their families in previous generations.

During the Civil War there occurred an event which some believe was the first incident in the great feud. Asa Harmon McCoy, Randolph's brother, was one of the few Union sympathizers in the Tug Valley; only a few weeks after he came home from serving in the Union army, he was found shot to death in a cave in the mountains. Feud legend attributes his death to Devil Anse Hatfield or his uncle Jim Vance, both of whom were leaders of a Confederate guerrilla unit, the Logan Wildcats (named for Logan County, West Virginia). This incident, however, does not seem a likely catalyst for the full-fledged feud, because there were no reprisals and no further incidents for the next thirteen years. Later, during the feud, both sides denied that any events connected with the Civil War had caused the trouble between them.

By the late 1870s, when the feud began in earnest, both men were well-established members of the community. Old Ranel, then fifty-three years old, resided on the Kentucky side of the Tug near the banks of a creek known as the Blackberry Fork of Pond Creek. He and his wife, Sally, were known throughout the Tug Valley as "Old Ranel" and "Aunt Sally," not only by the McCoy relatives but also by everyone else in the community. Devil Anse was, at forty, somewhat younger and made his home opposite Old Ranel's on the West Virginia side of the Tug. Devil Anse's appearance—tall, with stooped shoulders, a black beard, and a prominent hook nose—substantiated his reputation as a formidable figure in the community. In addition to his role as a guerrilla leader in the war, Devil Anse was known as the best horseman and marksman in the valley.

In the fall of 1878, Old Ranel became convinced that Floyd Hatfield, a cousin of Devil Anse, had stolen one of his hogs. Instead of reaching for his rifle, as the mountain stereotype would suggest, Old Ranel complained to the nearest justice of the peace. Because Floyd Hatfield resided on Old Ranel's side of the river in Kentucky, the hog case was tried there—among McCoy's own friends and relatives. The local judge attempted to ensure an impartial trial by choosing a jury that was exactly balanced, six Hatfields and six McCoys. But despite the careful choice of jurors and the favorable jurisdiction, Old Ranel lost the case. He lost not because of the Hatfields, but because one of the *McCoy* jurors voted against him.

Still, this outcome did not drive Old Ranel to violence; he grumbled but accepted the verdict. However, two of Old Ranel's nephews, Sam and Paris McCoy, were not quite so acquiescent. A year and a half later, still incensed at the outcome of the trial, they got into a fight with one of the witnesses against their uncle—a fight that ended in the witness's death. Feud stereotypes might lead us to expect that the Hatfields would set out after the McCoys with guns in their hands and murder in their hearts, but instead they obtained warrants and arrested the two McCoys. What happened then surprised even the McCoys. When Sam and Paris were tried on the West Virginia side of the river—with Devil Anse's own brother as judge—they were acquitted on grounds of self-defense.

In the same year that Sam and Paris were acquitted, the events of the feud took a romantic turn. At local election-day festivities, Johnse Hatfield, the handsome, fun-loving son of Devil Anse, and Roseanna McCoy, the dark-eyed daughter of Old Ranel, fell in love. He was a swaggering eighteen years old and she, not the sixteen of legend, but a demure twenty-one. Roseanna did not return home that day, but instead went with Johnse to live with the Hatfield family. The lovers did not marry, legend says, because Devil Anse refused to allow it; he was adamantly opposed to his son's marrying a McCoy. Roseanna stayed with Johnse long enough to become pregnant but, ultimately, she was unwilling to accept the continuation of an illicit relationship. She left the Hatfield home to live with her aunt. One day she discovered that three of her brothers planned to ambush Johnse, arrest him on moonshining charges, and take him to jail. Heroically, she raced on horseback, with only the light of the moon to guide her, over the rough, mountainous terrain to warn her lover's family of the danger. Her timely warning allowed Devil Anse to rescue his son from the McCoy captors, but he still would not allow the couple to marry. Roseanna's infant died, but the worst was yet to come; she discovered that Johnse had married her cousin, Nancy McCoy. (No one has explained why Devil Anse would be so opposed to Johnse's marriage to Roseanna, but not to Nancy, who was a daughter of the murdered Unionist Asa Harmon McCoy.)

The next event of the feud also took place on an election day—a day usually dedicated to merrymaking and socializing as well as politics. Tolbert McCoy, a twenty-eight-year-old son of Old Ranel, somehow—the details vary depending on the account—became involved in a scrap with Devil Anse's brother Ellison Hatfield. Shouting such pleasantries as "I'm hell on earth!" McCoy lunged at Hatfield with a knife; when Ellison defended himself with a large rock, two more McCoy sons joined the battle on behalf of their brother. One of them produced a gun and shot the unfortunate Ellison, who had, by now, been stabbed over two dozen times. As Hatfield lay wounded but still alive, the local judge took charge. He instructed three constables to arrest the three McCoys and shepherd them off to the nearest jail in Pikeville, Kentucky. When the McCoys expressed a desire to stay and fight, he warned that Devil Anse (who had not been present) might well kill them.

The judge's assessment of the situation was sound. Hearing of the fight, Devil Anse soon organized an unofficial posse. Overtaking the constables and their prisoners on the way to Pikeville, they took charge of the McCoys and forced them to return to the Tug River and then across to the Hatfield side. Miraculously, Ellison Hatfield was still alive, and Devil Anse told the McCoy assailants that if Ellison lived, so would they. In an abandoned log schoolhouse near the mouth of Mates Creek, the death vigil began. The boys' mother and Tolbert's wife came to see them and to beg Devil Anse for mercy. At one point, Anse seemed to agree to return the boys to Kentucky alive. However, when Ellison died the next day, Devil Anse was not in a merciful frame of mind. He and about twenty others took the McCoys back to the Kentucky side of the Tug (just across the river from present-day Matewan), tied them to some pawpaw bushes and, in ritualistic fashion, shot them in cold blood.

Although a Kentucky court issued indictments for Anse Hatfield and twenty of his supporters, for five years no action was taken to extradite or arrest them. Old Ranel did not attempt violent retaliation but pursued his grievance through legal channels. He made frequent trips to the county seat and nearest town, Pikeville, attempting to convince a friend and distant relative, a lawyer named Perry Cline, to help. In 1887, five years after the pawpaw bush killings, he succeeded. Cline agreed to intercede and persuaded the governor of Kentucky to offer rewards for Devil Anse Hatfield and the others involved. The state of Kentucky began extradition proceedings. The result was a dramatic escalation of the feud. Private detectives invaded the mountains attempting to capture the feudists, increasing the level of violence. Kentucky posses, led by the flamboyant "Bad" Frank Phillips, crossed the river into West Virginia, where they killed Jim Vance, Devil Anse's uncle, fought a pitched battle with a West Virginia posse on the banks of Grapevine Creek, and captured nine Hatfield supporters. One of these was Devil Anse's older brother, Valentine. In retaliation, the state of West Virginia offered rewards for the McCoy "invaders," but the Hatfields planned their own revenge. On New Year's Day, 1888, they attacked the McCoy home, burning it to the ground and killing two of Old Ranel's children. His wife, Aunt Sally, was knocked down and beaten after she ran out of the house in an attempt to reach her daughter Alifair, who lay dying in the snow.

This incident created a national sensation. With rumors emerging from the mountains that entire communities were in arms, fighting pitched battles and threatening to burn the nearest towns of Pikeville and Logan Courthouse, the governors of both West Virginia and Kentucky sent personal emissaries to investigate the situation. Both announced preparations to send in state militia units to restore the peace. These plans were discontinued, however, when the emissaries returned with news that only a few families were involved and that the valley was calm. Feud violence had ended, but the court cases and newspaper coverage had only begun. Governor E. Willis Wilson of West Virginia, outraged because Kentucky officials had ignored proper extradition procedures and kidnapped West Virginia citizens, obtained a writ of habeas corpus from a U.S. district court in Louisville, and he even went there to argue the case in person. Because the prisoners had been seized illegally from West Virginia, he contended, they must be returned and due process followed for their extradition. Wilson lost his case in the district court in Louisville, and he appealed it to the Supreme Court of the United States; on 14 May 1888, that court denied the writ of habeas corpus and upheld Kentucky's right to retain and try the prisoners.

In September 1889 the Hatfield supporters were tried in Pikeville and convicted of murder. Eight were sentenced to life imprisonment but one, Ellison Mounts, who was convicted of the murder of Old Ranel's daughter Alifair, was hanged the following February. Although there were dire predictions about what Devil Anse, in his thirst for revenge, would do, none came to pass. Anse did not gather his men together and ride into Pikeville, burning, pillaging, and raping as he went. Nor did he attack any of the many McCoys living on the West Virginia side of the river. In fact, despite numerous rumors, there were no further incidents. After twelve years and as many deaths, the feud was over.

Despite the drama of these events and the national attention they attracted, we still lack the answers to such crucial questions as why the feud started, stopped, restarted, and stopped again. There are many opinions as to the causes, of course. In the hundred years since the feud there have been innumerable magazine and newspaper articles (both fiction and nonfiction), several novels, and four historical studies devoted to the feud. Out of these, two major interpretations have emerged. The first, and still the most prevalent, holds that the feud and the culture from which it emerged were anachronisms in modern society. That is, they represented a primitive way of life which had somehow been preserved in much the same way that prehistoric fossils are preserved. The quaint, idiosyncratic speech, folk dress, log cabins, and plaintive music of the mountain people, as well as a propensity for indiscriminate violence, set them apart from the rest of us. This was, wrote one sociologist, a "retarded frontier" and the mountain people "our contemporary ancestors."[2] The idiosyncracies of mountaineers were attributed to everything from genetic makeup to social isolation caused by the rugged mountain terrain. But whatever the background factors, the feud, according to these writers, was caused by the primitive and "uncivilized" nature of mountain culture.[3]

In Virgil Carrington Jones's still-classic 1948 work on the feud, the mountaineers were portrayed as stubbornly proud and loyal to their families, but with a misguided sense of honor. "The Hatfields and the McCoys," wrote Jones, "were high strung, honest, proud, perhaps a little too proud for the wilderness in which they eked out their meager frontier living."[4] Over the years, this stereotype became so powerful that respected historians accepted these assertions. Richard Hofstadter, in his book *American Violence*, summed it up this way: "In addition to . . . inherited hatreds, the poverty and isolation, the backward education and law enforcement of the area, led to sustained feuds."[5] His documentation consisted solely of Jones's book. Because there existed no other detailed studies of this or any other feud, Hofstadter's conclusion was based on the same popular, conventional wisdom on which Jones, who was not a historian but a journalist, had depended.

One source of that conventional wisdom originated in the newspapers and magazines of the time and was expressed in the first book ever published on the subject, one that was written even before the feud was over. This work, by *New York World* reporter T. C. Crawford, expressed the typical attitudes of the national press. Crawford attributed feud violence to a chain of circumstances beginning with the mountaineers' physical isolation from the rest of the country. He described the region as being "as remote as Central Africa." Like central Africa, he explained, there were no civilized institutions. True, there were churches and schools, but they were hardly worthy of the name. The "school houses," he concluded, "supply very meagre means of educating the children of the mountain people who live in this isolated region."[6] Although Crawford, as a newspaper reporter, admittedly was more interested in sensational rhetoric than in analysis, his conclusions differed little from a scholarly article that appeared in the *American Journal of Sociology* in 1901. The author of this study, like Crawford, admitted the existence of schools but assumed their backwardness, describing them as "of the pioneer type—one room, built of unhewn logs, benches without backs, no desks, maps, charts, or any of the other furnishings of a modern city schoolroom." Similarly, the church "is the most important social institution in the mountains," but was rendered ineffective by extreme sectarianism, which reflected the "ignorance" of the mountain people.[7]

The power of the stereotype is very much apparent in these examples; if the existence of schools and churches was admitted, then journalists and scholars pointed to the backwardness and irrelevance of those institutions. Inevitably, they argued, ignorance, isolation, and the lack of social institutions lead to idleness, absence of "industry," and a tendency to violence. As recently as 1978 another historian reiterated this one-dimensional analysis of feud causes. "The isolation of the Tug Valley fostered a prolongation of frontier conditions in which education and organized religion suffered." The result, continued this historian, was that "the mountain boy . . . often grew up untempered by strong parental or social discipline and with neither training nor example in self-control."[8]

Another Kentucky historian, in a recent book, acknowledged the problems created by the lack of educational and religious institutions but argued that the real cause of feuds was the extreme weakness of county governments and judicial processes.[9] These authors agree that mountaineers were socially and culturally deficient—and that deficiency fostered tendencies toward violence.

All these arguments reflect the assumption that violence and lawlessness were more or less routine in preindustrial Appalachian communities. Although there is no explicitly stated social or cultural theory, their implicit theory is that when economic, social, and cultural "progress" arrived—in the form of modern transportation, education, and religion—the feuds, like moonshining, would naturally fade away and the mountaineers would be transformed into normal, law-abiding, middle-class Americans like the rest of us. By this interpretation, traditional societies such as the one inhabited by the feudists certainly had romantic and appealing aspects, but they were fundamentally flawed until they had been assimilated into the economic and cultural system of industrial capitalism which prevailed in the rest of the country.

Some recent historians have suggested quite a different interpretation—not only of feud violence, but of the general nature of Appalachian culture before industrialization—which stands conventional wisdom on its head. John Alexander Williams and Gordon McKinney have both pointed out that southern mountain feuds increased rather than decreased in frequency and intensity in the 1880s, at the precise time that American industrialists began to exploit the rich coalfields of southern West Virginia and northeastern Kentucky.[10] The Hatfield-McCoy feud, along with a rash of others, occurred in this region at precisely that time.[11] From the Civil War to the early twentieth century, economic changes were transforming Appalachia from a region of self-sufficient and stable communities to one of dependency and poverty.[12] The mountaineers, argues McKinney, were confronted with the loss of control over their own economic and social environment. Unable to stop or even understand the process, they reacted with what outsiders perceived as "irrational violence." "No other group in the history of the United States," writes McKinney, "has faced such an onslaught in such a short period of time." Why, he wonders, weren't they "even more violent than they were?"[13]

Introduction

McKinney's viewpoint is a compelling one for social historians, influenced by E. P. Thompson and Eric Hobsbawm, who have emphasized the negative and exploitative aspects of industrial capitalism.[14] Such scholars question the old "progressive" view that traditional societies can only benefit from economic and social development. They assert that commercial and industrial capitalism often exert a negative impact, destroying the stable foundation of traditional communities and causing unprecedented poverty, social destabilization, and violence. Thus, in a startling reversal of entrenched assumptions about violent feuding, this new interpretation argues that "progress"—in the form of economic development and the imposition of strong but alien educational, religious, and political institutions—was a violent disruption of traditional culture and quite understandably caused the mountaineers to strike back in anger and frustration. Civilization, in the form of commercial and industrial capitalism, led not to the salvation of these communities, but to their destruction.

The striking coincidence in timing between feud outbreaks and the sudden capitalist transformation of the region is persuasive, especially when buttressed by studies of other forms of collective violence in the Appalachians such as whitecapping, Ku Kluxing, lynching, and homocide and crime rates. All these acts of violence increased in the last two decades of the nineteenth century and have been correlated with the capitalist penetration of the region.[15] David Thelen, writing about Missouri, has posited an ongoing conflict between the "modernizers" and the "traditionalists" which was provoked by such economic change.[16]

But how valid is this model in the specific case of the Hatfield-McCoy feud? Is there a connection between the events of the feud and the onslaught of industrialization? True, the feud was roughly concurrent with the coming of railroads and coal mines. The Norfolk and Western Railroad—the first to penetrate the region—was surveyed in 1888, the same year as the "battle of Grapevine Creek," and completed in 1892, two years after the hanging of Ellison Mounts.[17] But as the narrative of feud events has demonstrated, the targets of feudist violence were not railroads, banks, or politicians, as one might expect if resistance to economic change were the basis of the feud (and as David Thelen found in his examination of Jesse James and the Bald Knob vigilante movement in Missouri).[18] Not only did the Hatfield-McCoy feud seem to represent simply two ordinary mountain families fighting it out, but also the feud began in 1878, some ten years *before* the first railroad surveyors appeared in the region. James Klotter has also pointed out that accounts of other feuds began appearing in the newspapers in the decades before the industrialization of the region.[19] If the feud came first, then industrial capitalism could not have caused it. What did? The question is a critical one, which cannot be answered except by a detailed study of the community that produced the feud. Only then can we determine the relationship of the feud to capitalist transformation. As a beginning point for that inquiry, there are three aspects of the feud which suggest that neither model is entirely satisfactory.

Violence. Contrary to the legend, which claims that hundreds were killed over a period of decades, the real feud lasted only twelve years and caused only twelve deaths. Moreover, the number of people involved in the feud came nowhere near the entire community or the hundreds of legend; rather, it was less than forty on each side, for a grand total of eighty individuals. This was a fraction of 1 percent of the combined populations of Pike and Logan counties. While the older, "progressive" theory claims that feud violence was only a slight exaggeration of the "normal" state of Appalachian social relations, most residents of Logan and Pike counties did not accept violence as part of the normal course of events. They were shocked and frightened by the violent deaths that accompanied the feud. "We didn't know we lived in a place where such things could happen," commented one woman who had been a child at the time.[20] The recollections of people who were living at the time are confirmed by Pike and Logan county court records, which indicate that serious crimes such as murder and larceny were rare indeed. Verbal abuse and fighting seemed to be more common, but physical injury and murder were rare. In the 1870s and 1880s, the Tug Valley may have been boisterous and rowdy, but it was far from dangerous.

It is important to examine the tensions which so divided the two factions that they resorted to unprecedented levels of violence. When the focus of attention shifts from a preoccupation with feud violence itself to the underlying causes of the conflict, the problem of mountain feuding takes on new dimensions. Even though the number of people killed in the Hatfield-McCoy feud was not nearly as high as legend would have us believe, the level of violence *was* high relative to Tug Valley standards. If mountaineers were not "naturally" violent and lawless, then something unusual was happening within this particular community which drove a few individuals and families to resort to extreme measures. A common assumption has been that the underlying conflict was somehow related to family loyalty.

Family. For most of us, the very names of Hatfield and McCoy are symbolic of interfamily conflict. In fact, the older, "progressive" model of Appalachian society assumes that one of the causes of feuding is a primitive and excessive family loyalty. And accounts of the feud have reinforced our images of the West Virginia Hatfields and the Kentucky McCoys, each crouched on their side of the river and ready to leap at any member of the opposing family who dared venture across. Yet examination of the feuding groups raises questions about this assumption. The supporters both of the Hatfields and of the McCoys consisted of numerous individuals unrelated to those families; in fact, more than half of each group were unrelated to the feud leaders. More puzzling, there were McCoys on the Hatfield side and Hatfields on the McCoy side. For example, the juror in the hog trial who voted for the Hatfields and against his uncle Ranel was Selkirk McCoy; Selkirk later took part in the execution of Ranel's sons and was tried with the other "Hatfields" in Pikeville. When the Hatfield supporters were tried, six of the witnesses against them also bore the name Hatfield. Remember, too, that Hatfields and McCoys frequently intermarried, the most famous example being Johnse Hatfield's marriage to Nancy McCoy. Obviously, family solidarity does not carry quite the explanatory weight that feud legend implies. This is not to deny the importance of family in Appalachian culture, but only to suggest that there may have been some other factors defining feud alliances that were more compelling than family loyalty.

Timing. The feud lasted only twelve years, rather than the decades attributed to it by the legend. If one rejects the Civil War as the cause of the feud, as most scholars now do, then it began in 1878 with the hog dispute and ended in 1890 with the hanging of Ellison Mounts. Even within this period the feud was divided into two distinct phases, separated by a period of five years. The first phase lasted from 1878 to 1882; it began with the hog trial and ended with the ritual execution of the three McCoy boys. During this first phase, the feud remained entirely a local affair. For the most part, newspapers ignored these events and no one outside the Tug Valley seemed to care what occurred there. When indictments were issued against the twenty Hatfields involved in the killing of the McCoys, no officials in Pike County were willing to serve the warrants or pursue extradition. Left to their own devices, local residents were ready to let the matter end.

Five years later, those same officials in Pikeville, the county seat, vigorously renewed their prosecution of the case. Perry Cline, a lawyer who was also a friend of the new governor of Kentucky, used his influence to have the indictments reinstated, rewards offered, and extradition proceedings begun. This action brought a new energy and notoriety to the feud. In this second phase, private detectives invaded the region hoping to claim the rewards; "Bad" Frank Phillips organized posses and captured Hatfield supporters, a pitched battle was fought near Grapevine Creek, and the McCoy home was attacked. It was these events which came to the attention of the national press and the U.S. Supreme Court and furnished the basis of the legend.

It seems clear that the first phase emerged from the internal social and cultural dynamics of the Tug Valley community, and it is those dynamics which must be probed to reveal the roots of the feud. The second stage, however, was instigated primarily by the intervention of outsiders—officials in the town of Pikeville, which was not part of the Tug Valley community, and the governor of Kentucky—and must be approached differently. These outsiders certainly knew about the first phase of the feud, because Old Ranel for five years had bombarded them with requests for assistance. Why were they so uninterested in the feud in 1882, whereas by 1887 they appeared willing, even anxious, to intervene? Could the coming of the railroad and a new awareness of the rich coal and timber potential of the region have prompted, directly or indirectly, such intervention? The answers to these questions must be sought in the relations of the community to the world beyond its mountain barriers.

The two phases of the feud, then, require two different levels of analysis—one that focuses on the internal dynamics of the Tug Valley community and another on the community as it affected and was affected by regional and national patterns. These two levels of analysis suggest that although both the "progressive" model and the capitalist disruption model of feuding have something to contribute, neither by itself can fully explain the feud. In fact, all these tantalizing hints—the level and nature of violence, the confusion in family alliances, and the two distinct phases of the feud—suggest a complexity not usually associated with Appalachian communities. It is that complexity which this book seeks to explore.

PART ONE
The Feud as Community Conflict

· ·

1

Prologue: The Death of Asa Harmon McCoy

· ·

Most accounts of the Hatfield-McCoy feud begin with the death of Asa Harmon McCoy on 7 January 1865. McCoy had served in the Union army during the Civil War and had returned home to the Tug Valley in mountainous eastern Kentucky only a short time before he was killed by a Confederate guerrilla unit known as the Logan Wildcats. The guerrillas were led by William Anderson ("Devil Anse") Hatfield, who later became the McCoys' nemesis in the famous feud.[1] Because of this connection a folk tradition emerged which assumed that the feud was a continuation of Civil War hostilities.

This explanation, however, has serious flaws. Although Asa Harmon McCoy had indeed served in the Union army, most of his family—and especially his brother Randolph, the future leader of the McCoy feudists—were, like the Hatfields, loyal to the Confederacy. Many of the McCoys, including the notorious Randolph himself, even served with Devil Anse Hatfield in the Confederate guerrilla unit responsible for the death of Asa Harmon. Not only the Hatfields and the McCoys, but most residents of this remote border community supported the Confederacy.[2] It is likely that Asa Harmon's killing was not the result of divided loyalties within the community but was, instead, the expression of a consensus which branded him an outcast and a traitor. After his death, there was no attempt at retaliation, public or private—strong evidence that even Asa Harmon's family was not prepared to defend his behavior.

Despite evidence to the contrary, most students of the feud have continued to insist that a Civil War "legacy" was at the root of the feud. They have argued that, despite Asa Harmon's traitorous behavior, his family resented his killing by the Hatfields and bode their time for twenty years until a chance arose for revenge. The specific incident of Asa Harmon's murder, the argument continues, was not so important as the lawlessness and violence unleashed by the war. Because local courts and county governments were disrupted by the war, social disorder fostered habits of private violence and revenge that persisted into the postwar period, naturally leading to the feud outbreaks of the 1880s and 1890s. Thus the Civil War "legacy," for the feud, was less a specific incident than the general condition of social chaos bequeathed by the war.[3]

This second argument is just as flawed as the first. Although military activity, both regular and irregular, did prevent the normal functioning of the county courts during the war, this did not become a chronic condition. By 1866–67 county governments had been reinstituted in both Pike and Logan counties and were making an effort to catch up on business that had been neglected during the war—predominantly road building and tax collecting.[4] They also attempted to deal with damages to property caused by both Confederate and Union troops. Numerous cases were brought to the courts seeking damages for livestock, equipment, and foodstuffs that had been confiscated by the guerrillas.[5] Although it is unclear how some of these cases were settled, the main point is that, once the emergency was over, Tug Valley citizens reverted to the normal channels of authority. Even more significant, the crime rate returned to its almost negligible prewar levels.

Ironically, what the death of Asa Harmon McCoy reveals about the Tug Valley community is not disharmony and social chaos but a remarkable consensus and solidarity in the face of wartime disruption—a consensus that provided the foundation for successful reestablishment of local government once the war had ended. It was shattered only by the outbreak of the feud twenty years later. If we are to understand this famous conflict, then, we must begin by probing the nature of the Tug Valley community during the half century before the feud erupted.

The Tug River Valley home of the Hatfields and the McCoys contains some of the most beautiful terrain in the eastern United States. Today the scars of a hundred years of coal mining have all but destroyed the rugged grandeur of its narrow valleys, rocky streams, and precipitous slopes. But when the feudists were growing up the land was pristine and protectively sheltering of its inhabitants even as it challenged their ability to survive. Towering mountains obliterated the sun for many hours a day and impeded travel except along creek beds and rivers. The Tug River itself is shallow and rocky, making navigation perilous even for small boats; traversing the region was almost as difficult as living in it. Before white settlement, Indians frequently hunted the area for its abundant game and fish but avoided it as a site for permanent villages.[6]

Not until the early nineteenth century, almost two hundred years after the first British settlements in Virginia and Massachusetts, did the first white settlers, including the progenitors of the feudists, arrive in the Tug Valley. Most were part of a new wave of immigrants from Germany and Ireland, who had arrived in the colonies at a time when affordable land on the eastern seaboard was no longer available.[7] Their migration down the great Valley of Virginia was gradual; they often settled in one place for a period of seven to ten years before moving on.[8] Finally, around 1800, the migrants from such southwestern Virginia counties as Tazewell, Russell, and Montgomery—including William McCoy, Randolph's grandfather, and Valentine Hatfield, Anderson's grandfather—moved northwest into the eastern extremity of the new state of Kentucky.[9]

Both the Hatfields and the McCoys settled on the southern bank of the Tug River in what was soon to become Pike County, Kentucky. They had come for land and they found an abundance of it, not only available but inexpensive—2.5 cents an acre from the county court. However, the near-vertical nature of the mountain slopes rendered almost two-thirds of the land useless for farming; the only tillable land, the narrow strips along river and creek bottoms, was quickly claimed.[10] Less than thirty years later, crowded conditions caused the children of the original settlers to covet the still-vacant lands across the Tug River in Logan County, Virginia. Daniel McCoy, father of Randolph, and several of his brothers were among the first to move, obtaining property assessed as some of the most valuable in the county because of its proximity to the river. Here, on the Virginia side of the Tug, Randolph, his brother Harmon, and eleven siblings grew up.[11] Valentine Hatfield, Anderson's grandfather, followed in the mid-1830s; with twelve children, nine of them sons, Valentine needed plenty of land, and he found it on Horsepen and Gilbert creeks in northeastern Logan County.[12] Migration, for these families, was finally at an end. A century later their descendants could be found living along the very same hollows and creeks.

Indeed, the most striking characteristic of the Tug Valley community, especially in the half century before the feud, was its social stability. It was not just the Hatfields and McCoys who provided social continuity. Other families who later became famous for their role in the feud were also early settlers. Peter Cline and his five children settled on both sides of the Tug near a tributary still called Peter Creek.[13] Jesse Phillips obtained land on Johns Creek, where his grandson, "Bad" Frank Phillips, one of the most famous feudists, died and was buried in the Phillips cemetery in 1898.[14] Abner Vance, grandfather of Anderson Hatfield's mother and prominent feudist Jim Vance, as well as Nathan Chafin, father of Anderson's wife, were all among the original inhabitants of the valley.[15] In fact, families of virtually all the feudists were present from the earliest settlement period.[16]

Social cohesiveness was enhanced even further once the great migration of the early nineteenth century was over and newcomers slowed to a trickle. After 1840 westward migration bypassed the mountains as easterners rushed headlong beyond the Appalachians to obtain flat and fertile land in Ohio, Indiana, or Illinois. As wagons and foot travelers poured west on the National Road to the north or through the Cumberland Gap to the south, roads through and into the Tug Valley fell into disrepair. Apart from an occasional peddler, cattle drover, or circuit preacher, few outsiders visited the mountain hollows. The original families proliferated, intermarried extensively, watched each other's children grow up, and established complex kinship networks that defy the outsider's comprehension. Outside the valley the forces of market capitalism and industrialization transformed America, but geography and the more easily exploitable resources available elsewhere protected the valley's inhabitants from the disruption associated with economic development. They gradually created an insular society that supported an interlocking network of political, religious, and social activities. Although not unaware of events taking place outside the mountains, Tug Valley residents identified with their local, immediate environment of sheltering mountain ridges and narrow creek beds and their comfortably familiar set of family, friends, and neighbors. Indeed there was little reason to fear—or to hope for—any change in the physical, economic, or social environment.[17]

In the antebellum period a remarkable homogeneity developed from a variety of cultural backgrounds. Settlers were of different national origins—English, Scotch-Irish, and German, with a scattering of French Huguenots and others. Three families who later became prominent in the feud symbolize this diversity: the Hatfields were English, the McCoys were Scotch-Irish, and the Clines were German. All these families had relatives who moved on to become part of the mainstream migration to the Midwest and West, undermining the theory that the Scotch-Irish or Welsh chose to settle in the mountains for genetic or temperamental reasons. The imperatives of the mountain environment blended all cultural groups together, so that by the time of the Civil War their differences in house styles, farming, dress, religious worship, and even political allegiances were almost imperceptible.

The settlers had come to find land, and land was at the root of their society and culture. As the basis for economic survival as well as social status within the community, the importance of landholding reflected an eighteenth-century cultural heritage. The early migrants were not destitute deviants who sought escape from the responsibilities of farm work, family, or community activities— "squatters," as they became popularly known in history textbooks. Judging from the meticulous care with which the early land records of both Logan and Pike counties were kept, Tug Valley families placed immense importance on obtaining as secure a title as possible to as much land as they could afford. This proved no easy task in a region governed by Virginia laws, which had allowed tracts encompassing millions of acres, with no clear, fixed boundaries, to go to speculators for two cents an acre.[18] Still, the residents of the valley eagerly purchased tracts from speculators or applied for grants of "vacant and unappropriated" land from the county courts. An early Logan County surveyor's book, still on display at the county courthouse, with its exquisite three-color, hand-drawn maps, bears silent testimony to the significance of the land to Logan families. In addition to the surveyors' books, deed books from antebellum Pike and Logan counties demonstrate the care with which even minor land transactions between family members were recorded.

If the importance of land was an eighteenth-century heritage, the Tug Valley social structure, although based on hierarchical values, was much more egalitarian in practice than that of tidewater Virginia. In the mountainous terrain it was not possible to imitate the plantation system and its polarized society, and small farms predominated. In 1850 more that two-thirds of Pike and Logan County households owned their own farms.[19] But even the one-third of household heads who reported no landholdings do not represent a pauper class. Many such households consisted of young families like that of Randolph McCoy, who in 1850 was listed in the census schedules without property, although in fact he was living on his father's farm. Such households were part of the parents' domestic economy until such time as the children obtained their own land.[20] Thus most residents owned or could soon expect to own small, self-sufficient farms of 30 to 35 cultivated acres and 300 acres of "unimproved" land, often mountainsides too steep for anything but hunting or perhaps grazing cattle.[21] Although a few absentee speculators claimed thousands of acres, it was rare for actual residents to possess more than 1,000 acres. Jacob Cline, father of feudist Perry Cline, became an exception when he purchased 5,000 acres along Grapevine Creek in the 1830s. Devil Anse's father Ephraim, with 181 acres, and Daniel McCoy, with 200 acres, were more typical.[22] Still, some families, like that of Jacob Cline, were better off economically and therefore acquired the superior social status usually associated with large landholdings. Men such as Cline were identified in the census records with the title "esquire," indicating their position of esteem and respect in the community. Even though the social structure was egalitarian compared to more economically developed regions, residents observed a status hierarchy based on social distinction and landholding.

Nevertheless, whatever social differentiation existed, economic activity was virtually the same for everyone, and poverty was almost unknown. All families participated in a domestic semisubsistence economy that included cultivating corn, wheat, oats, tobacco, and vegetables. Men and women tended domestic animals such as cattle, swine, sheep, horses, and sometimes oxen. Women engaged in home manufactures for family consumption while men supplemented the family diet with the abundant wild game and fish.[23] Differences between an average and a wealthy family were not in quality of life but in quantity of land, animals, and production of home manufactures. The undiversified, subsistence economy of Tug Valley residents extended up and down the social scale. It sustained a premodern life-style of hard work alleviated by seasonal rhythms and individual flexibility, lack of distinction between work and recreation, and a sense of predictability.[24]

This subsistence or semisubsistence economy, however, did not preclude economic and social interaction—interactions that fostered a strong sense of community. If trade beyond the mountains was almost nonexistent, barter and market exchanges within the Tug Valley community itself were extensive. Families were productive economic units whose tasks were shared with relatives, neighbors, and friends more frequently than not. Hunting, fencing, planting, harvesting, horse trading, and house building were all tasks shared by men in the neighborhood; women got together for canning, sewing, and quilting. The many hours spent in common activities provided the opportunity for reinforcement of values as well as an extremely effective way to disseminate community information.[25] These informal networks of information and exchange, however, were not the only mechanisms for interaction. Such formal institutions as county court and church provided institutional structures for social cohesion and shared cultural values.[26]

County courts, the traditional form of local government in the South, were organized as soon as Pike and Logan counties were created by their respective states. The county court was at once an executive, legislative, and judicial body and the central focus for the ordering of community affairs from land distribution to poor relief. For the antebellum era, the minutes of Logan County Court sessions are not available, having been destroyed when the courthouse was burned by Union troops during the Civil War. For Pike County, however, the county court records, beginning in 1821, are still extant. They are a typical set of Appalachian county records; matters most commonly dealt with include laying out new roads, appointment of local residents to build and then maintain the roads, granting of tavern licenses and setting of prices, probation of wills and estates, appointment of guardians for orphans, provision for paupers, granting exemptions from taxes or road work, and making grants of "vacant and unappropriated" lands. The county courts oversaw almost all aspects of the lives of local residents.[27]

They were, however, only able to accomplish this thoroughgoing integration because of their autonomy. Although authority for the actions of the courts derived from the state legislatures, within those parameters local officials and residents exercised almost complete control over their communities. The justices who composed the county court were appointed by the governor, but only upon recommendation by local justices. In wealthier, more populated, and commercially oriented counties, the courts gradually became elitist, undemocratic, and even oppressive. But in remote mountain counties such as Pike and Logan, residents had a sense of autonomy and control over their own lives. Although, as Robert Ireland points out in *The County Courts in Antebellum Kentucky*, justices were usually drawn from the upper half of the social structure, in Logan and Pike counties this simply meant that the justices were known to, and were not so different from, most of their neighbors.[28] Conflict did exist, but it was handled at the local level between individuals who shared similar perceptions of authority and justice. As we shall see, the first phase of the feud provided several illustrations of the effectiveness of this system.

Functions of the courts also served to structure community activities; road building and maintenance is a good example. State laws of both West Virginia and Kentucky required all men over the age of sixteen to devote a certain number of days every year to road work, but it was the county court that appointed both the supervisor and the workers. The men designated for a road or section of a road were commonly those who lived there and were frequent users. In Pike County, it would be possible to construct a map of the neighborhoods in the county by compiling a list of road crews. For example, in 1866 Randolph McCoy was appointed "surveyor of the road from the mouth of the Blackberry Fork of Pond Creek up the same and across to Jerry Hatfield's and that he call on all hands . . . to aid him."[29] The following list of "hands" defines the group of people with whom Randolph McCoy had day-to-day contact, but it also suggests that those contacts were formal as well as informal.

The neccessity of road work and the formal designation of those responsible provided the kind of structure that cemented a sense of interdependence and community cooperation.

Yet for the Tug Valley, the county courts—which met in Pikeville or Logan Courthouse—were not always engines of community coherence because they divided the valley in ways that countered its social and cultural unity. At this point, it must be emphasized that the Tug Valley community was not identical with Pike and Logan counties. It is tempting to define southern communities using county boundary lines because court records, tax lists, deeds, and census returns all focus on the county unit. Sometimes, however, using the county as a unit of study obscures the reality of a natural geographic and social community. For the Tug Valley the matter is doubly complicated. The first and most obvious difficulty is the division of the valley not only by a county boundary (between Pike and Logan) but also by a state boundary (between Kentucky and West Virginia). But despite its status as a political divider, the Tug River actually functioned not as a barrier but as a conduit of communication and a focal point for the community. Even when this reality is acknowledged, however, the researcher cannot solve the problem by simply combining the records of Pike and Logan counties into a single unit for analysis.

The Tug Valley, in fact, occupies only a part of Pike and Logan counties; its separateness is emphasized dramatically by the towering mountain ridges that flank the river in parallel lines about twenty miles from each bank. To the north of this ridge in Logan County is the Guyandotte Valley, where the county seat of Logan Courthouse (also known as Lawnsville or Aracoma) is located. To the south of the ridge in Pike County is the valley of the Levisa Fork, where the county seat of Pikeville (originally Piketon) is located. The Guyandotte and Levisa Fork valleys were both difficult to reach from the Tug Valley, and they were economically and socially distinct as well. In 1895 West Virginia recognized this geographic reality by creating Mingo County, which encompasses the West Virginia side of the Tug Valley. Although Pike County has not been similarly divided, local residents today refer to the Tug Valley as the remote "backside" of their county. To study the Tug Valley community then, one must separate out those records of Logan County that pertain to its southern half and those of Pike County pertaining to its northern section and put them together. Only then will the real dynamics and functioning of the Tug Valley as a community begin to emerge.

For this reason as well as the remote self-sufficiency of the valley, even more immediate political entities—the election districts into which each county was divided—were the most meaningful and relevant political units. These small districts held yearly elections which not only carried out the formal political task of electing district officials but also functioned as the most important social event of the year. In the Tug Valley the election districts of Magnolia in West Virginia and both Pond and Blackberry in Kentucky were the centers of community political activity; elections in each of the three districts were attended by residents of the others. Beyond the de facto political integration of these districts, however, the nature of social interaction at elections compelled community conformity. Voting was viva voce, which meant that every voter had to step up before the assembled company and publicly declare his vote. Everyone in the community was fully aware, not only of everyone else's political beliefs, but of their status as landowners or tenants and their family connections. Men came to the elections prepared to state and defend their politics as well as their reputations, if necessary. They drank, ate, exchanged hunting and fishing stories, and— if they were young and single—swaggered boldly before the young women in attendance. Women, old and young, accompanied their menfolk to election day, bringing garden produce and domestic animals they wished to sell or trade. Thus, the election districts were important far beyond their political and judicial functions; they formalized the neighborhood networks that bound families together the rest of the year. It was no accident that several of the major events of the feud took place on district election days.

This pattern of internal social stability and local independence from outside political and economic influences was reinforced by a set of religious values which developed before the Civil War. For the early settlement period of the Tug Valley (1800–1840) there is very little documentation concerning religious organization or belief. If the early families were involved in the great Kentucky revivals of the first decades of the nineteenth century, they left no record of it. By the 1840s, however, churches did exist in the Tug Valley. In Pike County, the Old Pond Creek Baptist Church was located near the

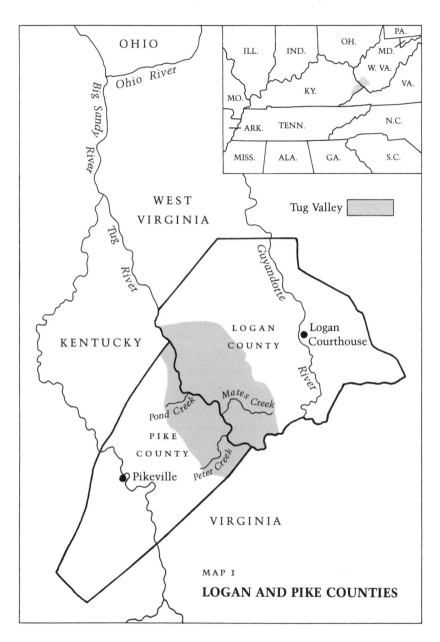

MAP I
LOGAN AND PIKE COUNTIES

Note: Logan County was part of Virginia until 1863, when West Virginia was created.

mouth of Pond Creek, a region populated by large numbers of both Hatfields and McCoys; several Hatfields as well as McCoys were members of this church.[30] A cousin of Devil Anse, who bore the same name but who lived on the Kentucky side of the river, was the minister. Preacher Anse was a respected and distinguished member of the community, also serving as Blackberry district's justice of the peace.[31] On the Virginia side of the river in Logan County, a Baptist church was built near present-day Matewan and was attended by one of Devil Anse's brothers. Although it is impossible to know how many families in the valley joined or attended these churches, it is apparent that mountaineers as a group were a religious people. Truda McCoy, who interviewed many Tug Valley residents in the 1920s, reported that the McCoys were very religious, particularly the women. It is these religious values which most cogently reveal the community's definition of itself and its relation to the world beyond the valley.

The churches were Baptist but identified themselves with a splinter group differentiated from mainstream Baptist churches. The Logan church attached "Primitive" to its Baptist identification; others with similar theological tendencies described themselves as "old," "original," "particular," "predestination," or "anti-missionary."[32] In the vernacular, they were known as "hard-shell." The separation between mainstream Baptists, who had done so much to proselytize Kentucky in the early nineteenth century, and this splinter group had taken place in the 1820s through the influence of charismatic frontier preachers such as Alexander Campbell, John Taylor, and Daniel Parker. Although many variations existed, the central cause of the division was differences of opinion on missionary activity.[33] The Primitive, or "old," Baptists objected to missionary work and the money collected for it. Their argument was twofold: first, since God had predestined each person's salvation or damnation long before he or she was born, it was both foolish and a violation of God's will to attempt conversions by persuasion; second, equipping, training, and supporting ministers for missionary work would create a wealthy, elite class of ministers, separate from their parishioners. Because the majority of Baptists were evangelical, this small group of objectors, mostly located in the southern Appalachians, came to be regarded even by Baptist historians as strange and bizarre reactionaries.

The Death of Asa Harmon McCoy

Because this Primitive or antimission predestinarian strain of religion flourished almost exclusively in remote southern Appalachian communities like the Tug Valley, it reveals the values and attitudes that prevailed in such an environment. Bertram Wyatt-Brown has pointed out that, rather than dismissing Primitive Baptists as a strange aberration, we would do well to study them for insights into southern regional folk culture.[34] Their emphasis on predestination suggests a cultural worldview that later writers on Appalachia have labeled "fatalistic"—a derogatory term implying a lack of ambition and faith in the American ideal of "progress"—but the fact is that similar beliefs were held by most Americans up until the nineteenth century. For example, belief in predestination was prevalent in colonial New England; indeed, it was not until the 1830s that New Englanders began jettisoning their predestinarian and nonproselytizing beliefs, a radical change provoked by the new openness and fluidity of society that accompanied market capitalism.[35] Because this economic transition had not penetrated remote Appalachian communities, mountaineers were not prepared to accept the shift to evangelical religion that permeated American culture. Further, in the 1830s and 1840s they became fearful of exploiting or being exploited by the commercial atmosphere and the money required to fuel a widespread missionary movement. It was then that the Primitive Baptist movement gained strength. By rejecting the overwhelming momentum of evangelical Christianity, which some historians have linked to the emergence of the middle class and a national market economy, southern mountaineers set themselves apart from and rejected the dominant American economic and social order.[36] By the 1850s, Tug Valley residents self-consciously perceived themselves as a separate community, independent from and diametrically opposed to an evangelical/commercial worldview.[37]

It is within this context of social stability, localism, and aggressive independence from both American and southern culture that the impact of the Civil War on the Tug Valley must be viewed. In no other way will the allegiances of valley residents during that conflict be understood. Despite the fact that Kentucky was a Union state and that West Virginia seceded from Virginia in order to become a Union state, most of the residents of the Tug Valley were adamant in their Confederate sympathies. The later feud leaders,

Devil Anse Hatfield and Old Ranel McCoy, were not unusual in actively fighting for the Confederacy. On the face of it, this behavior seems contrary to common assumptions about the loyalties of mountaineers during the Civil War. Most scholars assume that mountaineers tended to be loyal to the Union; indeed this loyalty is supposed to explain the secession of West Virginia from Virginia. Mountaineers, it has been said, did not own slaves and were unfairly treated by the planter elite of their states. Thus, it was "natural" for the mountaineers to support freedom and the Union. The fact is, however, that Logan County, like other central and southern West Virginia counties, remained violently opposed to the Union and to West Virginia's creation as a Union state. Logan Countians refused to participate in the statemaking process; they did not send delegates to the statehood conventions in Wheeling, and they refused to vote on the new state constitution.[38] Like other mountain counties, Logan residents possessed only a very few slaves and grew virtually no cotton, rice, or sugar. Thus, Logan's identification with the Confederacy must have been rooted in factors other than slavery. Similarly, Pike County was in the Union state of Kentucky, but most of its residents, particularly those in the Tug Valley, also supported the Confederacy.[39]

The majority of residents of Logan County and to a lesser degree Pike County believed that support for the Confederacy offered the most promise of preserving, not slavery, but their own independence and autonomy. In fact, they seemed convinced that the Confederacy, not the Union, stood for the continuation of the yeoman-farmer republicanism enshrined in the American Revolution. If the planter elite that led the South to war was fighting for a social and economic system based on slavery, that fact was not completely understood by residents of the Tug Valley. Harmon McCoy provides a good illustration of the point. Paradoxically, he was one of the few people who sympathized with the Union, but at the same time he was one of the few in the valley to own slaves.[40] Others in Pike County who sided with the Union also tended to be slaveowners and were slightly wealthier than their neighbors. Thus, in the Tug Valley, there existed a kind of reversal of national roles. A few wealthier residents who owned slaves cast their lot with the Union, while the majority of average farmers embraced the Confederacy as the defender of traditional liberties and local autonomy.

But why were Logan and Pike counties different from other mountain counties, which did follow the more familiar model and support the Union even in such Confederate states as North Carolina and Georgia? One key to understanding the mountain communities that did support the Union was in their social and economic relationship to the surrounding regions. By the 1850s, upcountry counties in Georgia and the Carolinas possessed railroads and therefore were already more commercially developed and thus linked to larger regional economic networks than was the Tug Valley.[41] Which side residents of these counties chose to support seemed to depend on the nature of their commercial links to the planter and regional economy. Dependence on and entanglement in the planter economy did not necessarily produce solidarity with the planters; mountaineers often perceived themselves as exploited and entertained considerable class animosity toward the planter aristocracy. That resentment, combined with their hostility toward the slave system, inclined them either to remain neutral or to support the North. The decision to reject an alliance with the South emerged out of the mountaineers' entanglement, both economically and culturally, with the dominant planter economy. Tug Valley residents, on the contrary, by the 1850s were becoming more and more socially and economically withdrawn from the rest of the country, South or North. The railroad-building spree of the 1850s had bypassed the valley and even regional trade was extremely limited. Ironically, this very independence from the plantation South may have allowed Tug residents to identify with it during the Civil War.

Tug Valley residents, in choosing the South, were not embracing the idea of southern nationhood so much as defending their autonomy. The alacrity with which mountaineers deserted the regular army to form guerrilla bands operating in their own region is further proof of the point. The Hatfields are good examples. In 1861 Devil Anse enlisted as a private in Company D, Forty-fifth Battalion of the Virginia Infantry; by 1863 he had become a first lieutenant in Company B, stationed at Saltville, Virginia. By December 1863 Devil Anse apparently deserted along with his brothers, Ellison and Elias.[42] In the absence of information as to why they deserted, historians have often assumed that the mountaineers simply wanted less regimentation and more opportunities to rob, steal, and plunder.[43] (It is instructive to keep in mind that no one ever makes such assumptions about American soldiers in the Revolution who regularly deserted in order to harvest their crops or to defend their local communities.) In the case of the Hatfields and McCoys, events back home offer a more plausible explanation.

Between 1861 and 1863, when these men were away from their homes, considerable fighting had occurred in the region, particularly around Pikeville. Union forces under the command of Col. James Garfield had been sent to secure the area from the Confederates under Gen. Humphrey Marshall. Pikeville itself changed hands several times and Garfield fought a skirmishing action near the mouth of Pond Creek, the heart of the Tug Valley.[44] On the Virginia side (West Virginia was not created until 1863) a Union force under Col. Edward Siber occupied the town of Logan and burned the courthouse.[45] Because the Confederacy could not afford to send a large army to defend the Tug region, the situation was critical. The Hatfields may well have deserted the regular army in order to return and defend their families and homes. It was not until 1864, by which time Devil Anse would surely have heard of the inroads of the Union army, that he organized his own irregular unit—the Logan Wildcats.

Although the objective of the Wildcats was to prevent such depredations, the band also carried on guerrilla warfare against its Union counterpart, the Kentucky home guard. Indeed, Harmon McCoy, as a member of the latter group, had been instrumental in spying on the Logan Wildcats and stealing their horses.[46] The Logan Wildcats skirmished with Union units both regular and irregular, not only in Logan County but also in surrounding counties; they also intimidated residents suspected of Union sympathies by stealing their horses, hogs, and cattle. Constant skirmishing and guerrilla activity throughout the war entirely disrupted local government. In both Logan and Pikeville, the county courts ceased to meet between 1861 and 1865.

But despite skirmishing between local guerrilla groups, the real contest in the valley pitted a majority of residents who were Confederate in sympathy against a formidable Union army supported by a few local sympathizers. From the perspective of Tug Valley residents, the valley was being threatened by outsiders—outsiders with the firepower and the manpower to destroy their community. That is why Devil Anse and his Wildcats were such heroes; their little band was all that protected the community from the enemy. From that perspective, it is easier to understand why Harmon Mc-Coy, first by his activities in conjunction with the home guards and then by his actual enlistment in the Union army, earned the bitter hatred of his neighbors.

In the postwar era this wartime solidarity was reinforced by a community sense of embattlement, of being under political siege from the outside. Logan County, for example, was forced to accept the provisions of the new West Virginia state constitution, which instituted a system of local government based on a New England township model.[47] The magisterial district of Magnolia, home of most of the Hatfield feudists, became a township, and its leading citizens were barred from voting or holding office because of their military service to the Confederacy.[48] Although the state government made some half-hearted attempts to enforce these restrictions, a few Logan residents defiantly continued to hold elections, serve as justices, and vote in violation of their own state constitution.[49] On the Pike County side of the Tug similar conditions prevailed, although some districts around the town of Pikeville contained significant numbers of Unionists who supported the Republican party after the war. But in the Tug Valley, residents were still solidly Democratic and, as in Logan, they continued to vote in spite of their Confederate military service.[50] Although inhabitants of the Tug Valley subverted the wills of their own state governments, they did so at the cost of becoming more self-consciously isolated than ever before.

Tug Valley residents, then, perceived themselves as different from and perhaps even in active opposition to the economic, religious, and political configurations, not only of the United States and the South, but also of their own counties. In a region devoid of railroads and market connections, rejecting the ideological tenets of evangelical Christianity, and isolated politically as Confederate hold-outs in Union states, Tug Valley residents reconstructed their community, almost defiantly, on traditions of autonomy and independence. What they had not yet realized, however, was that the economic forces unleashed in the rest of the country by the Civil War were soon to invade and change their community in far more profound ways than the war itself had done.

The Devil in West Virginia

· ·

The career of Anderson Hatfield illustrates the subtle alterations in economic and social patterns that were beginning to transform the Tug Valley in the years following the Civil War. Although not as sudden and dramatic as the massive industrialization of the 1890s, these changes gradually undermined economic self-sufficiency and social autonomy.[1] Although everyone in the valley experienced these changes to some degree, it was Anderson Hatfield who was on the cutting edge of that early, yet far-reaching, economic change. Ironically, the individual who, for modern Americans, embodies the very essence of traditional mountain culture was, in his own time, a powerful agent for its transformation. Long before the outbreak of the feud, Anderson Hatfield played a highly visible and controversial role in his community, one which served to confirm his reputation as a "Devil."[2]

Valentine Hatfield, Anderson's grandfather, was the original Hatfield settler in Logan County but not in the Tug Valley; that distinction belonged to Devil Anse's own father Ephraim. When Valentine and his family—seven of them grown sons, already married—arrived in Logan County in the mid-1830s, they established themselves on Horsepen and Gilbert creeks, tributaries of the Guyandotte River. The Guyandotte was the next river valley north of and roughly parallel to the Tug Valley. Two of Valentine's sons, however, did not remain with the rest of the family but moved to the Tug Valley and settled along Mates Creek. One brother, Ephraim, was the father of Devil Anse.[3] By the time Ephraim settled there and began raising his family—Anderson was born in 1839, not long after the move—the McCoys, Vances, Rutherfords, and Chafins had preceded him and claimed some of the most valuable lands near the mouth of Mates Creek. Ephraim's land was scattered, some of it near the mouth of the creek and some high up near its headwaters.[4] As his eleven children, including six sons, grew to maturity, Ephraim provided them with farms along the length of Mates Creek. As the family proliferated, the area became inexorably identified with Ephraim's branch of the Hatfield family.

During the years of Anse's childhood and youth, his father was one of the most trusted and respected members of the Tug Valley community. Known as "Big Eaf" because of his huge size—six feet tall and three hundred pounds—he nevertheless had a reputation as one of "the quietest men" in the valley. Anse and his brothers and sisters enjoyed the reflected prestige of their father's position as a local justice of the peace who handled conflicts between neighbors with a fairness and firmness respected throughout the district.[5]

As a boy, however, Anse began to earn quite a different reputation from that of his father and brothers—one based on his precociousness. According to one story, which may be apocryphal, after her son singlehandedly fought a catamount Anse's mother remarked approvingly that he "was not afraid of the Devil himself," and the nickname stuck.[6] G. Elliot Hatfield, who grew up in feud country and knew some of the participants, cannot unequivocally confirm that the nickname was rooted in Anse's childhood, but he believes that it was.[7] It is certain, however, that Anse early became one of the most accomplished marksmen and horseback riders in the region, thereby earning the admiration and emulation of his peers. His "hobby" of capturing and training bear cubs as pets, which he continued into adulthood, only enhanced his reputation.[8] Perhaps it was this sharp difference between Anse's temperament and that of his father that made the epithet "Devil" seem especially appropriate.

The alacrity with which Anse seized leadership at the outbreak of the Civil War was in character with his previous reputation. At the war's onset Anse was just coming of age and was courting Levicy Chafin, the daughter of a neighboring farmer. They were married in 1861, but within weeks Anse, along with many of his brothers, cousins, and neighbors, joined the Confederate army.

When he and his friends deserted in 1863 and returned home to form an irregular unit to defend the Tug Valley, Anse was clearly their recognized leader.[9] When the war was over, Anse's reputation in his community had already reached legendary proportions and would have been difficult to live up to. But that was not his only problem.

In a society where a young man's father was his chief economic resource as he approached adulthood, Anse Hatfield apparently was at odds with Ephraim. After he married and had children of his own—thirteen of them—Anse chose names for them that honored relatives and friends he admired—a common pattern in the valley. His first son, born during the Civil War, was named after a comrade in the Logan Wildcats, Johnson McCoy.[10] The next son was named William Anderson after Anse himself but was nicknamed "Cap," probably after Anse's rank in the Confederate army. Others included Robert E. Lee Hatfield and E. Willis Wilson Hatfield (the West Virginia governor who defended Anse in the feud). Notably absent was the name of Anse's own father, Ephraim. Since two of Anse's older siblings followed tradition and named their firstborn sons Ephraim, and since Anse himself named his first daughter Nancy, after his mother, this omission hints at active hostility between father and son.[11]

Confirmation of such hostility is to be found in Big Eaf's failure to provide land for only one out of his six sons—Anse. On the surface it is difficult to understand the reasons for Big Eaf's behavior. After the war was over, as Anse settled into adult married life, he showed all the usual signs of following in the family tradition of community leadership. His oldest brother, Valentine, had already made significant strides in that direction, marrying into the prominent Maynard family and receiving from his father a piece of land on nearby Beech Creek. Elected justice of the peace in 1870, Valentine, for eighteen years, served in that position as creditably as his father had.[12] Anse's younger brothers, Ellison and Elias, also followed the family pattern; they married and settled on tracts of land obtained from their father on tributaries of Mates Creek.[13] Ellison, a large, handsome, physically powerful man, had won a heroic reputation in the Civil War, having served at the Battle of Gettysburg, and was greatly admired by the young women of the Tug Valley.[14] Elias was most like his father, quiet and more thoughtful than his brothers.[15] Anse's youngest brothers, twins Smith and Patterson, were still young at the war's end, but they soon married and acquired farms from their father.[16] All the brothers were respected members of the community and frequently served in public office.

After the war Anse, too, seemed to settle down to farming and his expected role in community activities. He built a house on land owned by his father on Strait Fork of Mates Creek and was even able to acquire a second piece of land from his wife's relatives.[17] By 1870 Anse had been appointed deputy sheriff and, along with community leaders such as Dr. Elliot Rutherford, was actively promoting education in his district. Apparently funds were available but no school existed, nor had a teacher been engaged. Rutherford, who spearheaded the movement, brought the case to the county court, supported by the Hatfields. After Elias Hatfield offered to donate property and build the school, the court ordered the Magnolia district committee to hire a teacher.[18] The school, built on Mates Creek, functioned for a time, but it had been abandoned by the time it played a role in the famous feud twelve years later. Elias Hatfield subsequently built another school on his own farm near the mouth of Mates Creek, and Devil Anse served as trustee.[19] But by 1870, despite conforming to the rituals of adulthood, Anse had not achieved the economic and social success of his brothers. The house he lived in and the land he farmed would never be his; in fact, Anse did not have to wait for Ephraim's death to discover that he would not inherit any land. As early as 1866 Ephraim had deeded the Strait Fork farm, where Anse lived, to Ellison.[20] But whatever Anse's personal friction with his father, it was exacerbated by a more general crisis facing the Tug Valley.

For Anse and many other young men who, like him, began settling down after the war, the traditional patterns of existence were becoming more and more elusive. In the two generations since the settlement of the valley, large families such as Anse's had rapidly expanded the population. Young men returning from the war cleared land and built their homes further and further up the mountainsides in increasingly remote hollows. Although the Tug Valley was sparsely populated by comparison with other regions, this growth in population was beginning to limit the amount of wild game which had been an essential part of the mountaineers' life-style and sustenance. Not only was game becoming scarce, but politicians in distant state capitals, in the name of conservation, began enacting laws restricting hunting and fishing.[21] In Pike County the court records were filled with prosecutions for poaching.[22] This outside interference with a mainstay of the Tug Valley's self-sufficient economy caused both hardship and resentment.

Federal laws taxing the sale of liquor further escalated the problem. First in the aftermath of the Civil War, and again in the 1880s, the federal Treasury Department made concerted efforts to enforce the law, sending agents into remote areas; these agents asked mountaineers to inform on their neighbors' activities in the brewing and sale of liquor. Mountaineers had traditionally made and sold spirits and considered such taxation infringement of their rights.[23] Yet their only resistance was passive—hiding stills, evading contact with strangers, and submissively paying fines when caught. Anse, along with many of his neighbors, was periodically summoned to court in Logan to stand trial for "retailing"; when he lost a case, he simply paid the $10.00 fine and continued to make spirits.[24] External interference such as this increased the general wariness of outsiders, but its more immediate and practical effect was to thrust more and more onerous and, from the mountaineers' point of view, needless obstacles in the way of achieving economic viability.

Although externally imposed game and liquor legislation created hardship and annoyed the valley residents, there was a more serious economic problem. The supply of tillable land could not match a rapidly expanding population still fundamentally dependent on agriculture for survival. Between 1850 and 1870 the percentage of Logan County households that could claim no land of their own rose from 30 percent to 50 percent.[25] This meant that half of all heads of household were tenants on someone else's land or farm laborers, a startling increase in only twenty years. In Anse's family, the effects of this economic crunch were felt not only by Anse but by the entire family. Anse's brothers, though above average for the valley in landholdings, illustrate the difficulties fathers were facing in trying to provide for their sons. None of Ephraim's sons except Anse— a special case detailed in this chapter—and Elias equaled in their lifetimes the land assets of their grandfather or their father.[26] All faced the prospect that the land available for their own children

TABLE I

Population Growth in Pike and Logan Counties, 1830–1890

	Pike and Logan Counties		Tug Valley[a]	
	Population	% Increase	Population	% Increase
1830	6,357			
1840	7,876	24		
1850	8,985	14		
1860	12,322	37		
1870	14,696	19	4,139	
1880	20,330	38	6,053	46
1890	28,470	40	8,678	43

Source: U.S. census, population schedules for Logan County, Va. (1830–60), Logan County, W.Va. (1870–90), and Pike County, Ky. (1830–90), NA.
[a]Pike and Logan counties were divided into districts only beginning in 1870; therefore that is the first year that the Tug Valley region can be distinguished from the rest of the two counties. Logan County districts that were part of the Tug Valley included Magnolia, Hardee, and Lee. The Pike County districts in the Tug Valley included Pond, Blackberry, and Peter Creek.

would not meet bare survival needs. Ellison Hatfield's land is a case in point. His wife Sarah described Ellison's two tracts of land on Mates Creek as "rather unproductive, and . . . nearly the whole . . . is rough mountainous land and wholly unfit for cultivation." The worst problem, however, was that the land could not be divided among the nine children, as "one-ninth . . . would not only be almost wholly unproductive, but could be sold for a mere pittance."[27] It was a dilemma faced by many families—even prosperous ones such as the Hatfields—in the 1870s and 1880s.

So when Devil Anse, at the age of thirty, found himself with four children (eventually he would have thirteen), facing a frustratingly barren future, it was not merely the result of his own personal problems with his father, but part of a broader demographic crisis in the valley. But just as Anse's dilemma emerged from a combination of his own unique personality and general forces of economic change, the solution he found required the juxtaposition of his own bold-

ness of temperament with newly available economic opportunities—opportunities thrust upon the Tug Valley by industrializing
America's need for timber.

Marketing timber was not a new idea. In the years after the war
many valley farmers began logging their otherwise useless slopes,
floating rafts to local merchants who would then move them on to
Cincinnati or Catlettsburg.[28] Devil Anse simply proved to be more
energetic and aggressive in the timber business than his neighbors—just as he had been in fighting Yankees during the Civil War.
Not content to work as a hired hand for neighboring farmers, Anse,
with his usual boldness, decided to start his own company even
though he did not possess the land or equipment for such a venture.
By 1869, in partnership with his brother-in-law, he had formed a
company and hired a crew.[29] His own land was not, of course, sufficient to support such an extensive operation, but he also had the
use of tracts owned by his brothers, Valentine, Elias, and Ellison. If
Anse neither possessed the landholdings so necessary to the preservation of social status nor pursued public office to gain the respect
of his neighbors, he did exhibit an ambitious determination to
make the most of any available opportunities. So extensive did
Anse's timbering become that most of his brothers and sons became involved, eventually making it the primary family business.
Nothing indicates just how much the timber trade came to be identified with the Hatfields better than the fact that a well-known
log-rafting song—"We're floatin' down Big Sandy / We're floatin'
with the tide / A hundred yaller poplar logs / Oh, Lordy, how they
ride"—was named after his eldest son, Johnse.[30]

From a modern perspective this ambitious entrepreneurial activity appears innovative and thoroughly progressive—an appropriate response to the scarcity of tillable land and wild game. But Tug
Valley residents did not always perceive it in such a light. Despite
the fact that small-scale timbering was widespread, it was feared as
risky, speculative, and conducive to dishonesty. Margaret McCoy,
mother of Randolph McCoy, revealed her own uneasiness when she
concluded that her husband's involvement in "what is generally
termed" the timber business would contribute to his economic and
moral "break up."[31] As if to confirm these fears, Logan and Pike
court records of this era are riddled with cases of trespass and damage, in which neighbors accused each other of illegal timber cut-

ting. Where once wooded mountain slopes had been proudly owned yet open to all for hunting and fishing, now neighbors became hostile and possessive about their boundary lines. Previously, the external pressures of religion, politics, fish and game laws, and liquor taxes had served to strengthen and reinforce the bonds of community, but the new externally generated market for timber caused divisiveness and bitter litigation between neighbors and kin. Just such a case pitted Devil Anse Hatfield against his neighbor, Perry Cline.

In 1872 Devil Anse filed a lawsuit against several of his neighbors, including Perry and Jacob Cline. (Perry and Jacob were brothers of Asa Harmon McCoy's widow, Patty.) The bill of complaint stated that the defendants had entered lands belonging to plaintiff Anderson Hatfield, "cutting, destroying and hauling away valuable timber."[32] This type of suit was not unusual; what made it notable was the amount of damages—$3,000—claimed by Hatfield. In order to pursue the case in court, Anse was required to give bond for twice the amount of the suit, or $6,000. Because he had insufficient land or property to give such a bond, he had to find supporters who would. Four came forward: Dr. Elliot Rutherford, George Steele, William McCoy, and Richard Phillips.[33] Their support indicated a confidence in his ability to win such a suit. Realistically, however, only one—Elliot Rutherford—could show that he owned property worth nearly the amount of the bond. A steadfast friend of the Hatfields, Elliot Rutherford was a physician and merchant, well respected in the community; no less a reliable source as Dun and Bradstreet reported in 1878 that Rutherford had been "in practice 30 years" and was "good" because he owned a "farm and has money besides and estate worth from $5,000 to $7,000."[34] This support, moral as well as financial, was so important to Devil Anse's ability to prosecute the case that six months later, when his fifth child was born, Anse named the boy Elliot Rutherford Hatfield.[35]

The facts in the dispute are difficult to recover. The case never went to trial, eventually being settled out of court, and so detailed records are not available. It is difficult to imagine why Perry Cline would cut timber from Anderson Hatfield's meager holdings when he himself possessed over five thousand acres of land that had been willed to him upon his father's death in 1858.[36] This inheritance had insured that nine-year-old Perry and his brother Jacob would be among the wealthiest landholders in the Tug Valley. Indeed, their father Jacob had gone to considerable lengths to secure his sons' legacy. Recognizing the confusion over boundary lines that plagued western Virginia, Cline had purchased this particular five-thousand-acre tract twice and recorded both deeds in the courthouse.[37] Moreover, he had moved to Logan County and established his home on the land that stretched along both sides of Grapevine Creek, a tributary of the Tug. Here Perry Cline grew up, probably impressed with the heroic stories of Devil Anse's exploits in the war; for a brief time, apparently, Cline and his brother worked on Anse's timbering crew.[38] Perry and Jacob Cline are listed in the 1870 federal census as Anse's nearest neighbors.[39] It would appear that Cline had enough timberland that belonged to him; perhaps boundary lines were unclear and the timber cutting on Anse's land was accidental. We may never know.

There must have been some basis for Anse's charges. He had the backing of some of the valley's most respected citizens, and the case ended with an out-of-court capitulation on the part of Cline. Within two years after Anse filed his suit, Cline had left Logan County for Pikeville, Kentucky; he probably realized that he had lost the case long before a settlement was finalized in 1877.[40] That settlement required that Cline deed over to Devil Anse "All the Lands that was willed to P. A. Cline by Jacob Cline sr., his father, said Land being and lying on Tug River in Logan County, West Virginia containing 5000 acres more or less."[41] In a remarkable reversal, Perry Cline had been impoverished and driven from the county while Anderson Hatfield emerged as one of the largest landholders and wealthiest men in the Tug Valley.

One aspect of this case is especially notable. Despite the fact that a settlement was not reached until five years after the original complaint was made, all the parties concerned, as well as most observers, seemed to assume that not only would Anse Hatfield win, but that he would win by obtaining what was widely known in the community as "the Cline land." Almost immediately after filing the suit, Anse began to borrow money from local merchants using the land as security; he even made a contract with Pond Creek merchant John Smith to deliver timber cut from the Grapevine lands.[42] All this took place before he had any legal title to the land.

Local merchants and Tug residents apparently thought he had justification for obtaining the five thousand acres, but that justification is not clear from the written record available to historians.

One explanation for Anse's triumph in this case rests on theories of Appalachian culture or, at the very least, Hatfield tendencies to terrorism and violence. When Perry Cline later wrote to the governor of West Virginia arguing that Anderson Hatfield should be extradited to Kentucky for feud crimes, he referred to the time when he himself had been a neighbor of Anse, claiming that ". . . these men has made good citizens leave their homes and forsake all they had, and refuse to let any person tend their lands."[43] The implication here that Anse drove Cline away and dominated the Tug community solely with violence or threats of violence is not borne out by county court records. Anderson Hatfield spent a great deal of time in court, most of it as a defendant in moonshining, debt, or trespassing cases. Neighbors, merchants, and tax collectors all appeared unafraid to fight Anse in court, where they more often won than lost. Anse was intimidating enough to have earned the appellation "Devil," but no one seemed to fear violent retribution when he was defeated in a court of law. In fact, community consensus was that though Anse might be a formidable opponent, he was "financially honest."[44] Had Perry Cline had grounds for fighting Anse in court, he presumably stood a good chance of winning.

The feud would eventually offer Perry Cline the chance for revenge, but for the moment Anderson Hatfield had triumphed. Never one to wait for opportunity to knock, Anse seized the initiative. At the same time he filed the suit against Cline, Anse set his crew of hired hands to logging the five thousand acres on Grapevine Creek. The boundaries of the land roughly followed the tops of ridges which surrounded the tiny creek, a watercourse so tenuous that it dried up for most of its length every summer; this creek offered even less fertile bottom land for farming than most other tributaries of the Tug such as Mates, Thacker, Beech, and Sulphur creeks. Only the prospect of marketing the virgin stands of poplar trees that abundantly covered the steep slopes on either side of the creek rendered the land valuable. In 1872, when the suit began, the land was valued at twenty-five to thirty cents an acre in the Logan land tax book; this valuation reflected its near worthlessness as farmland. By the time the case was settled in 1877, the land had tripled in value to ninety cents an acre. The county, as well as Anse, was beginning to realize the economic potential of timber.

Still, the difficulties of cutting, hauling, and marketing the timber were enormous. Without a swift-running, deep watercourse near at hand on which to float the logs, roads had to be cut, oxen and strong lines obtained to haul the timber, and supplies for the workforce purchased. For Anse Hatfield, beginning with virtually no capital, the task was considerable, yet he showed no signs of hesitation. On 29 July, three months after instituting the lawsuit against Cline, Anse negotiated a contract with merchant John Smith at the mouth of Pond Creek. The contract, in the form of a trust deed, stipulated that Anse and his employees could obtain supplies on credit, both personal and business, from Smith's store. In return Anse promised to deliver to Pond Creek six to ten thousand feet of poplar logs not less than 28 ½ inches in diameter "and bindes the timber over to John Smith for true payment of their debts that John Smith holds against them." Apparently Smith trusted Hatfield enough to provide all the supplies he needed until the next year when the logs would be delivered. As extra security, however, Anse bound "all his lands and cattle over to John Smith" until all his debts were paid.[45] If Anse did not deliver the timber, John Smith would take everything he owned. But Anse did not seem worried about the risks involved. Despite the fact that he was illiterate and could not read the contract himself, Anse made his mark and went to work cutting timber.

That Anse had embarked upon a large-scale commercial enterprise is attested to by the number of men—nearly thirty—hired between 1872 and 1874 and by the long list of supplies charged in Smith's store.[46] While the involvement of many farmers in the timber trade was limited to cutting only a small number of logs to supplement their subsistence farming, Anse's commitment was much more entrepreneurial and was undertaken at the expense of farming. This shift in emphasis from farming to timbering is demonstrated by his need to purchase corn in 1873.[47] A list of personal items charged at Smith's store also reveals Anse's interest in what might, in the mountains, be considered luxury items—fancy bonnets and combs for his wife and daughters, gold watches, and "fine" boots, frock coats, and hats for himself and his men. This lavish expenditure for clothes and personal possessions indicated a concern with appearance that reflected his desire to enhance his status in the community.[48] With such conspicuous signs of success, Anse became for his "hands" in the timber business a symbol of hope, showing a way out of the economic bind in which they found themselves. Anse, with his boldness, vision, and energy, gave them a livelihood and a leader to admire as well. His Civil War reputation seemed only to be enhanced by the economic initiative he demonstrated in the postwar period.

Early in his entrepreneurial career, however, Anse discovered that it took more than hard work and energy to survive in a commercial world. When he delivered the timber to John Smith's Pond Creek store, Anse was surprised to find that his version of the account balance differed greatly from Smith's. In fact, Anse was convinced that Smith owed him $3,000 more than the merchant was willing to pay. He concluded that he had been cheated. Contrary to popular images of the wronged mountaineer, however, Anse did not gather his men together and run Smith out of the valley at gunpoint; rather, on 1 June 1874 he initiated another lawsuit, this time against John Smith.[49] Although his suit against Perry Cline had not yet been settled and he was still periodically summoned into court for moonshining, Anse confidently filed his complaint.

The case was tried before a jury in the town of Logan in October 1874. Although the trial record is spotty and incomplete (there was no transcript kept), summaries of the testimony indicate that the jurors were most concerned, not with the disputed $3,000, but with whether Anse had delegated his employees to pick up and charge supplies at Smith's store. Anse did not deny this practice and apparently the jury found it reprehensible, for within a few days they not only exonerated John Smith but ruled that Anse owed Smith $500.[50] This decision, a severe blow to his business prospects, brought with it a host of serious financial consequences. The sheriff proceeded to attach Anse's timberlands for payment of the court's judgment, his lawyers sent him a bill for $400, and two Logan merchants sued for a debt of $600.[51] Apparently undaunted, Anse took measures to protect his lands, business, and employees: he mortgaged the five thousand acres to Logan merchants Nighbert and Altizer for $1,500, thereby raising the money to pay the judgment; he once again enlisted the aid of Elliot Rutherford, who paid half the lawyers' bill while Anse executed an IOU for the other half; finally, he sold part of his property on Mates Creek—the only property to which he had legal title.[52]

Even as he avoided financial disaster, Anse went on the legal offensive in both the cases that were so important to his future success. In 1876 his suit against Perry Cline was still pending. Although Cline was now living in Pikeville, Anse pushed the suit toward a trial. At the same time, he appealed the jury's verdict in the suit against John Smith. By spring 1877 both of these cases had turned in Anse's favor. For unknown reasons, Perry Cline capitulated and, in order to pay the damages, deeded to Anse his entire inheritance of five thousand acres on Grapevine Creek.[53] At the same time the circuit court overturned the verdict against Anse in the Smith case and agreed to submit it to arbitration.

During July and August 1877 the arbitrators proceeded to call witnesses in the Hatfield vs. Smith case. Unlike the first trial, a complete record of testimony was preserved in nearly—if not quite—verbatim form. Although the arbitrators were merchants from Logan town and, like the earlier jurors, unsympathetic to Anse's case, they heard more evidence and overruled his objections less often than had been done in the first trial.[54] The record of testimony is a rare and remarkably revealing document, illuminating the confusion in both procedures and values that resulted when traditional societies confronted the unfamiliar legal complexities of a market economy.

The major dispute between Smith and Hatfield was more clearly delineated in the second trial than it had been in the first. The discrepancy between the accounts of Smith and Hatfield turned on the price of logging and the cost of personal supplies charged by John Smith. Both parties agreed that Anse had delivered the timber on time and in the amount he had promised. But the other part of the agreement had stipulated that Anse would obtain the supplies he needed at Smith's store and the merchant would charge them to the Hatfield account. Anse claimed that Smith had verbally agreed to mark up the supplies only 25 percent above his own cost, but that in fact he had charged Anse 50 to 100 percent more. Smith first denied that he had marked up the goods more than 25 percent; when contradicted by witnesses he fell back on the argument that the 25 percent figure appeared nowhere in the written contract, and therefore he could mark up the goods according to his own judgment. But had there been an oral agreement? When pressed on this question, Smith waivered and finally admitted, "there may have been some talk like that."[55]

The problem was more than a question of witness veracity; it reflected a fundamental conflict between an emerging culture of commerce and a culture of traditional relationships and obligations. A culture of commerce required that contracts be inviolable, enforceable without reference to the circumstances surrounding the agreement, whereas traditional cultures took into consideration the appropriateness of the bargain to customary rights and obligations—in short, the fundamental fairness of the contract.[56] Although Devil Anse was experimenting with entrepreneurship, he was at a disadvantage in the world of commerce. Not only was he illiterate, but he still thought and behaved in the terms of an oral, face-to-face culture. For Anse, an oral agreement—because it simply verified the fairness of the agreement—was just as much a part of the bargain as anything that was written and his perception was still shared by most of the farmers in the Tug Valley. The sanctity of contract, abstracted from social or cultural context, was a novel concept. Thus, confronted with evidence that Smith had deliberately cheated Hatfield, but that Anse had indeed signed a contract which, narrowly interpreted, allowed that to happen, the arbitrators were puzzled as to just what their response should be.

During the trial, Anse's disadvantaged position became apparent. Because he could neither read nor write, the contract had been written by John Smith, who had summarized it orally. Witnesses such as the venerable Dr. Rutherford confirmed that John Smith had indeed committed himself to the 25 percent figure and then routinely charged Anse 50 to 100 percent profit. In addition, Smith had admitted to several people, including Dr. Rutherford, that he had actively sought ways to inflate the balance of Devil Anse's account so that he would not have to pay the agreed-upon price for the timber. In the face of such practices, Anse's confidence that he would eventually receive a fair judgment from the court seems, from a modern perspective, naive and unrealistic.

This merchant-farmer conflict was certainly not unusual in the post–Civil War South, where the crop-lien system systematically impoverished small landholders and tenant farmers, both white and black, over the next three decades. An environment with an almost cash-free economy and a largely illiterate population created many exploitative situations, which were exacerbated by the new legal ideology. What is surprising, perhaps, is that mountaineers like Anderson Hatfield challenged these practices, not with violence and guns, but with legal action and a strong sense of moral outrage coupled with confidence that justice would indeed be forthcoming. In his study of Missouri in this same period, David Thelen conceptualizes the problem as a disagreement over "ownership of the law." Traditionalists expected the law to uphold customary rights and obligations, while modernizers saw it as a mechanism for protecting economic development and profits. In Missouri, when it became clear that the modernizers "owned" the law, traditionalists resorted to violence to prevent the courts from functioning.[57] This had not yet happened in Logan County, and in Hatfield's case the conflict had not yet become violent.

At the end of a long, complex trial, held in places as diverse as the Mates Creek schoolhouse, the homes of witnesses, and the courthouse, the arbitrators reversed the original verdict, although clearly with some reluctance. Being merchants, they seemed caught between the desire to uphold a narrow interpretation of contract and the undeniable evidence that John Smith had deliberately lied to Anse. The case was further complicated by the fact that both principals were in some sense entrepreneurs. John Smith, however, was closer in style to the Logan merchants. He operated a general store, loaned money, and acted as a timber broker for local farmers; he kept regular hours, was educated, and spoke the language of commerce. Devil Anse on the other hand, despite the scale of his timber operation, was still an illiterate farmer who hired employees from among family and friends. He kept no books and relied on family and friendship obligations when it came to payroll and profit sharing. This made his evidence in the courtroom seem scattered, confused, and sometimes contradictory. The arbitrators, after hours and days of confusing testimony, caustically remarked that the evidence was "a little unclear." What stands out in this case, however, are Hatfield's dual roles: by comparison with other farmers he was a successful if overly aggressive entrepreneur; whereas from the perspective of town merchants, he was a backwoods bumpkin who had timber to sell and could be exploited.

The arbitrators' decision was something of a compromise. In an award far smaller than Anse's original damage claim, they ruled that John Smith owed Anse a total of $350. This amount, it should be noted, was less than the bill Anse's lawyers had submitted for the first trial. Officially, therefore, Anse had won his case, but in practice he suffered a serious financial setback. Yet Anse made no further attempt to challenge the verdict; it proved difficult enough to collect the $350 from Smith, who, at least six months later, still refused to pay the judgment. The record does not conclusively state whether Anse ever collected anything from Smith.

But despite his loss (legal victory notwithstanding, it *was* a financial loss), Anse was not inclined to retreat, and he did not waste energy on regrets or reprisals. His tangled financial affairs needed attention, especially now that a clear and legal title to the "Cline land" was in his hands. Although he chose not to register the deed at the Logan County Courthouse—probably to avoid paying taxes— several of his creditors heard about the deed and sued him for outstanding debts. In the spring of 1878 Logan town merchant George Lawson sued for $300 which he claimed Anse owed him for purchases at his store. In the bill of complaint, Lawson said he had heard that Anse owned five thousand acres of land but was trying to avoid creditors and tax collectors by not registering the deed.[58] At the same court session, Anse's lawyers from the Smith case sued for payment of their fees; they admitted that $200 of the $400 bill had been paid but they wanted the balance immediately. In several remarkable depositions submitted in these cases, Anse readily admitted that some of the debts were "just" while others were not. His statements and actions indicate his intention of somehow paying off the debts he considered just.[59]

One method of raising money was to sell off some of his recently acquired property; this would also have the effect of protecting him from court attachments when judgments were rendered against him by the court. By the end of 1877 Anse had sold two tracts of land to relatives who were also associated with him in the timbering business. One small tract of 150 acres went to Floyd Hatfield, a son of Anse's uncle John, who had acquired no land of his own to pass on to his children. Floyd had worked for Anse on the timber crew, and Anse sold him the land for the bargain price of fifty cents an acre.[60] This transaction enabled Floyd, who was a sharecropper on a Kentucky farm, to become a landholder and move his family back to West Virginia, where he had grown up. The other tract, consisting of 1,500 acres on the Wolfpen Fork of Grapevine Creek, went to Anse's uncle Jim Vance, his mother Nancy's brother.[61] Over the next dozen years Devil Anse sold numerous tracts from the Grapevine land to his relatives and friends.[62] Completing these transactions enabled Anse to pay off some of his debts and solidify the bonds of loyalty between himself and some of his followers. By the fall of 1878, Anse was back in good financial shape. He negotiated a new timber contract, this time with Mates Creek merchant George Lawson—the same Lawson who had recently sued him. Apparently Lawson thought Anse's timber operation was dependable and extensive enough to produce a good profit.[63] In spite of his many setbacks, Anse Hatfield had not accepted defeat. Handicapped by illiteracy, inexperience, and lack of capital, he prevailed through sheer will and determination.

Thus the old image of feuding mountaineers as ignorant, backward representatives of a culture frozen in time must be laid to rest. The epithet that became attached to Anderson Hatfield, Devil, if it did not originate in his commercial activities and aggressiveness, was sustained and reinforced by them. Anse was both respected and feared because of his Civil War record, but the behavior that ultimately marked him as different from his neighbors was his aggressive, though legal, economic maneuvering. Although most neighbors would admit his honesty, that virtue paled in the face of his unexpected exercise of economic power. Nevertheless, Anse never went beyond acceptable community parameters. His successful claim to the five thousand Cline acres seems to have been viewed even by Perry Cline as acceptable, if perhaps not entirely justified. Whatever wrong the young Cline might have done in trespassing on or violating Anse's territory hardly seemed to warrant driving him from the valley, dispossessed of his family inheritance. By the same token, Anse's financial maneuvering—mortgaging land to which he didn't hold a clear title, then using the money to pay one creditor while borrowing from another, and finally suing respected merchants—was not clearly wrong, but it was inappropriate, brash, and grasping in the context of traditional culture.

Anse's determined drive for economic success, even when it offended neighbors and kin, was all too appropriate for someone with the appellation "Devil." Individuals dissatisfied with their place in the community social structure who pursued profit at the expense of friends and neighbors violated implicit community traditions of conformity and cooperation. Individual ambition was seen as selfish, worldly, and ungodly. The Primitive Baptist faith, with its emphasis on the devil as a real person actively at work corrupting individuals, was pervasive in the valley. As we have seen, members of both the McCoy and Hatfield families belonged to this denomination; Devil Anse's own cousin was a preacher in the Pond Creek church. In the Calvinistic world of the Primitive Baptists, characterized by fatalism and suspicion of change, Anse Hatfield's arrogant flaunting of his own economic success and social mobility was reprehensible. Not only did he buy expensive clothing for himself and his family, but he made no secret of his sarcastic contempt for traditional religious values. These values equated preoccupations with money, pride, and status as worldly, and worldly matters were not simply in a separate catagory from religious ones—they were, by definition, indications of being in league with the devil.

In 1889 Anse quipped half seriously and half tongue in cheek: "I belong to no Church unless you say that I belong to the one great Church of the world. If you like, you can say it is the devil's Church that I belong to."[64] The joke about belonging to the devil's church was perhaps a play on words indicating he belonged to *his own* church. Such a remark was the ultimate expression of selfishness and contempt for both his community and God. In his statement the connection between worldliness and the devil is explicit, and Anse admits, albeit humourously, his liaison with both.

Although Anderson Hatfield's activities appear modern, his concept of the world nonetheless was shaped by traditional values. If he had been a fully modern man he would have attempted to defend his activities as perfectly justified both legally and morally. Most Americans in the late nineteenth century would have called Anse's motivations "individualism," "free enterprise," or "ambition" and would have seen no reason why he should be estranged from community or church. In Middle America, capitalists were the pillars of most churches. But in the Tug Valley, those values had not yet taken root. The community was still more traditional than modern; it bore a greater resemblance to the America of the seventeenth and eighteenth centuries than to that of the nineteenth.[65]

So Anse admitted to a preoccupation with worldly pursuits that clearly, by his own admission, linked him with God's active opponent. Yet, though he spurned the literal religious beliefs of his neighbors, he continued to accept community standards of behavior, taking pains to defend his honor and honesty. He stridently insisted that he "never told any lies," "scrupulously" paid his debts, and was always "hospitable."[66] Even so, Anse accepted the community opinion that his economic activities placed him in opposition to traditional canons of cooperation—placed him, in fact, in the devil's camp—but he was not willing to relinquish his position and status within the only world he knew.

Anderson Hatfield occupied an anomalous position in his community. He was a budding entrepreneur, but he was also a man whose outlook and value system had not transcended traditional values. Eagerly engaging in worldly commerce and using the profits to acquire fancy clothes in which to flaunt his new status, Devil Anse nevertheless jokingly admitted his cooptation by the devil. Admired by his followers and feared by his enemies, Devil Anse had the respect—sometimes grudging—of both groups. That combination of fear and respect had thus far prevented any violent challenge to his activities. However, because his neighbors were not afraid to confront him in court, it is apparent that Devil Anse was not considered a dangerous renegade, but rather someone who operated on the margins of, but still within, acceptable parameters. Despite the handicaps of illiteracy and inexperience, the economic future for Anse and his "boys" looked bright. Then one of the "boys" became entangled with Randolph McCoy in a dispute over a hog.

The Devil Challenged

• •

At the time the feud began in 1878, Randolph McCoy was fifty-two years old, living on the Blackberry Fork of Pond Creek in Pike County. Thirteen years had passed since the murder of his brother Harmon, with no sign of animosity between his family and the Hatfields. On the surface there appeared to be little reason for a feud between Randolph McCoy and Devil Anse Hatfield. As we have seen, Anse had no lack of enemies; Perry Cline was the most obvious, but he had moved out of the valley and had no role in the initial phase of the feud. Others such as John Smith and George Lawson, who were tangled in court cases against Devil Anse, were more likely candidates to trigger some wider conflict. Yet the one person who seemed to hate Devil Anse the most—Randolph Mc-Coy—had no obvious reason for doing so. To understand his behavior, one must understand the history of Randolph McCoy's family within the Tug Valley community.

   In the early settlement period of the Tug Valley, the McCoy family was not very different from any other family, including the Hatfields. William McCoy, Randolph's grandfather, had arrived in the region during the first decade of the nineteenth century, bringing a large family of ten sons and two daughters. Four sons continued the migration westward, but the other eight children remained in the region. The six sons who remained in the Tug Valley settled on both the Kentucky and West Virginia sides of the river just to the north and south of present-day Matewan.[1] Because they settled the area slightly earlier than the Hatfield family, the McCoys obtained larger and more valuable grants of land right on the Tug. These tracts provided both larger amounts of farmland and easier access to transportation. The biggest grants, totaling 1,500 acres, went to the eldest McCoy brother, Samuel, who was the father of Sally McCoy, Randolph's first cousin and future wife.[2] Of all the McCoy brothers, Samuel acquired the most land, but the others were far from poor. By 1860 John, Randolph, Samuel, Joseph, and Daniel— all the brothers except Richard—owned acreage well above the average and were worth about $1,000 each.[3] As a family they were better situated than the Hatfield brothers, whose lands were further up the mountainsides.

It was Daniel McCoy, the father of feudist Randolph, who first began to be perceived as somewhat deviant. By the end of the Civil War, Daniel was beginning to exhibit behavior that embarrassed the rest of his numerous family, his wife, and his children. In 1867 Margaret, his wife of fifty years, left her husband and filed a divorce suit, which was granted by the Logan County Court in 1872. Although divorces were not unusual in the valley, one in which the parties were over seventy years old and had been married fifty years was. Claiming that her husband had "driven" her from their home, Margaret filed a request for support; Daniel responded with a countersuit for divorce. His statement denied that he had driven her from the house or refused to share "all the means that he has accumulated." He further insisted that she had abandoned him "without any provocation whatever."[4] Daniel's countersuit was an attempt to avoid support payments to his estranged wife, and it prompted Margaret to submit a lengthy petition documenting the course of their marriage.[5]

Margaret married Daniel McCoy in 1817, when she was sixteen and he twenty-six. Between 1819 and 1846 she gave birth to thirteen children, all of whom lived to maturity. This did not seem unusual to her, as she began her petition by remarking that she and Daniel "for many years lived happily together and in a state of prosperity according to their condition, blessed with a small amount of property and as *common* [my italics] in this country they had a good lot of children which were raised up in the usual way."[6] What she did regard as unusual was Daniel's lack of responsibility toward her and the children.

Within five years after their marriage, according to Margaret, Daniel "complained of being sick and unable to do anything in the

way of assisting her, during which time the whole duty of supporting herself and family devolved" upon her. For thirty years Margaret worried constantly about providing food and clothing for her
family; she stayed up every night until after midnight, knitting,
spinning, weaving, carding, and sewing, making all her own, her
children's, and "even" Daniel's clothes. What Margaret was complaining about here was not so much these domestic activities,
which all mountain women performed, but their extent. Margaret
felt that Daniel should have purchased some of these items, especially the "sleeves" for his own shirts. To keep her family in what
she called "good" clothes was a task beyond any one human being,
yet she felt compelled to justify her inability to keep pace with her
domestic tasks. Because her husband did not fulfill his responsibilities, it was necessary for her to work in the fields planting and
harvesting. Daniel, she lamented, was "always dilatory and im-
provident." Often, she said, the harvest would not be enough for the
family, and she would have to raise money for such necessities as
wheat and corn by weaving and selling cloth. Worse, she was forced
to hire someone to do such farm chores as clearing land and split-
ting rails while Daniel was "idle or asleep."[7]

The petition documents Margaret's insistance that Daniel was
lazy and irresponsible as a farmer, worker, and provider, but her
greatest complaint was his lack of respect for her as a partner in the
marriage. The entire second half of the petition is taken up with
details of Daniel's insults, neglect, and failure to pay attention to
her wishes in decisions involving the family economy. One gets the
impression that Margaret would have endured the long hours of
hard work and Daniel's laziness, if only he had treated her with
respect. The best example of this relationship involves Daniel's
dealings in land, the family's most important asset. In the 1840s,
when Daniel and Margaret needed to buy farmland for their growing family, it was no easy task raising the $100 purchase price. Mar-
garet had "raised a snake-bitten colt with her own hands which
went as payment for $60.00 on the purchase of a piece of land . . . at
a time when they were very poor." Another time Daniel, in his
laziness, "turned out a lot of Pigs to die," which she rescued, raised,
and eventually sold for $50.00. This money also went toward the
purchase of a piece of land.

Both the economic problems and Margaret's patience, however, reached a culmination in the years immediately following the Civil War. At that time Daniel, like many other valley residents, was attracted by the prospect of quick cash and "went into what is generally termed the timber business, that is cutting and hauling saw-logs for market." Margaret's tone here is disapproving and reflects a suspicion that this endeavor was risky, speculative, and not quite respectable. In Daniel's case, the temptation to dishonesty triumphed. "He cut a huge quantity of timber," said Margaret, "upon lands belonging to the heirs of John Lawson dec'd, well knowing the same to be upon lands other than his own." When she "remonstrated" with her husband "for doing so great a wrong and one that would involve him in a law-suit and eventually break him up," he "became very angry." Nevertheless, Margaret proved entirely correct in her fears. John Lawson and his family were among the largest landholders and most influential merchants in Logan County. They were not likely to allow Daniel to make away with their land's most valuable resource. In 1867 they took him to court and won the case. As a result, Daniel was forced to sell his own land to pay off the debt. Margaret was "bitterly opposed" to the sale of the "whole farm," arguing that with the help of their grown children they "could manage" to pay the debt. This way, she said, they would only need to sell about forty acres of their two-hundred-acre farm.[8]

Daniel's response was insulting. He declared that "she had contraried him long enough," and that she could not prevent him from selling the entire farm. Daniel's problem was that, in fact, she *could* prevent him from selling the land. When any deed was registered in the county clerk's office in Logan or Pike, the clerk was required to speak to the wife separately from her husband, explain the transaction, and obtain her mark or signature of agreement. This practice was meant to protect wives from just such a maneuver as Daniel was attempting. The requirement caused a crisis in their marriage. Daniel pressured Margaret to "make her right to it [the sale]." When she steadfastly refused, Daniel told her "privately" that "he never intended to live with her anymore, called her an old fool," and ordered her to leave their home. Margaret did just that, but says in her deposition that she intended only "to stay with some of her children who were married" until reconciliation. Daniel, however, was furious. He "followed her and took her horse from her, saying that if she would make her title to said land she might keep the horse." Margaret's resentment and bitterness at this degrading attempt to buy her off with a horse is poignantly evident in her petition. She would have consented, she said, "but for the brutal manner in which she was treated."

Margaret argued that, contrary to Daniel's professed desire for her return home, he had indeed "driven" her from their home, and furthermore, at the present time he had "no home left to which to take her, not for himself, much less for her." As part of the divorce settlement Margaret did eventually give her consent to sell the land. She lived out her life as a domestic servant on the Pike County side of the Tug, while Daniel moved in with their daughter and her husband in Logan. The court apparently thought it was Margaret who had grounds for the divorce, which it granted after hearing from several of the children and neighbors. According to Margaret, the youngest son, James McCoy, had agreed to testify in her behalf, but Daniel had persuaded him to refrain from making a deposition by giving him a cow.[9] James's desire for the cow apparently overcame his obligation to testify for his mother; but perhaps he knew she would get the divorce without him since everyone in the valley was aware of Daniel's irresponsibility as a husband and father. There was no mention of Randolph—now forty-five years old and living on Blackberry Creek—in the divorce case; apparently he preferred to avoid the whole matter.

Margaret and Daniel McCoy were not, of course, typical of married couples in the Tug Valley or in Appalachia. Yet, from the genuine poignancy of Margaret's petition, we can discern much about the expectations for a "normal" marriage relationship. There was no mention of "love" or "compatibility." Margaret approached the marriage almost as a business partnership tempered by affection. She expected to have children constantly and to work hard—washing, spinning, cleaning, and even planting and harvesting. In return she wanted Daniel to do his work—clearing land, chopping wood, hunting. When he failed do these chores, Margaret regarded it as a violation of the agreement implicit in their marriage. Still, negligence alone was not enough to cause separation or divorce; the real catalyst was Daniel's refusal to treat her as a partner in family decision making. When he made irresponsible decisions, acted the tyrant, and threatened her, Margaret knew that in the eyes of the community she had the right to a divorce.

The attitude toward marriage that was common in most of seventeenth- and eighteenth-century America—which viewed marriage as a domestic partnership in which husband and wife were responsible for well-defined and separate, yet equally important, tasks in farming and raising a family—still prevailed in the Tug Valley. This did not mean, however, that women in nineteenth-century Appalachia and colonial America enjoyed a "golden age" of equality. In both situations, women saw themselves and their roles as subordinate to their menfolk, but that subordination was embedded in a hierarchical social structure that transcended gender relations. Given the limits of the social order, women had rights outside and beyond those that might be arbitrarily granted by husbands or fathers. Wives were clearly subordinate to their husbands, but men did not not have a license of absolute power over women. The customs and traditions of the community provided a modicum of insurance that both parties would fullfill their expected roles. Fundamentally this partnership had little to do with intangible feelings of love and romance but was based in duty and responsibility. There was, of course, a wide range of behavior within the acceptable parameters. Husbands and wives performed their duties and responsibilities to a lesser or greater degree and there was much gossip among neighbors as to the acceptable limits for deviation. But it was clear in the case of Daniel and Margaret McCoy that Daniel had exceeded the limits, not only in his behavior toward his wife but in his treatment of their children.[10]

The most important function of a father in an agricultural subsistence society such as the Tug Valley was not emotional or psychological sustenance, but economic and social support. A father provided land for a start in life and social status commensurate with his own standing in the community. Quality of parenthood was judged by these criteria almost to the exclusion of others. In return, of course, children were expected to care for their aged parents. Personality differences, annoying characteristics, and just plain cantankerousness could all be forgiven if fathers provided their children with even a modest start in life. The federal population and agricultural census schedules, as well as countless deed books in

Pike and Logan counties, reveal the efforts of fathers to live up to this standard. As children came of marrying age—usually between twenty and thirty for sons—fathers divided up the family holdings to provide each son and sometimes each daughter with a viable farm. In the Tug Valley this practice was becoming more and more difficult as families continued to produce eight to twelve children apiece. Daniel McCoy and his brothers were more fortunate than most valley families in their share of fertile lands—more fortunate, as we have seen, than Ephraim Hatfield and his brothers. Daniel's brothers, John, Samuel, and Randolph, all grew to old age surrounded by grown married children and grandchildren, forming what came close to subcommunities within the valley. The names of these McCoy brothers recur so frequently in census lists that it is extremely difficult to distinguish one family from another as generations of children and grandchildren received the same names.

There is, however, one notable exception. Virtually no McCoys carry the name Daniel. Not one of Daniel's thirteen children chose to name their sons after him. Few remained living near to him after they had married. In the deed books of Logan County, Daniel is conspicuously absent from the index—he never settled a piece of land on his married sons or daughters even though they were beginning to form their own families in the mid-1840s. By the end of the Civil War the two oldest sons had disappeared from the valley entirely; one took his family to Missouri and nothing was ever heard from him again. Of the five sons who remained, three (John, Samuel, and James M.) were impoverished and landless throughout their lives.[11] Two of Daniel's sons, Randolph (the future feud leader) and Asa Harmon (the Civil War Unionist), escaped poverty through fortuitous marriages. Harmon married Patty Cline, daughter of one of the valley's largest landholders, Jacob Cline; he moved to Peter Creek and inherited a farm from his father-in-law.[12] This was an accepted way to improve one's financial situation and gain status in the community.

Randolph, or Ranel, advanced his standing in a similar manner. In 1849, at the age of twenty-four, he married his first cousin, Sally McCoy. This in itself was not unusual, as there were many first-cousin marriages in the valley. But Sally was the daughter of Samuel McCoy, economically the most successful of all the McCoy brothers. At first Ranel and Sally settled down on land owned by

Daniel in Logan County. The 1850 census shows them living next door to Daniel, renting a fifteen-acre farm. But apparently Sally's father was aware that Randolph was not likely to get anything from his own father. If he cared about his daughter's economic and social future, he must have been upset by this marriage. Evidence that he decided to help the couple himself is found in the will he left at his death in 1855.[13] By this will Sally inherited some of her father's lands on the Blackberry Fork of Pond Creek in Pike County, not his best lands along the fertile Tug River bottom—those went to his sons—but some three hundred acres of mountainous woodland. With this prospect, Ranel and Sally, who by now had four children, moved across the Tug to Kentucky. The fact that none of Daniel's children benefited from his property bears out Margaret's charge in her divorce complaint that Daniel would not "share his means with herself or the children." Thus, long before Margaret left her husband and filed a divorce petition, relatives and neighbors in the Tug Valley must have been aware of Daniel's deviant behavior.

Despite the obvious fact that Daniel's children were not fond of him, they nevertheless seemed to emulate some of their father's behavior patterns. Community gossip undoubtedly attributed the children's deviancy to family traits. Harmon, Randolph's brother, had successfully raised his financial status by marrying Patty Cline, but he lost standing in the community by supporting the Union in the Civil War. As we have seen, his death did not cause great indignation or concern among his relatives or neighbors.

During the Civil War Randolph followed community consensus by aiding and abetting the Confederate raiders led by Devil Anse Hatfield, thus avoiding the disgrace brought upon the family by his brother Harmon's Union activities. But during this period, Ranel was involved in two court cases that identified him with his father—one directly and one indirectly. In the court case referred to by Ranel's mother in her divorce petition, involving Daniel's illegal cutting of timber, Ranel was also named as defendant.[14] Ranel's experience with timbering, unlike that of Devil Anse, was fraught with anxiety, danger, and family tensions. Instead of providing new opportunities for prosperity, timbering led to diminished economic and social status for Daniel McCoy's family. At the same time, it created an internal family conflict. Ranel's mother's conviction that timbering was not only speculative but led directly to dishonesty was amply justified by Daniel's behavior. Furthermore the court case, by breaking up the family farm, led directly to Daniel and Margaret's divorce. Randolph had reason to suspect anyone involved in commerce and timbering of dishonest, disruptive, and antisocial intentions.

Another court case suggests that though Ranel might have rejected his father, he seemed to be earning a similar reputation for foolishness and irresponsibility. In this second case, which was of quite a different nature, both Ranel and Sally were accused by their cousin, Pleasant McCoy, of "malicious gossip." Apparently Ranel and Sally told their own children, as well as numerous relatives and friends, that cousin Pleasant "had intercourse with a cow." In the tradition of many premodern cultures, valley residents were ever protective of their reputations and honor and did not hesitate to sue when they felt slandered. Although the outcome of this case is unknown because the records have been lost, it seems significant that some of Ranel's own family thought he was both "malicious" and a "gossip."[15] Did they shake their heads and instruct their children to avoid Old Ranel and Aunt Sally, concluding, "like father, like son"?

Other fragments of evidence support this assessment of Ranel's marginal position in the community. Although the Pike County Court records list many McCoys who served in minor county offices—district justices of the peace, road surveyors, and administrators of wills—Old Ranel was rarely entrusted with any of these positions. He appears infrequently in the county records at all, with one notable exception. In January 1880 several of Ranel's neighbors, in their capacity as viewers of a new road that ran up the Blackberry Fork of Pond Creek and over the mountain ridge to connect with a road along the Hatfield branch of Blackberry Creek, reported that the road was finished and ready to be opened—except, that is, for the portion running through the land of Randolph McCoy, who apparently was not making the required contribution to road work. The court ordered the completed portions of the road opened and summoned Ranel "to appear in the Pike County Court . . . and show cause if any why said road shall not be established."[16] Ranel never answered the summons and the case was continued every month all through the year 1880, finally simply disappearing from the court minutes in 1881. Did Ranel object to the road? Was it ever opened? The record is silent.

A second fragmentary bit of evidence concerning Randolph's local reputation is found in the federal census of 1880. When the local census taker made his rounds in the spring of 1880 recording names of all family members, he listed Ranel in an unusual way. Aunt Sally McCoy was placed at the top of the household roster, in the position always reserved for the head of the family; Old Ranel's name appeared below hers.[17] This was a form rarely followed in Pike or Logan counties; in the rare cases when it was used, the man was usually noted as having some mental or physical disability. In Ranel's case no such explanation is given. A check of the census schedules for 1850, 1860, and 1870 reveals that Ranel was listed in the usual way as head of the family. In 1880 Ranel was fifty-five years old. Were some of his well-known peculiarities becoming more pronounced, enough so that the census taker, a local official and a neighbor, almost without thought made Aunt Sally responsible for the family? Truda McCoy, in her book about the McCoy side of the feud, lends credence to this theory. "At the head of the McCoys was Ranel," she says, "and at the head of Ranel was Sally with her insistent pleadings to wait—always wait."[18] As one historian has concluded, "Randall combined a morose nature with a tendency to talk about his troubles with all who would listen."[19] If such was the case, then Ranel was indeed following in the footsteps of his father.

Thus in 1878, when Old Ranel rode over the ridge to the Tug River and began raving to neighbor Tom Stafford and the justice of the peace, Preacher Anse Hatfield, that his sow and pigs had been stolen by Floyd Hatfield, the matter was not quite so simple as one man's word against another.[20] Ranel's word was suspect, but on the other hand, if the old man were disregarded entirely, he was likely to go on haranguing relatives and neighbors forever. It was probably with some impatience to satisfy Ranel and get the matter settled quickly that Justice of the Peace Anderson Hatfield organized a trial at his home on the Hatfield branch of Blackberry Creek.[21]

There is no extant written record of the trial; only legend remains. All sources agree, however, that despite his Hatfield name, Preacher Anse was trusted by both sides. When he attempted to satisfy both parties to the dispute by choosing a jury of six Hatfields and six McCoys, he revealed two very important aspects of the case. First, not all Hatfields were regarded as enemies by Old Ranel

McCoy, and hindsight shows that it was Devil Anse he most hated. Secondly, Old Ranel's animosity toward this specific group of Hatfields predated the hog dispute; otherwise the justice of the peace would not have found it necessary to balance the two families on the jury. Whether or not an actual theft had been committed, this episode must be put in the context of previously existing hostilities.

Old Ranel's bitterness may have grown out of his friendship with Perry Cline, whose land Devil Anse had finally won in the court case six months before. If Devil Anse was resented by most of his neighbors for his ruthless legal and entrepreneurial maneuvering, Old Ranel's friendship with Cline added a personal dimension to his bitterness. Moreover, as everyone in the vicinity was aware, Old Ranel was far more likely than most community residents to talk—endlessly and loudly—about grievances, whether real or imagined. Thus it is no wonder that when Old Ranel challenged the Hatfields by accusing Floyd of hog theft, the neighbors held their breath wondering how Devil Anse would react. But who was Floyd Hatfield, and why did Old Ranel identify him with the Hatfields he hated rather than the many Pike County Hatfields whom he trusted? Floyd, in fact, resided near Stringtown on the Kentucky side of the river and was married to the daughter of Randolph's cousin Nancy. This familial and geographic connection with the McCoys has, in the past, confused students of the feud who have never been able to explain why this first overt hostility was aimed at Floyd, rather than at Devil Anse or someone in his immediate family. The key lies in Floyd's economic ties to Devil Anse.

Floyd was the son of Anse's uncle John and thus only a cousin of Devil Anse, but he had been employed on the timber crew since 1870. By 1877 Anse had become a large landholder; Floyd was the first to buy property from Anse on the West Virginia side of the Tug, and in 1878 he was just preparing to move there. Moreover, Floyd and Ellison Hatfield, Devil Anse's brother, had married sisters and were frequent hunting and fishing companions. Floyd's links to and respect for Devil Anse were most evident in 1877—the same year he bought land from Anse—when Floyd named a newborn son Anderson.[22]

By 1878 Old Ranel must have been well aware that Floyd had bought land from Anse and was preparing to move to Logan

County. Can it be coincidence that the hog dispute occurred just at this point? Old Ranel's charge that Floyd was a thief came at the precise moment when the community was pondering whether or not Devil Anse and his "boys" were all thieves—whether of land, trees, or hogs. Within this framework of community suspicion, Old Ranel's friendship with an embittered Perry Cline could have prompted this challenge to Devil Anse and his cohorts. Yet Ranel did not accuse Devil Anse himself; perhaps Floyd was an easier target because he was one of the few of Devil Anse's "crew" who lived on the Kentucky side of the Tug, where Old Ranel would encounter him almost daily and thus be reminded of the injustices perpetrated by Devil Anse and his "boys."

Although Devil Anse himself did not participate in the trial, nor was he even present, his "boys" reacted as though they considered Old Ranel's attack on Floyd an attack on all of them. Floyd's allies in the hog trial were two individuals who proved instrumental in Old Ranel's loss of the case. The first was witness Bill Staton, who insisted that the disputed hog belonged to Floyd. Because Staton was the son of Ranel McCoy's cousin Nancy, some writers have been puzzled by his support of the Hatfields. But careful study of the sources reveals that Staton lived on the West Virginia side of the Tug, in the same neighborhood as the Hatfield brothers. His closest friends were Floyd Hatfield and Anse's brother Ellison, each of whom was married to one of Staton's sisters. So it is not surprising that Staton, despite his McCoy family connections, took the Hatfield side.[23]

The second key person in the trial was a juror, Selkirk McCoy. A nephew of Aunt Sally McCoy, he was unrelated to any of the Hatfields. But according to tradition, he voted against his uncle Ranel. Most students of the feud have agreed with Randolph's own assessment that Selkirk was, for some incomprehensible reason, a traitor. As with Floyd, what has been overlooked is Selkirk's economic connection to Devil Anse. Selkirk, along with his two sons, had worked on Anse's timber crew since 1872.[24] Selkirk's relationship to Anse, like Floyd's, was an advantageous one. The 1870 federal census schedules show Selkirk living in Pike County and owning no property; by 1880 he owned 120 acres of land and was listed as a next-door neighbor of Ellison Hatfield on Mates Creek.[25] Despite his McCoy name, then, Selkirk's loyalties belonged to Devil Anse.

When the verdict was in, Randolph McCoy complained vociferously but did not himself foment private retaliation. Yet the next events of the feud demonstrated that Ranel's obsession with the "thievin'" Hatfields could lead to violence. Although Ranel grumbled and threatened, he shied away from actual violent action. The next generation, however, were not like their father and grandfather—grumble, complain, and threaten, but do no real physical damage. In the aftermath of the hog trial two of Ranel's nephews, Sam and Paris McCoy, initiated the first violence of the feud.

Sam and Paris, unlike Old Ranel, resided on the West Virginia side of the Tug, near the home of their grandfather, Daniel McCoy. Their father, Samuel, was Daniel's fifth son, six years younger than Ranel. He, like Ranel and Harmon, got nothing from his father; unlike them, he did not marry a woman who could provide land and status. The 1860 census schedules show him working as a farm laborer and living in the town of Logan Courthouse with his wife and four children.[26] Sometime between 1860 and 1870 Samuel died—his wife appears as a widow in 1870. He may have been killed in the Civil War, but there is no direct evidence for this. Subsequent census and tax schedules indicate that the family remained landless, the three sons hiring out as farm laborers to support their mother.[27] By 1878, the year of the hog trial, Sam and Paris, the two sons who would become entangled in the feud, were seventeen and twenty-three years old. Very little is known of Paris, but Sam had already gained a reputation as a squirrel hunter—on one occasion he shot one hundred in a day. Hunting, to be sure, was an important part of the domestic economy, but to spend most of one's time shooting squirrels instead of doing the necessary farm chores marked even a young man as odd. Donating the squirrels for a church supper, as Sam did, was not enough to redeem him; all the friends and relatives "were just a little bit ashamed of Squirrel Huntin' Sam for his 'queerness.'"[28]

For two years after the hog trial, legend asserts that some of Ranel McCoy's sons and his nephews Sam and Paris sparred verbally and, on occasion, physically with both Bill Staton and Selkirk McCoy.[29] It is not at all clear why this animosity persisted, considering that Sam McCoy later wrote in his memoirs: "If I ever had a friend in the world Ellison Hatfield was. In fact all of them were good to me."[30] Sam was referring to the Hatfield group that included Bill

Staton and Selkirk McCoy. Nevertheless, on 18 June 1880, a fight occurred in Logan County between Sam and Paris McCoy and Bill Staton which resulted in Staton's death. Although there were no witnesses, everyone seemed to know who had been involved. Paris was arrested within a month and was tried in Logan County in September. Sam was not brought in until two years later, in the spring of 1882. Several McCoy relatives from both sides of the river testified against each defendant but, surprisingly, they were both acquitted on grounds of self-defense.[31]

The acquittal occurred at a time when Anse's brother, Valentine, was president of the county court and the Hatfield brothers exercised considerable influence in the judicial system. For the first time Anderson Hatfield became involved in the hostilities, which were rapidly growing into a feud. Ironically, he did so as a peacemaker. Although no written documentation survives, legend says that Devil Anse persuaded Valentine and the other judges to acquit Sam and Paris in hopes of preventing an escalation of violence. Whether he did so or not, the boys were acquitted by a Hatfield court. Though perplexing to later students of the feud, Anse's efforts at peacekeeping in 1880 were based on good reasons, rooted in his preoccupation with his timber business and its defense in the courts. He already had enough problems.

Whatever the reasons for the acquittal, Old Ranel and his sons were not mollified by the outcome. Their behavior in the next event of the feud—the famous romance between Old Ranel's daughter, Roseanna, and Devil Anse's son, Johnse—reveals their obsessive hatred of Devil Anse. At the same time, the incident demonstrates that the feud was not taken quite so seriously by the McCoy women.

In 1880 Roseanna McCoy was twenty-one years old, just about an appropriate age for marriage in the valley. She was supposed to have been beautiful, but feud legend may have embellished that attribute just as it lowered her age to fifteen or sixteen. Photographs show her as an attractive, somber young woman. The romance that developed between Roseanna and Johnse Hatfield on that election day in August 1880 was not an unusual one. Johnse was a virile, swaggering eighteen-year-old looking for women and adventure. All accounts agree that they were equally attracted to one another, spent the day together, and ended up by going home together—that is, to Devil Anse's household.[32] Although Roseanna must have heard many tirades against Devil Anse from her father and brothers, they did not affect her attraction to Johnse. The attraction may have been enhanced by the fact—which must have been plain to everyone—that Devil Anse's sons were prospering while, in contrast, her own father and brothers possessed little land for either timbering or farming. Several of her brothers, who were all in their twenties, rented their farms or worked as farm laborers; their futures seemed bleak indeed. Johnse's apparently bright prospects matched his dashing good looks and optimism.

Feud legend insists that Devil Anse, out of sheer vindictiveness toward Old Ranel, prevented his son from marrying Roseanna. It is just as possible that his refusal may have been based on Old Ranel's cantankerous reputation. But he did welcome her into his home; this act, coupled with his efforts to cool the feud, suggest that Devil Anse may not have been the one responsible for the nonmarriage. It was probably Johnse's, and perhaps even Roseanna's, choice not to marry. This would not have been unusual in the Tug Valley, where many young men and women met, romanced, even had children without an official wedding. As John Campbell pointed out in his early-twentieth-century study of the mountaineers, "There are not a few men and women in the Highlands living as husband and wife who have never been married by any legal form."[33] They were rarely ostracized or condemned by their neighbors. Gossip aplenty there may have been, but the rigid and judgmental sexual morality of Victorian America had not yet taken hold in Appalachia.

When the two young people parted company six months later, that, too, was not unusual, although Roseanna was then pregnant. We have no way of knowing whether Roseanna or Johnse broke off the relationship; legend has assumed that Johnse made the decision, leaving Roseanna broken-hearted and humiliated. She may have been broken-hearted, but it is highly unlikely that she would have been overwhelmed with humiliation. The census schedules show many cases of young, unmarried women with children living with relatives, most often their parents. It was not a disgrace. Roseanna's own mother, Aunt Sally McCoy, had had a child before she married Ranel in 1849 at the age of twenty. This child, a daughter named Josephine, was thirty-one years old in 1880 and had two illegitimate children of her own. It seems just as plausible that, when Roseanna discovered Johnse's numerous flirtations and affairs with other women, she may have decided to leave him and return to the home of her parents.[34]

Although legend asserts that Johnse and Roseanna were forced apart by the feud and by Devil Anse's refusal to allow their marriage, Johnse's subsequent behavior does not bear out this claim. He had already been flirting, and possibly having sexual relationships, with other women before Roseanna departed. After she left, he still attempted to see her, but he also increased his pursuit of others —particularly Roseanna's cousin, sixteen-year-old Nancy McCoy. Nancy was the daughter of murdered Unionist Harmon McCoy, but apparently neither she nor her four brothers yet perceived the feud as involving them. When Johnse began to court her by asking to carry her books home from school, Nancy was surprised and flattered. His good looks and rakish behavior, to say nothing of his money and family reputation, made him attractive to many of the young women in the neighborhood. Less than six months after Roseanna had left, on 14 May 1881, Johnse and Nancy were married.[35] There is no record or even legendary claim that Devil Anse objected to the marriage, nor did Nancy's mother and brothers— strong evidence that the feud had not been as devisive in the community as legend would have us believe. Ranel, it would appear, was having difficulty persuading anyone other than his own sons and his two nephews to take his vendetta against Devil Anse seriously. In the end, Johnse and Nancy's marriage came to a bitter end, not because of the feud, but because Johnse continued his flirtations and sexual activities in spite of the strong-willed Nancy's attempts to make him into a responsible husband. After seven years she abandoned the effort and, taking their two children, moved back to Pike County.[36]

What made Roseanna's case tragic was not Johnse's infidelity or Devil Anse's behavior, but the treatment she received at the hands of her own father. Some accounts say that Roseanna never returned home, that she knew better. Others, notably Truda McCoy, insist that she did return home for a time, but that Old Ranel either ignored or punished her. What we do know is that before her baby was born, Roseanna went to live with her Aunt Betty in Stringtown. Apparently her mother and brothers were not so unbending as her father, for they visited her frequently. When the baby died young of the measles, Roseanna was put in the position of a spinster aunt, residing in relatives' households when they needed help during a crisis—the illness of a child, for example. Although she returned home to care for her mother in the aftermath of the destruction of the McCoy home on Blackberry Creek, Roseanna never felt welcomed by her father. Just before her death in 1889, Roseanna, according to Truda McCoy, told her mother the reason for her depression. "It was Pa. Ever time Pa looked at me, I couldn't stand the hate in his eyes."[37] Roseanna's emotionally shattering experience was caused by her father's failure to behave with the expected parental solicitude. As John Campbell observed, "if the daughter with an illegitimate child does not marry, she lives, ordinarily, with her parents and her child is brought up as their other grandchildren, seemingly without discrimination."[38] Ranel, like his own father Daniel, apparently cared more about himself and his obsession with complaining and gossiping than about his family. One can readily imagine the neighbors shaking their heads and quietly expressing their sympathy for Roseanna's plight. What were parents for if they would not comfort and protect children in trouble?

Johnse and Roseanna's romance was not a cause of the feud, nor was it especially relevant to later developments.[39] Writers wishing to heighten the drama of the feud and make it appealing to middle-class audiences played up the "star-crossed lovers" aspect. To middle-class America, with its rigid moral values and its obsession with sentimental love and illicit sexuality, the "mountain Romeo and Juliet" story became the single most intriguing part of the feud. What the romance does reveal in a very dramatic way is the greater amount of sexual freedom enjoyed by mountain women as well as the surprisingly tolerant attitudes toward premarital sexual relationships and illegitimacy. Furthermore, for all their undeniable deference to men, the McCoy women—Roseanna, Nancy, Margaret, and Aunt Sally—demonstrated considerable self-esteem, independence, and assertiveness. These qualities are accentuated when contrasted with the insecure defensiveness of Old Ranel and the other men in the family. For an analysis of the feud, however, the most important revelation is the confirmation of Old Ranel's reputation as an annoying nuisance who was incapable of shouldering his responsibilities to family and community.

If, up to this point, there was still some question whether a feud really existed, the election-day fight of 1882 crystallized alliances on each side and escalated the violence to a frightening degree. It forced both Devil Anse and community residents to take the McCoys more seriously as a real threat to the peace of the valley. Still, it was not Old Ranel himself who resorted to violence but three of his sons, Tolbert, Pharmer, and Randolph, Jr. ("Bud"). These were not mere boys, but grown young men. The oldest, twenty-eight-year-old Tolbert, had been married for a year and had not lived at home for at least three years; the 1880 census records him as living with another family and working as a farm laborer. His brothers were nineteen and eighteen and still lived with their father on Blackberry Fork.[40] They were part of a very large family; Ranel and Sally had produced sixteen children—an extraordinary number even by valley standards.[41] Half of these were sons, and it must have been oppressively clear from the beginning that even if Old Ranel had been willing to provide for his children, as his own father had not, the three hundred acres of mountainous woodland inherited from Sally's father would not suffice. It was apparent that Ranel's sons, like so many others in the valley, would have to fend for themselves. The oldest five, James, Floyd, Tolbert, Samuel, and Calvin, had already left home by 1880; two hired out as farm laborers while the others sharecropped on small farms nearby. In a culture where economic survival and social status still depended on the ownership of land, the stigma of hiring out or sharecropping was a greater disgrace than premarital sex or illegitimate birth. Old Ranel's sons had more cause for shame than their sister Roseanna.

Nevertheless, many other young men in the valley found themselves in the same social and economic predicament in the 1880s. What made Ranel's sons different was the added burden of being Ranel's children and Daniel's grandchildren—thus tainted as irresponsible and foolhardy. Moreover, they had endured Ranel's carping most of their lives and, probably for at least ten years (since Devil Anse Hatfield began his lawsuit against Perry Cline), had been constantly regaled with bitter accusations against Devil Anse and his family for stealing, bullying, refusing to pay debts, and caring for nothing but money. Perhaps to young men growing up in such an atmosphere it seemed that their own dismal economic prospects could be attributed to the undeserved success of people such as Devil Anse Hatfield.

Tolbert McCoy, who in 1880 and 1882 took the lead in antagoniz-
ing Devil Anse and his family, exhibited the same foolhardy behavior as his father and grandfather. In the fall of 1880, only a month
after his cousin, Paris McCoy, had been acquitted of murder in Logan County, Tolbert managed to get an appointment as special
deputy in Pike County, enlisted his brother Bud's help, and arrested
Johnse Hatfield for carrying a concealed deadly weapon.[42] This had
to be a trumped-up charge, because most men carried weapons for
hunting, if nothing else. His sister, Roseanna, who had by now left
Johnse, heard of the plan to arrest him and hastened to warn his
father. When Devil Anse rescued his son from Tolbert's custody, he
did so, for someone with his reputation, with remarkable restraint.
Tolbert himself described the incident to the sheriff of Pike County
this way: Anse and his gang "came all together upon them armed
by force and . . . took from them custody of . . . Johnson Hatfield,
released him, and took the . . . McCoys into custody as prisoners,
kept them as prisoners for a long time, cursed and abused them."[43]
In sum, Anse and his followers overwhelmed Tolbert and Bud, took
their guns away, and made insulting remarks; no physical injury
occurred but the psychological humiliation must have been excru-
ciating. Tolbert hurried to the Pike County justice of the peace and
insisted that warrants be issued for the arrest of Anse and all his
men. When, three months later, Elias and Floyd Hatfield were arrested in Pike County as a result of this warrant, community residents became alarmed. This might be pushing Devil Anse too far.
Two of Tolbert's own cousins, Reuben and Sylvester McCoy, came
forward to testify in defense of the Hatfields.[44] No one, even his
own relatives, it seemed, was on Tolbert's side.

Humiliated once again, Tolbert was spoiling for a fight. Even
Truda McCoy, whose book defends the McCoys, characterizes Tol-
bert as "always looking for trouble."[45] When election day rolled
around in August 1882, he was indeed looking for trouble—specifically trouble over money and unpaid debts. Tolbert kept badgering
"Bad Lias" Hatfield to pay off an old debt for a fiddle. "Bad Lias"
was not Anse Hatfield's brother Elias, nor was he a Mates Creek
Hatfield at all. Anse's brother was known in the community as
"Good Lias." "Bad Lias" was a Pike County Hatfield, the brother of
Preacher Anse. This Pike County family of Hatfields was usually
on good terms with all the McCoys; in fact, in the 1889 trials, five

of them testified as McCoy witnesses against Anse and his family. Thus, Tolbert's attempt to pick a fight originated more with his general bad feelings over money matters than in a specific grievance against Anse Hatfield and his crew. This obsession with debts and money indicates the anxiety experienced by the younger generation of the McCoy family. When Bad Lias insisted that he had paid his debt some three years previously, Tolbert threatened violence but was restrained, first by Constable Matthew Hatfield, then by Preacher Anse. As "Squirrel Huntin'" Sam later reminisced, "strife and ambition were high" that day.[46]

As the day wore on, Tolbert returned again and again to badger and threaten Bad Lias. Finally Devil Anse's brother, Ellison Hatfield, intervened; he seemed to think he could stop the fight. His method, however, was to distract Tolbert by shouting "I'm the best god damn man on earth."[47] As might be expected, this did not produce a calming effect on Tolbert; quite the opposite, he suddenly turned on Ellison, his rage heightened by the audacity of Hatfield's interference. Ellison was everything Tolbert was not: a large, physically strong man; a war hero; a respected officer of the law in Logan County; a landholder; and, most important, Devil Anse Hatfield's brother. All the stories drummed into Tolbert by Old Ranel must, at that moment, have congealed into an irrational fury. The Hatfields cheated and lied but they were successful, feared, respected, and admired. Tolbert was going to give them what they deserved. Wildly, blindly, brutally, he stabbed Ellison at least a dozen times. If his brothers had not come to his aid, however, Tolbert might have been killed then and there. Ellison was a big man and physically powerful; even with multiple stab wounds he was able to pick up a large rock and could easily have killed Tolbert had it not been for Pharmer and Bud McCoy. While Bud aided Tolbert with his own knife, Pharmer picked up a gun and shot Ellison, ending the fight but not killing him.[48]

This event sent shock waves through the community. Not only was the level of Tolbert's rage and violence an abnormal one, but everyone recognized that Devil Anse and his family would surely retaliate. However reluctant he had been previously to participate in a feud with the McCoys, this challenge could not be ignored. Those present at that election-day fight scrambled for a solution before Devil Anse, who had not been present, could hear of the fight and rally his forces. Thinking quickly, Preacher Anse Hatfield, as justice of the peace, instructed two Pike County deputies to arrest the three McCoys and take them to the Pikeville jail. There, at least for a while, they would be safe. When Old Ranel and his sons objected that they were themselves "fighters" and had "old axes and things to fight with," Preacher Anse tried to impress them with the seriousness of the situation. He "told them the Hatfields might come with a company of men and kill them."[49] Thus admonished, the boys obediently trudged off for Pikeville with constables Tolbert and Joseph Hatfield. Preacher Anse knew that Devil Anse had in the past shown respect for the letter, at least, of the law. There was reason to hope that he would allow the Pike County Court to handle the matter.

Of Ellison's brothers, only Elias was present at the election-day fight. He immediately took charge of his wounded brother and sent messages to Valentine and Anderson that Ellison was close to death. Since it was then late in the evening, it was not until the next morning that both Anse and Valentine arrived on Blackberry Creek. Anse went to see Ellison and arranged to have him taken back across the Tug to West Virginia, while Valentine and Elias proceeded up Blackberry Creek after the constables and their charges.[50] Apparently the constables had seen no need to rush, for they had stopped the night before for dinner at Floyd McCoy's home and then put up at John Hatfield's for the night. Thus the next morning they were only about a mile down the road toward Pikeville when Valentine overtook the party. What followed was curiously tame considering the stereotypical view of Appalachian violence. Valentine quietly began to argue with the constables about the legalities of the situation. Shouldn't the trial be held in the "district" where the crime had occurred, he asked them. Apparently Valentine appealed to the guards' sense of justice. One of them later testified hearing Valentine say that "he had not slepped [*sic*] any the night before and was tired and worn out and that he wanted them to go down to the south of the creek to have a trial. That he wanted to be near his brother and wanted to get the evidence of Dr. Rutherford and Old Uncle Wall Hatfield."[51]

Nothing illustrates the dilemma of all the participants in this strange drama more than their responses to this difficult situation. The guards and constables had been instructed by such a respected authority figure as Preacher Anderson Hatfield, the justice of the peace, to take the boys to Pikeville jail, but now they were being told by another justice, one just as respected in age and position, to cancel that order and return to the Tug Valley. Not only that, but his argument made good sense. Pikeville was not really a part of their community, and it did seem only fair that the three boys, whom everyone knew were guilty, should stand trial in their own district. They had no reason to assume that such a trial would be biased—the example of Sam and Paris McCoy's acquittal in Logan County was still fresh in their minds. And there had been dozens of witnesses to the attack on Ellison. Consequently, the constables made no resistance and decided to return with Valentine and their prisoners to the Tug River.

Upon reaching the home of Preacher Anse, they met Devil Anse and a group of twenty or thirty of his supporters. By then it was dinnertime and, while most of the crowd milled about outside the house, Preacher Anse invited the McCoy captors, Valentine, Elias, Devil Anse, and several unidentified others to eat dinner. Witnesses in the later trial do not report exactly what was said at the table, but the topic of conversation or argument was the procedure which should be followed from then on. Considering Preacher Anse's earlier position, he must have insisted that the boys should be sent off to Pikeville jail, whereas Valentine continued to insist on keeping them in the valley. Apparently Anse became impatient with the debate, for he stomped out and, assuming a stern, military bearing, he called on all the "Hatfields" to "fall into line."[52] Notice was being given that the debate was over; Devil Anse was signaling his readiness to use force to keep custody of the boys. At that point no one had the nerve to object, so Anse and his crew tied the boys in an old corn-hauling sled for the trip down to the mouth of Blackberry Creek, where they would cross the Tug River into West Virginia.

Confining the boys in the old, abandoned log schoolhouse at the mouth of Mates Creek, Anse waited to see if Ellison, miraculously still alive, would survive his wounds. Late that night the boys' mother, Aunt Sally McCoy, and Tolbert's wife Mary were allowed to see and talk to the prisoners. Aunt Sally, however, spent most of the time begging Anse to spare the boys, to send them back to Kentucky alive. She desperately tried to assure Anse that if only he would release the boys, Randolph would not organize a rescue party.[53] Aunt Sally was convinced that the Hatfields would listen to her tearful pleas, and there are some hints in the testimony that some of the boys' captors—perhaps even Valentine—were persuaded that they should allow the boys to be tried in Pikeville even if Ellison were to die.[54] Anse, however, after initially seeming to sympathize with Aunt Sally, remained steadfastly opposed. If Ellison survived, he said, the boys would be returned to the authorities in Pike County; if Ellison died, the boys would be killed. As they waited for news of Ellison's condition, Valentine used the time to ask questions of witnesses as to whether the youngest brother, Bud, had taken part in stabbing Ellison. Bud was eighteen, rather than sixteen as feud legend would have it, and according to witnesses he had indeed been in the thick of the fight.[55]

News finally came on 9 August, forty-eight hours after the election-day fight, that Ellison Hatfield was dead. What followed is the most famous incident of the feud: Anse and about twenty of his supporters took the boys back to the Kentucky bank of the river. Just a few feet from the river, opposite present-day Matewan, the boys were tied to some pawpaw bushes, blindfolded, asked if they had any final words, and then shot in cold blood. If Anse considered that justice had been done, he and Valentine also recognized the enormity and illegal nature of their actions. Although few in the group could read or write, one—Charlie Carpenter, the schoolteacher—could. He offered to write a group compact in which they all agreed to remain silent and protect each other from prosecution.[56]

Anse Hatfield had finally engaged in violent retribution against the McCoys. Yet he had acted reluctantly. Even so, it was an action that none of Ellison's other brothers seemed willing to take. Smith and Patterson avoided the matter entirely, while Elias and Valentine argued for a less harsh retribution. But Anderson had overcome the most obstacles in establishing his status and social authority. The difficulties he had overcome to achieve his position made him the most defensive of all his brothers—the one Hatfield least likely to let a challenge so serious as the killing of his brother go unpunished.

In those forty-eight hours between the stabbing of Ellison and his death, the community had been in a suspended state of shock. Old

Ranel raced to Pikeville to get official help, but few in the valley dared interfere. Much as Devil Anse may have been resented or hated, Tolbert and his brothers foolishly had tempted fate. Just as the community had uneasily accepted Anse's legal right to the five thousand acres he had won from Perry Cline, it now accepted the retribution that followed the murder of Ellison.

In September, the Pike County Court indicted Anse and twenty others for the murder of the McCoys, but no attempt was made to serve the warrants, extradite the Hatfields from West Virginia, or arrest them.[57] In 1882 Ranel's neighbors urged him to let the matter rest. A crude sort of justice, after all, had been done. To antagonize Devil Anse any further would be to invite violence of frightening proportions. The Tug Valley community was making the best adjustment it knew how to a volatile situation. Of course, in a small area such as the Tug Valley, where everyone knew each other, the collective will was often tacit. In this case, community consensus was that it was best to live with the results of the McCoys' foolish challenge to Devil Anse and to arrange matters so that the feud would not continue. Devil Anse's past reluctance to engage in indiscriminate violence provided some hope that such an outcome was possible. The most difficult problem would be to quiet Old Ranel's shrill demands for retaliation. Actual evidence on this question is scant, but Truda McCoy argues in her book that it was Aunt Sally who pleaded with Old Ranel to refrain from any action.[58] Truda McCoy attributes this to Sally's devout religious nature and her aversion to violence, which may have been true, but it is also highly likely that relatives and neighbors supported her efforts to restrain her husband. Whatever the mechanisms, this restraint proved effective for the next five years, until the feud was resurrected by individuals and forces beyond the control of the Tug Valley community.

Family, Justice, and Violence
in the Tug Valley

· ·

The killing of the three McCoys marked the end of the first phase of the feud. When violence erupted for the second time five years later, it would become the focus of national publicity, spawning the folklore and stereotypes that have been associated with the feud ever since. Because of the notoriety of the feud in its later phase, incidents and behavior from that period are often attributed to the first phase, confusing both narrative and analysis. Truda McCoy's book, based on oral histories collected in the 1920s and 1930s, often makes this error, demonstrating that even the participants' memories could be distorted by the passage of time and colored by the notoriety surrounding the second phase. Before examining the second phase of the feud it is important to analyze just what its initial events reveal about this still traditional, but hardly static, community. What new perspectives have emerged regarding the issues of family loyalty, the role of the judicial system, and violence in traditional Appalachian culture?

FAMILY

Family loyalties consistently have been employed to explain the Hatfield-McCoy feud or, indeed, all feuding; the strength of family ties, according to convention, has prompted Appalachians to ignore the merits of a situation, "rationality," and the proper role of the law in solving conflict. Thus, feuds are assumed to have been per-petuated for generations—to have gone on, in fact, after the partici-pants have forgotten the original cause. Yet this study of the most famous feud in American history challenges that assumption. Al-though Randolph McCoy and a few of his relatives opposed Devil Anse, they could not persuade numerous other McCoys in the Tug Valley to come to their aid. In fact, just the opposite occurred: the majority of McCoys remained neutral, and several of them sided with Devil Anse and his family. Selkirk McCoy voted against Ran-dolph, Nancy McCoy married Johnse Hatfield, and several other McCoy cousins testified against Sam and Paris McCoy. In fact, most McCoys in the Tug Valley seemed averse to exhibiting the vengeful family loyalty we have come to expect of Appalachians.

On the Hatfield side, the same pattern is apparent. When Devil Anse summoned his supporters after the attack on Ellison, only a handful of them (six out of thirty-one) bore the Hatfield name—all were sons or brothers of Devil Anse except for Floyd, a cousin. But an analysis based only on surnames could be misleading—many others with different surnames might be cousins, uncles, nephews, or other relatives. A check of these genealogical connections re-veals that eight more Hatfield partisans were kin, making a total of fourteen relatives among Anse's supporters. Still, this constitutes less than half the group (see Table 2). If family connections really did determine feud loyalties, then surprisingly few of Devil Anse's relatives appear as his supporters. Even such close relatives as his two youngest brothers, Smith and Patterson, all his uncles, and doz-ens of his nephews and cousins were absent from the roster. Not only were many Hatfields neutral, but on occasion they supported the McCoys; Preacher Anse, who testified against his cousin Devil Anse in the later trials, is the most obvious example. U.S. census schedules for 1880 reveal that there were thirty-seven Hatfield households in the Tug Valley which did not contribute a single member to the feud. Apparently, family solidarity is not a sufficient explanation for feud alliances.

Careful study of other Appalachian feuds will, I believe, chal-lenge conventional wisdom that "irrational" family loyalties and grudges produced gratuitous violence. Because early feud publicity stressed that such conflicts were "wars of extermination," between families, other possible causes were never investigated.[1] Occasion-ally contemporaries did raise objections to the blood vendetta for-

TABLE 2

*Kin and Economic Relationship of Hatfield Supporters
to Devil Anse*

Name	Kin Relationship	Economic Relationship
Carpenter, Charlie	none	schoolteacher, Mates Cr.
Chafin, John	brother-in-law	timber crew
Chafin, Moses	''	''
Chafin, Tom	''	business partner
Chambers, Tom	none	timber crew
Christian, Dan	none	timber crew
Christian, Moses	none	bought land from Anse
Elem, Frank	none	farmhand
Ferrell, William	none	timber crew
Hatfield, Cap	son	timber crew
Hatfield, Elias	brother	timber crew
Hatfield, Ellison	brother	timber crew
Hatfield, Floyd	cousin	bought land from Anse
Hatfield, Johnse	son	timber crew
Hatfield, Valentine	brother	business partner
Mayhorn, Dock	nephew-in-law	timber crew
Mayhorn, Plyant	nephew-in-law	timber crew
Mayhorn, Samuel	none	timber crew
McCoy, Albert	none	timber crew
McCoy, Lorenzo Dow	none	timber crew
McCoy, Selkirk	none	timber crew
Messer, Alex	none	timber crew
Mounts, Ellison	cousin	none
Murphy, Joseph	none	business partner
Staton, Bill	none	?
Staton, John	none	?
Steele, Ralph	none	business partner
Varney, Andy	nephew	timber crew
Varney, Lark	nephew	?
Whitt, Dan	none	timber crew
Whitt, Jeff	none	?
Total = 31	Kin = 14 (45%) Not kin = 17 (55%)	Business = 26 (84%) None = 1 (3%) Unknown = 4 (13%)

Sources: Commonwealth of Kentucky v. Valentine Hatfield, KSC; Hatfield, "Genealogy of the Hatfields," in *The Hatfields,* pp. 175–201; John Smith's account book, chancery court case file no. 27, CCCO; deed books (1877–88) and land tax books (1870–88), LCC; U.S. census, population and agricultural schedules for Logan and Pike counties, 1870, 1880, NA.

mula. In 1889 the *Louisville Courier-Journal* printed a letter from a participant in the Howard-Turner feud in Harlan County. Upset by the many news stories claiming that the feud originated before the Civil War and that all the Howards were warring with all the Turners, the informant recounted another version. He claimed that the quarrel's origin was as recent as 1883. Furthermore, there were in the county many different families with the name Howard or Turner; two of the Howard families were involved, but on different sides! It was a rare effort to correct popular misconceptions about Appalachian feuding and suggests the Hatfield-McCoy feud was not unique in its blurring of family alliances.[2] A recent historian has also raised questions about the role of family loyalty in Appalachian violence. Lynwood Montell, in *Killings*, analyzes fifty killings which took place over a half century in one Appalachian community and concludes that the conflicts which produced the killings were not familial but individual; members of the victim's or the assailant's family were almost never drawn into such disputes. Responsibility for revenge or retaliation rested with individuals, not families.[3] Thus, the assumption that family loyalties in Appalachia were excessive and irrational may be entirely unfounded.

But if unquestioning family loyalty did not motivate Devil Anse's supporters, what did? Of the numerous Hatfield kin residing in the valley, what prompted the few that did so to rally to his support? And what factors influenced individuals not closely related to Anse to declare their allegiance? Table 2 attempts to identify the common denominator among Devil Anse's supporters in the feud's initial phase. It confirms the pattern that emerged in Randolph McCoy's attack on Floyd Hatfield in the hog dispute: resentment of Devil Anse's land and timber operations. Although less than half (45 percent) of an identifiable thirty-one supporters were related to Devil Anse, twenty-six—or a striking 84 percent—were tied to or dependent upon him through land purchases or timbering. This economic connection seems to have been a crucial factor in choices made by Hatfield relatives. Smith and Patterson Hatfield, for example, were never connected with Devil Anse's timbering business, and they consistently avoided involvement in the feud as well; brothers Valentine, Ellison, and Elias, who *were* timbering partners, also became deeply entangled in the feud. The pattern established by Hatfield families in the Tug Valley also holds true for those not closely related to Devil Anse. Table 2 shows that fourteen of the seventeen supporters who were unrelated were nevertheless tied economically to Devil Anse. If they had purchased some of the "Cline land" from Anse, they were dependent on the finality of the court litigation over that land, and if they worked on the timber crew, they owed their livelihood to him. Charlie Carpenter, the schoolteacher on Mates Creek—because Anse and his brothers Elias and Ellison had donated the land for the school, forced the district to hire Carpenter, and provided most of the students—must be regarded as economically bonded to Devil Anse as well. Taking into account all of Anse's supporters, related or unrelated, then, it is apparent that the most compelling motive for actively supporting Devil Anse in the feud was economic, not genealogical. This interpretation is underscored by the inclusion of three McCoys—Selkirk and his sons Lorenzo Dow and Albert—in the roster of Hatfield activists. According to John Smith's list of Devil Anse's timber employees, Selkirk and his sons were the *only* McCoys ever employed by Anse; they were also the only McCoys to become actively involved in feud violence on the Hatfield side. (Although several other McCoys testified for the Hatfields in various court proceedings, I have not included them because they were not involved in feud violence.) One must conclude that the feud was not a family feud in the conventional sense of that term; in fact, what was being challenged by the McCoys was a set of competitive economic activities carried out by one particular group of people centered around Devil Anse Hatfield. Yet, despite the evidence that the Hatfield group was defending rational economic interests, not only historians but the feudists themselves repeatedly characterized the conflict as a "family war."

That the challenge to a social and economic threat was couched in terms of family grudges and loyalties is not really surprising. Since the first settlement of the Tug Valley, the primary organizing principle of the community had been the extended family. Mountain ridges defined family groups, agriculture and hunting were family work routines, and social status as well as economic survival depended upon family affiliation. When timbering came into prominence after the Civil War, that too was organized around existing family units. In many traditional societies servants and employees who were dependents of the head of household were also considered family and both sides had reciprocal responsibilities and obligations which far exceeded the exchange of wages for labor. In the same way, Anse's timber "hands" were identified not simply as employees but as *Hatfields*.

The cultural process through which such economic and social networks were conceptualized as "family" helps to explain why historians have been led astray in their understanding of feud dynamics. Taking the participants' convictions about family at face value, historians have diligently attempted to trace family relationships and been repeatedly frustrated—partly by the presence of McCoys on the Hatfield side, and vice versa, and partly by the fact that, in the Tug Valley, almost everyone was at least distantly related. Thus, Floyd Hatfield (of the hog dispute) was married to Old Ranel McCoy's cousin, but Floyd himself was a cousin of Devil Anse. What has become apparent is that in such a case the determining factor for Floyd Hatfield was his economic bonds to Devil Anse. Although conjugal and blood relationships may be traced with ease, more important but less accessible to historians are the social networks so obvious to community residents that they are taken for granted.

The case of Selkirk ("Kirk") McCoy is the best example. Kirk had fewer actual family ties to Devil Anse than most other valley residents. Yet legend persists, passed down from generation to generation, that Kirk was "more a Hatfield than a McCoy!"[4] The most oft-cited reason is that he had married a Hatfield and was influenced by his wife. However, genealogical research proves that Selkirk's wife was completely unrelated to any Hatfields—indeed, she had closer family ties to the McCoys.[5] The fascinating aspect of this misleading oral tradition is the assumption on the part of contemporaries that the feud was indeed a family conflict. Everyone recognized that Kirk McCoy, despite his name, belonged to Devil Anse's network. What was not clear, even at close range, was the economic and social basis of that relationship. But because in the valley's cultural world a loyalty network was defined by the term "family," Kirk McCoy *had* to be a Hatfield; the easiest way to explain or justify his "Hatfieldness" was to remember (erroneously) that he married into the Hatfield family.

Another reason given for Kirk's Hatfield allegiance is his betrayal of the McCoys at the hog trial. He should have voted with the

McCoys, goes the rationale, but because he did not he was from that point on considered a Hatfield. It seems clear that the notoriety of the feud in the national press and its prominence in the thoughts of valley residents during the later second phase created some distortions. According to this analysis, the feud itself created the division between the warring groups rather than reflecting preexisting social conflict, making the feud both cause and consequence and requiring no other explanation than its existence! Both these after-the-fact rationales for Selkirk's behavior have tended to obscure economic and social relationships that shaped both the community and the development of the feud, but they do offer glimpses of a fascinating process in the creation of folk tradition. The fact is that the presence of Kirk McCoy in Anse Hatfield's timbering crew six years before the hog trial and his residence in the heart of Hatfield country near the headwaters of Mates Creek made him "really a Hatfield" long before the hog dispute. This reality, however, did not prevent his neighbors from conceptualizing his actions in the feud as the result of "family" loyalty.

In Appalachia in the late nineteenth century, as in most traditional cultures, "family" was a socially constructed institution only partially based on blood and conjugal ties. Families represent groups of people bound together economically, geographically, and socially. In a community where the majority of people are likely to be related by blood or marriage, family identifications sort out and define the social units. Each family unit is then characterized in some way—"smart," "ambitious," "hell-raisers," and so on. Family members who do not fit are the exceptions that prove the rule. Thus, Selkirk McCoy's Hatfield loyalties only brought into bold relief and confirmed the identification of the "true" McCoys. As Carlene Bryant has shown so conclusively in her study of a modern Appalachian community, *We're All Kin*, actual blood and conjugal relationships cannot accurately describe the way in which families are conceptualized by the community. Residents reported to her that "blood is thicker than water," and that inheritance of family traits determined character and behavior. However, when Bryant compared charts based on genealogical relationships with residents' conceptualization of family history and present family relationships, the two were radically different. Close relatives who, by genealogical standards, should have been part of the family grouping were absent or were identified with another family, while individuals only distantly related or entirely unrelated were unabashedly incorporated into the "family."

Examples of this phenomenon in the Hatfield family are numerous. Frank Ealem, who was employed by Elias Hatfield and lived in his home, was regarded as a "Hatfield," as were Kirk McCoy, French Ellis, Charlie Carpenter, and many more of Anse's supporters. Family units in the Tug community were based partially, if not primarily, on existing social reality rather than on "blood." As Bryant points out, however, mountaineers "thought that these relationships *are* kinship—they are 'natural' similarities and bonds, believed to result from a common biological heritage or to be expressed through marriage."[6] In the end, this social construction of family is what "explains" Tug Valley residents' assumption that someone like Selkirk McCoy *must* have married a Hatfield.

As social, economic, and even political units, these families, like modern-day nations, were vital to individual self-identification. They generated intense loyalties, fueled rivalries among themselves, and were thought to possess a "character" all their own. Today we assume the existence of national traits—the American character versus the French character or the Russian character—but in nineteenth-century Appalachia, Tug Valley residents assigned such traits to families. Like modern nations, the traditional family was a social construction based on geography and ideology—although that ideology tended to be implicit rather than explicit. One contemporary historian of the Big Sandy Valley, for example, described the Hatfields as "noted for physical development and strength, and, while by no means ignoring scholastic learning, depend largely upon common sense to carry them through." The Pike County Hatfields were seen as religious, politically active, and more intellectual than their cousins across the river.[7] And we have seen how Daniel McCoy's family had acquired a reputation for malicious gossip and foolhardiness.

Although hindsight allows historians to perceive the social and economic dimensions of Devil Anse's network, he and his contemporaries experienced the resultant stress in terms of a clash between families. Most students of the feud have uncritically accepted this rhetoric and sought diligently to explain the feud through a family loyalty that appears "irrational" to the modern

sensibility. The same difficulties are met in attempting to understand political conflict in seventeenth- and eighteenth-century
America, which was ordinarily organized around extended family
groups; eighteenth-century Virginia and New York are particularly
acute examples.[8] But the same pattern of family conflict in Appalachia has only served to clinch the stereotype of irrationality. Inevitably, it makes the mountaineers appear somewhat stupid, because
our present-day culture does not sanction war based on family
pride, however much it may approve of war rooted in national pride.
However, just as twentieth-century Americans use nationalistic fer-
vor to both complement and mask economic motives, nineteenth-
century Appalachians were passionate about defending their family
honor, which in the case of the Hatfields and McCoys had an important economic and social component.

Any social conflict in nineteenth-century Appalachia was likely
to be expressed as family conflict, not from a lack of alternative
community institutions, but because families defined the contours
of social, political, even religious organization. However, the economic conflict apparent in the feud is not the "real" conflict only
masked by family loyalty. Rather, the economic conflict operated
through and within families constructed by social necessity. The
two were intertwined in the Tug Valley in a way that twentieth-
century Americans have difficulty comprehending. This same pattern of the integration of family with other institutions is illus-
trated by the mountaineers' approach to the legal system.

LAW AND JUSTICE

As we have seen in Devil Anse's struggle with the courts over his
timbering contract, the new legal ideology had not yet fully penetrated Logan County. Although new concepts of law were beginning
to be adopted by certain segments of the population, during the
feud's first phase the functioning of the courts was still largely determined by a more traditional system of judicial authority, and it
is that system which is so well illuminated by the events of the
feud. The tensions and violence in the Hatfield-McCoy "family"
feud strained "peace and dignity," according to official court records, but not enough to shatter the structure of authority.[9] By now

it must be apparent that mountaineers spent a great deal of time in court settling all kinds of differences—over boundaries, gossip, debt, and divorce, but only occasionally theft or murder. Far from ignoring the legal system, Tug residents appear to have been quick to resort to litigation, sometimes over slights and insults which seem, from a twentieth-century perspective, trivial. This pattern was not unique to Appalachia; it is reminiscent of all colonial America, especially the Puritan towns of New England. In that culture as in the nineteenth-century south, Michael Hindus points out, crimes against "order and morals" were much more common than crimes against property.[10]

This absence of property crime in a largely illiterate culture that was virtually without police, jails, or other forms of coercion indicates the strength of social authority, both formal and informal. The courts were used to mediate disagreements that we would define as private matters. Put another way, it appears that the Tug Valley residents committed fewer crimes than those in modern communities, but they spent more time in court. Their willingness to abide by the decisions of the local judicial system reflected a confidence that the justice meted out would approximate community consensus and parallel the informal authority structure of family and neighborhood. In a community the size of the Tug Valley, everyone could be—and usually was—aware of the circumstances and individuals involved in any case being considered by the county or circuit court. Frequently family members or neighbors were judges, jury members, or witnesses. No one was an objective bystander. In such an atmosphere "blind justice," the ideal of modern impersonal society, was not a real (or desired) possibility—there was too much familiarity. Yet mountaineers respected the letter and spirit of the law as well as a kind of commonsense justice based on familiarity. Although family conflicts were often fought out in court, private blood vendettas were rare. Respect for an abstract, written, legal tradition came from a strong eighteenth-century English heritage, which endured remarkably well in spite of an illiterate oral culture.

The strength of both structures, the formal and the informal, could create a dilemma for the mountaineers when they conflicted with one another. When the written law conflicted with a commonsense notion of fairness, how would the problem be resolved without damage to one or the other system? These conflicts fall into three categories: (1) the absence of objective judges; (2) the indivisibility of specific evidence in a case from its social context; and (3) the question of jurisdiction, which was peculiar to the Tug Valley. Let us take these problems one at a time.

Both Pike and Logan counties were composed of smaller subdivisions, usually called precincts, voting districts, or magisterial districts. The Tug Valley consisted of three districts—Pond Creek, Peter Creek, and Blackberry—on the Kentucky side of the river, and one—Magnolia—on the West Virginia side. During the 1880s parts of Magnolia were made into the Hardee and Lee districts. These areas were quite small: Magnolia had only 158 households in 1880; Hardee was somewhat larger with 393. Pond Creek district had 203 households. The small size of these districts insured that everyone not only knew the local justice but was acquainted with his idiosyncracies and biases. Each justice handled cases in his own district and several times a year might be called upon to sit on the county court in the town of Logan or Pikeville. As noted earlier, during the feud's first phase Preacher Anderson Hatfield was a justice in the Pond Creek district while Valentine Hatfield, older brother of Devil Anse, served as justice in Magnolia. Family connections were taken for granted. Valentine Hatfield, for example, was cousin or uncle or related by marriage to so many Magnolia families that disqualification on the grounds of family relationships would have rendered the whole system inoperable; no one in the district would have been any more impartial. In spite of these connections—or perhaps because of them—district residents expected justice from Valentine Hatfield. And he was in something of a difficult position, because most of his neighbors knew almost as much about his cases as he did.

The results of this kind of situation were apparent in one of the events connected with the feud, the trials of Squirrel Huntin' Sam and his brother Paris for the murder of Bill Staton. When Staton's body was found in the woods, the assumption was that the McCoy nephews had committed the crime. As justice, Valentine Hatfield swore out warrants for their arrest and appointed two special constables to find the suspects. One was his own brother, Elias Hatfield, a good friend of the murdered Staton. No one was surprised by this integration of personal and public interest; it was not only unavoidable but, from the perspective of local residents, desirable in such situations. When the two McCoys were arrested and tried, several prominent McCoys in both Pike and Logan counties testified against the brothers, but they were acquitted nevertheless. Records of the trials did not survive, but there is enough evidence to confirm that the acquittals were granted on the basis of self-defense. Somewhat more speculative is the rumor, repeated in several books on the feud, that Devil Anse influenced his brother to let the boys off in order to avoid escalating the feud.[11]

In either case, however, the results of the trials are surprising from a modern perspective, which assumes that justice could not have been achieved with such a conflict of interest. If Sam and Paris really acted in self-defense, it is surprising that a Hatfield-controlled court allowed it to come out. Why didn't the Hatfields simply lynch the boys, or at least take revenge by convicting them of murder? If Sam and Paris ambushed and murdered Staton in cold blood—as seems possible, considering their threats over a long period—then the Hatfield court was using the legal system to obtain some long-term objective such as reducing the probability of future violence. But the most likely possibility is that the court was well aware of community opinion that both the Staton brothers and the McCoys were equally guilty of threatening, baiting, and inviting trouble. The Hatfield court simply recognized that consensus and attempted to achieve a compromise between the letter of the law and the spirit of fair play. This case illustrates a positive side to mountain justice that is often overlooked in our almost automatic condemnation of the personal nature of justice in traditional communities.

Another dilemma is demonstrated by numerous cases in which the verdicts seem to have been decided well before the trials and the legal form seems nothing but a ritual. In fact, what occurred was a balancing of formalities with commonsense justice. In small communities where people, families, and events were all well known to everyone, no single case could be separated from common knowledge of the participants' reputations, any previous crimes, and the surrounding circumstances. Still, the mountaineers valued the legal process, and they spent a great deal of time making sure that it was followed. Numerous examples of this commitment involved none other than Devil Anse himself, the most oft-cited illustration of a mountaineer who flaunted his contempt for the law. One example, the civil lawsuit between Perry Cline and Devil Anse, has already been examined in detail. Another, not connected with the feud, was Devil Anse's role in an 1870 murder case.

A black man known as "Negro Mose" had been murdered by one Riley Samson—shot through the stomach, according to the grand jury indictment in the April term of the Logan Circuit Court. At the time, Samson was an employee in Devil Anse's timber operation.[12] However, Devil Anse was also serving as a deputy sheriff; in that capacity he arrested Samson and brought him before Justice Evans Ferrell. Samson did not deny shooting Mose, but he claimed that the black man was a Union soldier who had been hiding out in the mountains trying to kill former Confederates, especially Devil Anse Hatfield. Devil Anse's brother, Ellison Hatfield, testified that Mose was "an armed enemy to southern soldiers," and another Magnolia resident claimed Mose "was in arms with the Yankees and was waylaying the roads to kill the rebels as they passed in the county of Logan. . . . I saw him one time come down to the road armed when it was nearly dark." Devil Anse topped off the case with his own testimony. "One Enock Casady informed me," claimed Anse, "that a negro called Mose had offered him, Casady, twenty-five dollars to kill me. I then reported that fact to Col. H. M. Bently, then commanding officer of this section of the state in the Confederate States army and that said negro was also reported to be in arms and Col. Bently ordered him to be killed." Ignoring the fact that the war had been over for five years, Devil Anse confidently stated that "negro Mose was killed in obedience to this military order and that said Riley Samson was a regular soldier" carrying out orders! On the strength of this evidence, Justice Ferrell found Samson not guilty and released him from custody.[13]

Apart from the fascinating testimony that assumes the continuation of the Civil War, this case illustrates the relationship between the community and the law. In a lawless environment the case would never have appeared in the records at all. A black man, said to be armed and out to kill former Confederates, was lurking in the mountains and threatening Logan citizens. Given the prevalent racism and fear of strangers in the mountains, it would not have been surprising if the black man had been shot or hanged with no fanfare or legal niceties. This solution would have informally satisfied the mountaineers' need for "justice," but it would have ignored the formal legal system. Instead, the negro was killed, an indictment issued, an arrest made, and a hearing held. It was not a meaningless charade, but rather a ritual that reaffirmed for the mountaineers the effective functioning of the system. That the law was in many cases bent to conform to public biases may be obvious with hindsight, but we know that such distortions of supposedly impartial laws are common in our own society as well. The important thing is that mountaineers thought of themselves as law abiding, and the court system was respected as essential to the smooth functioning of mountain communities. As long as the law was embedded in the local customs and traditions and reflected community values, Tug residents would go to great lengths to observe the social authority symbolized by the courts. Vigilantism or an extralegal system could only be justified when external forces imposed an authority that seemed to violate local custom. This did happen later in the feud.

Another dilemma caused by the social context impinging on the legal system could arise when community consensus recognized that, although a person was technically guilty, the crime itself was not a serious violation of community norms. Respect for the law required a verdict of guilty in these cases, but judges and juries tended to compensate with extremely light sentences or fines. This appears to have been a frequent situation in assault and battery cases where the defendant was found guilty and fined one cent.[14] Did the juries believe the victims deserved a beating? Were both parties drunk and not responsible? Reasons are never given in the court records, but because it is obvious that "real" cases of assault and battery warranted much higher fines, there must have been some rationale. Again the important point, in the light of the modern image of hillbillies, is the mountaineers' need to observe legal forms.

Devil Anse was involved in a similar case after the feud was over. He had moved his family to Island Creek near the town of Logan and owned property near that of a large mineral and lumbering company, which was owned by timber and coal barons in Philadelphia. Ironically, in a turnabout of the earlier Perry Cline case, this company sued Devil Anse for trespassing and damages; they claimed he had been cutting timber on their land. The jury found

Devil Anse guilty, as he admitted he was, but his punishment consisted of an order to stay off the land in question and a fine of one cent. Apparently, when the jury was forced to choose between a local villain and an alien one they had no trouble choosing sides![15] The judgment honored the letter of the law while at the same time expressing the jury's opinion as to the justice of that law.

The question of law and justice did encounter one problem peculiar to the Tug Valley. The valley was, socially and economically, a coherent community, yet legal jurisdiction was divided between two different states, Kentucky and West Virginia. This unusual setup became a major factor in the later phase of the feud, but it also caused problems in the early stages. Criminal cases involving the arrest and incarceration of the accused had to be taken to the county seat—either Pikeville in Kentucky or Logan Courthouse in West Virginia. Neither Pikeville nor Logan Courthouse was really part of the Tug community, but in the 1870s Logan Courthouse was not a threatening place for the Hatfields; they served in county as well as district positions and felt they were, if not on friendly, then at least on familiar ground. Pikeville was another matter entirely. Few people from the Tug Valley were in positions of influence there, and those that were seemed especially hostile to Devil Anse. One example after 1874, of course, was Perry Cline. Thus, when in 1880 Tolbert McCoy had himself appointed deputy constable and arrested Johnse for carrying a concealed deadly weapon, Devil Anse could not allow his son to be taken to the Pikeville jail. Legal formalities had to be put aside, and that is exactly what Anse did, as gently as possible, only verbally abusing poor Tolbert.

The most serious instance, and the one that led to the shocking violence of the feud's first phase, was the problem of justice in the wake of the 1882 election-day fight. Tolbert McCoy and his brothers stabbed Ellison Hatfield on the Kentucky side of the Tug River. This meant they would be taken by Pike constables to Pikeville jail and tried there. When Valentine Hatfield found out what had occurred, he rushed to the scene, well aware that Tug Valley justice was unlikely in Pikeville. Later, during Valentine's trial, several witnesses testified that Valentine sought to convince the Pike constables that it was "necessary" to hold the trial in the "district" in which the crime was committed. By "district" he did not mean the distinction between the Kentucky or West Virginia side of the river but rather referred to the Tug Valley as a unit. The constables did not resist; they dutifully turned around and started back toward the Tug. Most valley residents would have agreed in principle with Valentine that justice had to be local justice, and that was not available in Pikeville.

Devil Anse was in a difficult position. When his brother died of his wounds, Anse couldn't depend on justice from the Pikeville courts, but the crime had not been committed in Logan County. The legal forms for which he had in the past shown so much respect would now, of necessity, be violated. Nevertheless, from his statements to bystanders it seems that he attempted to justify this breach of legal authority to himself and others. By making retribution contingent upon his brother's life and by questioning witnesses as to the involvement of the McCoy boys, he was holding a rough facsimile of a trial. This procedure was convincing to his neighbors because they knew as well as he that the boys had committed the crime. The final decision to execute the boys on the Kentucky side of the Tug was calculated to protect both Devil Anse and his neighbors from the consequences. If they had been killed in Logan County, some of Anse's West Virginia neighbors might have complained and brought the case to court. But the river was a real boundary, as Anse was aware; he probably realized that he could avoid arrest by Kentucky officials much more easily than by West Virginia ones. He was right: on 14 September 1882 indictments against Devil Anse and twenty others were issued by the Pike County Court, but Pike officials made no attempt to arrest Anse or to start extradition procedures in the state of West Virginia. Recorded on the warrant was the fiction that Anse could not be found. Because of the mountaineers' demonstrated need to settle most matters in court, this inaction in a murder case is strong evidence that even local officials in the McCoys' home district had concluded that the McCoy boys were as much to blame for the feud as the Hatfields. To be sure, the feud had reached unusual heights of lawlessness and violence, but not because of the absence of a legal system or contempt for the law. Quite the contrary, an arbitrary political boundary had prevented the community from resolving the conflict with customary local mechanisms.

Because the Tug Valley was, in spite of the burgeoning timber industry, still very much a precapitalist, premodern society, the system of law reflected the personal nature and values of its culture. Those values centered on honor and shame in a family and community milieu. The legal system was expected to uphold more than equity in money, property, and debt, and more than straightforward preservation of order; it was expected to uphold the good name and reputation of its citizens and to preserve the status quo. This expectation is apparent in the plethora of cases concerned with slander, breach of peace (usually this meant "profane swearing"), and assault and battery. As in the case of Tolbert McCoy versus Hatfield's "gang," which he charged with "confederating" to harass him, many assault and battery charges did not involve serious physical injury, but rather cursing, shoving, and pushing, or otherwise inflicting humiliation. It was for *humiliation* that Tolbert demanded redress from the courts.

With such broad expectations, the law could not be confined to facts or evidence presented in the courtroom. The total picture—that is, common knowledge of family background and individual history and reputation—were crucial ingredients in judicial decisions. Such a system was integral to the structure and values of the community, and it necessarily dealt with private, interfamily as well as intrafamily arguments. To argue that this was a flawed, imperfect system is to argue that the entire culture, with its personal, subjective values, was inferior to our bureaucratic, impersonal ideal. This is exactly what has happened; writers have blamed feud violence on the personal nature and subjectivity of the culture. The assumption which followed was that altering the culture of the mountaineers would prevent feuds and violence. What we have seen in this investigation of the first phase of the feud, however, is that the level of violence was exacerbated by an externally imposed, arbitrary boundary line that prevented the local authority system from legally adjudicating the case. In short, altering and interfering with mountain culture by imposing a political division on a socially cohesive community escalated the feud rather than prevented it.

VIOLENCE

Aside from the cases that made it into the judicial system, what was the extent of fighting and violence in mountain culture? Perusal of county court order books will easily correct the misapprehension that mountaineers ignored the judicial system.[16] These records cannot, however, tell us how much violence there really was. Some court records are spotty or missing altogether; most important, the existing records don't tell us how many instances of assault and battery or homocide were not reported or how many were settled at the district level and therefore never appear in the records. Quantification is impossible in such situations. Yet reminiscences of the Hatfield-McCoy feud make it quite clear that actual murder in the Tug Valley was rare enough so that incidents such as the killings of Bill Staton, Ellison Hatfield, and the McCoy brothers had a shocking impact. The daughter of Joseph Simpkins, a business partner of Devil Anse, put it this way: "My family didn't know they were living in a land where such things occurred; in fact, it was unusual to hear of such things."[17] In 1889 and 1890 Logan's first newspaper reported only two murders. Most court time was spent on cases involving the carrying of concealed weapons or the illegal sale of liquor.[18] One participant in the feud, Mose Chafin, later told a grandson that Devil Anse's younger brother Smith was "ashamed" of "some of the Hatfields," insisting "he wasn't raised that way."[19] Apparently, the limited violence Devil Anse engaged in was unacceptable to some of his own family.

This is not to argue that the mountaineers in the period before industrialization were paragons of peace and restraint. Far from it: their culture was raw, boisterous, and rowdy. Young men especially bragged, swaggered, and regaled listeners with tall tales of their hunting and shooting feats. Drinking, swearing, and fisticuffs abounded, especially on festive occasions such as court and election days. This was attested to by the number of occasions on which young people—men and women—were brought into court and charged with disturbing religious worship, breach of the peace (profane swearing or threatening to injure someone), or "slander." This type of personal crime, as opposed to property crime such as theft, was rooted both in the eighteenth-century Virginia heritage of most of these Tug Valley residents and in the nature of a personal, face-to-face culture. It is remarkable that in such a boister-ous milieu there was so little real, physical damage. As historian Elliot Gorn points out, despite chronic fighting "most backcountry-men went to the grave with their faces intact, just as most of the southern gentry never fought a duel."[20] Thus, the brutal stabbing of Ellison Hatfield on election day in 1882 was not the normal out-come of a brawl but a shocking act of violence.

Still, it seems that brawling and gunfighting *were* becoming more common in the 1880s. The number of young men who earned ap-pellations such as "dangerous" or "bad"—men who drank too much and too often and terrorized their neighbors with threats and guns—was perceived as a problem. This trend was dramatized by the two families that concern us here. Randolph McCoy's sons were much more ready to insist on proving their worth with force than was their father. Randolph himself may have complained and threatened, but he ultimately shunned actual violence. Anderson Hatfield, too, as the feud's second phase more clearly demonstrates, was much more apt to consider violent action as a last resort, whereas his sons, particularly Cap, readily turned to violence.

If there is an explanation for the generational increase in violence it may be found partly in historical development and in the circum-stances peculiar to each generation in the Tug Valley. The Hatfields and McCoys exemplify the pattern. Devil Anse's and Randolph's children were the third generation of the families who settled the valley. The first generation had come in the 1820s and 1830s and had not been dependent on family for land. Grants from the state and county courts were plentiful and cheap. Both Ephraim Hatfield and Daniel McCoy had preempted valuable lands throughout the 1840s and 1850s. For their children—the second generation—things were not so easy. Randolph McCoy and Anderson Hatfield had to depend on their fathers' acquisitions. Because Daniel lost all his land in a lawsuit, his children did not benefit; they were less fortu-nate than most second-generation sons such as Ephraim's—Valen-tine, Ellison, Elias, Smith, and Patterson. (Anse, as we have seen, was an exception.) Although they could acquire adequate land from their fathers, they could never equal the fathers' economic status. But another avenue was open to them. This was the generation that had the opportunity to earn its status by fighting Yankees in the Civil War. Anse and his brothers, Ellison and Elias, and Randolph

McCoy all took part in an event that enshrined them as heroes in their community. Unfortunately, their sons had neither the economic opportunity of their grandfathers nor the heroic opportunity of their fathers.

The frustrations of the third generation did not become apparent until the 1870s and 1880s when they came of age—the age when they should have become independent landowners in their community. In 1882 Tolbert McCoy was twenty-eight and his seven brothers ranged from thirty-two to eighteen, while their cousins, Sam and Paris McCoy, were twenty and twenty-five. None owned as much as a single acre of land.[21] The family of Harmon McCoy provides another dramatic example of the problems facing this younger generation. Harmon, as we have seen, rose above poverty when he married Patty Cline and inherited land from her father. He and Patty had six children, four of whom were sons, before Harmon was killed during the war. The daughters married well-to-do men— Johnse Hatfield and William Daniels—but the sons had to divide their father's inheritance. They were still property holders, but each owned only a small fraction of their father's moderate acreage. All the sons earned reputations as "bad" or "dangerous" men—the kind to be avoided by the neighbors—*well before* they became involved in the feud.[22] All these young men fit Elliot Gorn's description of young men who had "few material resources and less social power," and who chose to prove their worth to themselves and to each other by fighting.[23]

This generational pattern may also help to explain the response of Devil Anse and his timbering "family" to the challenge of the McCoys. The young men on the timber crew were in the same predicament as Devil Anse's own sons before his acquisition of the Grapevine lands; they had little prospect of owning land or raising their status in the community. This situation was all the more frustrating because, as Table 3 shows, these young men were not used to poverty or to being on the lowest rung of the social ladder. Tracing the parents and grandparents of Hatfield's supporters back to 1850 reveals that most were well off compared to the general population.[24] In 1850, when about 30 percent of all families in Logan County were landless, only 20 percent of the families of future Hatfield feudists owned no land. By 1870, however, when the percentage of landless families for Logan as a whole had risen to over 50 percent, the Hatfield families had narrowed the gap, with 41 percent owning no land. While for the county as a whole the percentage of landless households had risen by only two-thirds between 1850 and 1870, the percentage of Hatfield families without land had doubled. This means that the Hatfield group was being pushed into poverty at a faster rate than the general population of the county. Therefore, Devil Anse's acquisition of land and his timbering business came as welcome opportunities to relatives and neighbors facing a future with a lower standard of living than their parents. Between 1870 and 1888, Devil Anse's acquisition of the Cline land made his group, once again, materially better off than most Logan County families. Nine of Hatfield's supporters, including Floyd Hatfield and Uncle Jim Vance, were purchasers of Grapevine lands.[25] During the 1880s, when the number of landless households for the county as a whole remained static at 45 percent, the figure for the Hatfields shrank to only 23 percent, reflecting the dissemination of the Grapevine land among Anse's supporters.

Astonishingly, Devil Anse had managed to return his supporters to the slightly privileged positions their families had held a generation before. This accomplishment is all the more impressive when one considers that Hatfield families consistently produced more children than the county norm. The average household size in the county remained at approximately 6 from 1850 through 1880, whereas the Hatfield families' household size ranged from 7.0 to 8.1, always larger than most neighboring households by 1.5 to 2.0 persons. In this context, the economic gains of Hatfield supporters are even more impressive.[26]

The willingness of Anse's "boys" to support and defend their leader no matter what was asked of them is understandable in the light of what they owed him. The McCoys' attack on Ellison Hatfield, in such a context, must have seemed like an attack on all of them. When Anse invoked his military heroic image and demanded that all *Hatfields* "fall into line," he was appealing to their sense of manhood and honor—attributes rooted in land ownership and social status. More than twenty—with names as varied as McCoy, Messer, Mayhorn, and Whitt—complied.[27] The moment resonated with pride, courage, honor, and loyalty, but it also revealed a desperate attempt to preserve the gains Devil Anse had won for them. That desperation fueled the physically active nature of their culture and accelerated it toward the unusual degree of violence apparent in the feud.

The Feud as Community Conflict

TABLE 3

Families without Land:
Comparison of Hatfield Feudists to Logan County

	Families of Hatfield Feudists	Logan County Households
1850	20%	30%
1860	42	35–47[a]
1870	41	52[b]
1880	23[c]	45[d]
1890	18	n.a.
1900	n.a.	75 (Mingo Co.)[e]

Sources: U.S. census, population and agricultural schedules for Logan County, 1850–80, and population schedules for Mingo County, 1900, NA; land tax books, 1880–88, LCC.

[a]Computation from the 1860 population schedule results in a figure of 47 percent. The 1860 agricultural schedule, which seems more carefully done and is, I believe, more accurate, produces the figure of 35 percent.

[b]The Tug Valley districts of Logan County (Magnolia and Hardee) yield a figure of 47 percent. I have used the figure for all of Logan County because in 1870 several families of Hatfield supporters lived in Logan district, although by 1880 they had moved to the Tug Valley.

[c]This figure reflects tax list data through 1888, in addition to the population and agricultural schedules for 1880.

[d]The Tug Valley districts of Logan County yield a figure of 43 percent. I have used the entire county figure simply for the sake of consistency.

[e]Mingo County was created from Logan County in 1895. It encompasses the Tug Valley district of Logan County. The sharp rise of landless households in 1900 reflects the transition of mountaineers from farmers to wage laborers in the coal industry. In 1900 the number of landless households in Logan County was 62 percent.

CONCLUSION

Although the Hatfields and McCoys were, in this early phase of the feud, a small proportion of the Tug community, they were playing out community-wide sentiments.[28] The same scenario was taking place in many southern Appalachian communities, if one is to take the appearance of numerous feuds all over the region as an indication. Because we know that similar economic conditions, the decline of traditional or "slash and burn" agriculture, and the beginnings of the timber trade were being repeated in community after community, the rash of complicated "family feuds" at the same time can hardly be coincidental. Indeed, the Hatfield-McCoy feud has often been used as an example of a different kind of feud, one *not* involving merchants, markets, and politics. Whereas most other feuds occurred in towns, the reasoning goes, the Hatfields and McCoys fought in the most rugged, remote terrain, untouched by economic competition or ambition. Theirs has been regarded as a "pure" feud, the one which most clearly emerged from America's frontier past.[29]

Close examination has revealed the fallacies in this conception. Even in the early phase of the feud, one of the participants—Anderson Hatfield—was an incipient entrepreneur; despite his illiteracy, he was a shrewd, ambitious, aggressive, protocapitalist who counted on contracts, lawyers, and courts to protect his interests. As such he inevitably violated community expectations of cooperation and conformity, although in Devil Anse's case the issue was blurred because he had already earned a reputation in the war as aggressive and formidable. Still, population growth and a scarcity of tillable land, coupled with opportunities in timber cutting, created the role and Anse eagerly stepped in. If he had not, there were many others in the community ready to do so; one was Randolph McCoy's father, Daniel McCoy, who lost his farm in an unsuccessful attempt at timbering. Devil Anse's personality and war experiences simply gave him an edge.

Community response to the changing economy was ambivalent. Attracted by the opportunity to shore up a sagging standard of living, yet disturbed by the necessity of competing with neighbors, most valley residents attempted to have it both ways. They tentatively put a foot into the timber business by hiring out part time on a timber crew or by attempting to cut timber on their own land. At the same time they shrank from the complexity and dangers of contracts and legal agreements; Devil Anse's experience with merchants shows that their fears were well grounded. The result was a widespread acquaintance with the timber business accompanied by wariness—the attitude expressed by Margaret McCoy when she accused her husband of "going into what is generally termed the timber business." Although the neighbors may have been envious of Devil Anse and jealous of his profits, another response was disapproval and fear. He was living proof that success in the market economy resulted in taking advantage of one's neighbors. It meant, in a way, that one had "sold out" to the devil, deserting the company of God's people, who relied on cooperation. Jealousy, admiration, and fear merged into the silent hostility so well expressed in the sobriquet by which the community knew Anderson Hatfield— "Devil."

Mostly the resentment was passive, but it was there, waiting to be expressed by someone with an incorrigible, cantankerous temperament. This role, in the Tug Valley, was tailor made for Old Ranel McCoy. But, as in the case of Devil Anse, much more than temperament was involved. In a community of large families and a declining land supply, Old Ranel's family was in an extremely precarious position. Because of an advantageous marriage Old Ranel possessed enough land to place him among the respectable in the community, yet respectability was tenuous for his eight sons. This was even more true for Ranel's ardent supporters, his nephews Sam and Paris McCoy, whose prospects were considerably bleaker than those of his own sons. The future for all these young McCoy men was a choice between getting into the ever more competitive timber business, out-migration, or a lifetime as hired laborers or sharecroppers. None of these alternatives were likely to produce a placid mental state or tranquil social relations. The anxiety produced by this conflict tipped a naturally boisterous culture to malicious violence. If Old Ranel's family had not been around to express antagonism to Devil Anse, others would certainly have done so. However, the combination of Old Ranel's temperament with his particularly vulnerable economic and social position made his family the vehicle of resistance rather than Devil Anse's more obvious enemies. In expressing the resentment of the community toward Devil Anse, Old Ranel was also expressing its suspicion of the market values gradually penetrating the valley's isolation.

The social conflict that made up the first phase of the feud was due neither to an inherently violent culture nor to conscious or unconscious reaction to industrialization. Rather, it emerged from the unfolding of a set of social, economic, and cultural factors present from the settlement period of the valley. These factors consisted of a limited supply of tillable land, a high birth rate, and strong family values that deterred out-migration and defined status in terms of family reputation. These internal factors were complicated by external influences such as the new opportunities created by the demand for timber and the intervention of federal and state authorities in hunting, fishing, and whiskey production. In attempting to deal with all these circumstances, the mountaineers adopted a variety of solutions. Anse Hatfield aggressively seized the new economic opportunities; Perry Cline migrated to the nearest town, became a professional, and joined the modernizers; and the McCoys lapsed into anger and resentment. But these personal choices did not solve the problem; rather, they exacerbated competition and hostility. Yet in spite of all these individual efforts, the economic trajectory of the valley was still downward. Unless something changed—massive out-migration or industrialization, for example—Tug Valley residents faced an increasingly bleak future.

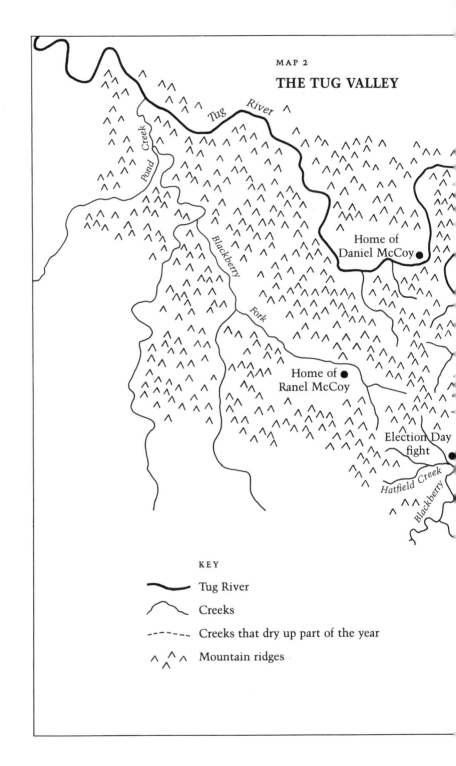

MAP 2

THE TUG VALLEY

Tug River

Pond Creek

Blackberry Fork

Home of Daniel McCoy ●

Home of ● Ranel McCoy

Election Day fight ●

Hatfield Creek

Blackberry

KEY

———— Tug River

⌒⌒ Creeks

------- Creeks that dry up part of the year

∧ ∧ ∧ Mountain ridges

N

Mates
Creek
First home of
Anse Hatfield

McCoy
boys
killed
School-
house

Thacker Creek

Beech Creek

Grapevine Creek

Devil
Anse's
second
home

Val
Hatfield
home

Peter Creek

Home of
Asa Harmon
McCoy

Two Worlds in Conflict
A Pictorial Essay

The World of the Tug Valley
Traditional Appalachia

Before the building of the railroad in 1889, the Tug Valley home of
the Hatfields and McCoys was rural and isolated. Virtually the
entire population of the valley subsisted by farming and perhaps
engaging in some rudimentary extractive pursuit such as logging
or gathering ginseng. No towns existed, and even the county seats
(Logan Courthouse for Logan County and Pikeville for Pike
County) were located beyond the mountain ridges which
surrounded and defined the valley. These photographs and
drawings portray the people, the activities, and the physical
environment of the Tug Valley in the years immediately preceding
industrialization.

1.
William Anderson
Hatfield, known as
Devil Anse. Of the
many photographs of
Devil Anse, this one
was probably taken
closest to the time of
the feud. (*Courtesy
West Virginia and Re-
gional History Collec-
tion, West Virginia Uni-
versity Library*)

2, 3.
Two likenesses of Ran-
dolph McCoy. Figure 2
is a drawing super-
imposed on the only
known photograph of
the feudist. Figure 3 is a
sketch done by a news-
paper artist when Ran-
dolph McCoy escorted
the nine Hatfield pris-
oners to Louisville to
appear in federal court.
The sketch appeared on
the front page of the pa-
per on 17 February
1888.

2.
(*Courtesy Leonard McCoy*)

3.
(*Courtesy* Louisville Courier-Journal)

4.
Old Ranel and Aunt
Sally McCoy, 1890. The
only known likeness of
Sarah McCoy, this
sketch appeared in the
*Louisville Courier-Jour-
nal* on 18 February
1890. (*Courtesy* Louis-
ville Courier-Journal)

5.
Valentine "Uncle Wall"
Hatfield. This drawing
appeared in the *Louis-
ville Courier-Journal* on
17 February 1888. Val-
entine was the older
brother of Devil Anse
Hatfield, a justice of the
peace in Logan County,
and a partner in Devil
Anse's timber business.
Unlike the other Hat-
field feudists, he volun-
tarily surrendered to
Frank Phillips. He was
subsequently tried and
convicted of the murder
of the three McCoy
sons and sentenced to
life imprisonment. He
died in the Kentucky
state penitentiary six
months later. (*Courtesy*
Louisville Courier-
Journal)

6.
Roseanna McCoy, date unknown. Although this photograph must have been taken when she lived in Pikeville, long after her role in the feud, it still reveals Roseanna's rural mountain background, especially when it is compared with the self-conscious posturing of Rebecca Scott Cline and Pauline Bowles (see figs. 28, 29). (*Courtesy West Virginia Department of Culture and History, Charleston*)

7.
Ellison Hatfield in his
Civil War uniform.
Devil Anse's brother
Ellison, a war hero, oc-
casionally served as an
officer of the law. When
he tried to stop a fight
on election day in Au-
gust 1882, he was at-
tacked by Tolbert,
Pharmer, and Randall
McCoy and stabbed
more than two dozen
times. When Ellison
died of his wounds two
days later, Devil Anse
and twenty supporters
executed the three
McCoys. (*Courtesy
West Virginia Depart-
ment of Culture and
History, Charleston*)

8.
Selkirk McCoy. This
drawing appeared in the
*Louisville Courier-Jour-
nal* on 17 February
1888. Sketches of all
the nine Hatfield sup-
porters were on the
front page of the paper
as they arrived in Louis-
ville for habeas corpus
hearings in federal
court. Selkirk McCoy
had been the first
"Hatfield" captured by
Frank Phillips in De-
cember 1887. Two of
Selkirk's sons were also
among the "Hatfield"
prisoners. (*Courtesy*
Louisville Courier-
Journal)

9.
Asa Harmon "Bud" Mc-
Coy, aged about thirty.
The son of Old Ranel's
brother Asa Harmon,
who fought on the
Union side in the Civil
War, Bud was born
about 1862 and, al-
though not involved in
the first phase of the
feud, he was wounded
in the "battle" of
Grapevine Creek. All of
his brothers and sisters
were involved in the
feud's second phase.
(*Courtesy West Virginia
Department of Culture
and History, Charleston*)

10.
Asa Harmon and Rhoda
McCoy on their wed-
ding day, 17 September
1907. This Asa Harmon
was the grandson of the
Unionist Asa Harmon.
Although taken a con-
siderable time after the
events of the feud, this
photograph demon-
strates that there were
still significant differ-
ences between Tug Val-
ley farmers and the Lo-
gan and Pikeville elite.
Compare the facial ex-
pressions and clothing
of the McCoys to those
of John R. Dils, Jr., J.
Lee Ferguson, Rebecca
Scott Cline, and Pauline
Cecil Bowles (figs. 25,
27, 28, 29). (*Courtesy
West Virginia Depart-
ment of Culture and
History, Charleston*)

11.
Evermont Ward, circuit
judge in Logan County,
West Virginia, in the
1870s. Ward was typical
of the local judiciary in
the years just before the
restructuring of the
county court system in
1881. He had no formal
education but was
easily accessible to
county residents and re-
spected for his fairness.
After 1881, circuit
judges usually did not
reside in Logan County
and were set apart from
rural mountaineers by
their wealth and educa-
tion. (*Courtesy Robert
Y. Spence, Logan, W.Va.*)

12.
Log house similar to
many Tug Valley dwell-
ings in the nineteenth
century. This photo-
graph was published in
the West Virginia *Wil-
liamson Daily News* on
2 August 1982 and
identified as the home
of Devil Anse Hatfield
on Beech Creek in Lo-
gan County. When I
purchased this copy in a
photo store in Pikeville,
Kentucky, it was identi-
fied as the James Madi-
son Thornbury home.
Whichever it actually
was, the house is very
much like the one
Devil Anse would have
inhabited. (*Courtesy
Paul B. Mays, Pikeville,
Ky.*)

13.
Pushboat on the Big
Sandy River, ca. 1900.
The Tug River is a fork
of the Big Sandy and
this scene would have
been a common one on
the Tug in the 1880s
and 1890s. The river
was too shallow and
rocky for larger vessels
such as steamboats, so
transportation, until the
coming of the railroad,
was confined to push-
boats such as this.
*(Courtesy Photographic
Archives, Alice Lloyd
College, Pippa Passes,
Ky.)*

14.
Heck White's mill, Lo-
gan County, West Vir-
ginia. A typical sawmill
for Logan County in the
1890s, it is probably
much like the one
Devil Anse hoped to
build when he peti-
tioned the county court
in 1880. *(Courtesy Rob-
ert Y. Spence, Logan,
W.Va.)*

15.
Uncle Dyke Garrett as
a young man, ca. 1870.
Dyke Garrett preached
in Logan County and
the Tug Valley for sixty
years; he was the most
widely known and
loved preacher in the
region. Although for
most of his life Devil
Anse was not religious,
he and Uncle Dyke
were good friends. In
1911, at the age of sev-
enty-three, Devil Anse
consented to be bap-
tized by the preacher.
Uncle Dyke considered
it the triumph of his
life to have finally per-
suaded Devil Anse to
accept Christ. He was
still talking about it
just before he died in
the 1930s. (*Courtesy
Robert Y. Spence, Lo-
gan, W.Va.*)

16.
Claypool Church on
Huff's Creek, Logan
County, West Virginia.
This log church, built
in 1886, is probably
much like the one at-
tended by Devil Anse's
brother Ellison on Pond
Creek. (*Courtesy Robert
Y. Spence, Logan, W.Va.*)

17.
Typical logging scene in
southern West Virginia.
The size of this pile of
logs in relation to the
creek and the two men
on top convey some
feeling for the impact
such operations had on
the people and the envi-
ronment. (*Courtesy
West Virginia Depart-
ment of Culture and
History, Charleston*)

18, 19.
Neither of these logging crews are the Hatfields, but both scenes convey a sense of southern Appalachian logging operations in the late nineteenth century.
(*Courtesy West Virginia Department of Culture and History, Charleston*)

The World of Pikeville and Logan Courthouse
Victorian Appalachia

Not all of Appalachia was rural and isolated from the economic, social, and cultural influences of capitalism. Mountaineers who resided in the small but urbanized towns early saw their fortunes as bound to economic development and middle-class Victorian values. These photographs and drawings of town dwellers and their environment reflect their desire and economic ability to differentiate themselves from their rural neighbors and identify with middle-class America.

20.
Logan Courthouse, ca. 1890. Although a formidable mountain ridge separated it from the Tug Valley, Logan Courthouse was the nearest town and the county seat—the place Tug Valley families like the Hatfields went to transact legal affairs. The courthouse from which the town derived its name is in the center of the picture. (*Courtesy Robert Y. Spence, Logan, W.Va.*)

21.
The Logan County
courthouse, 1870–1904.
This was the court-
house that Devil Anse
knew so well—the place
where he exerted so
much power in the
1870s and so little in
the 1880s. Here his
brother Valentine sat on
the county court and
even, on occasion,
served as its president.
(*Courtesy Robert Y.*
Spence, Logan, W.Va.)

22.
Buskirk-Hinchman
house, ca. 1890. This
was the type of house
built by the new com-
mercial elite in the
town of Logan in the
1880s and 1890s. Emu-
lating the Victorian
middle class in other
parts of the country, the
owners of this house
had moved a consider-
able cultural distance
from Appalachians who
still inhabited the log
houses that were still
typical of the Tug Val-
ley (see fig. 12). (*Cour-*
tesy Robert Y. Spence,
Logan, W.Va.)

23.
Pikeville, Kentucky, ca.
1908. Pikeville was the
largest town and county
seat of Pike County.
Mountain ridges sepa-
rated it from the Tug
Valley as they separated
Logan Courthouse on
the West Virginia side
of the river. Randolph
McCoy and his family
came to live in Pike-
ville after the destruc-
tion of their home on
Blackberry Creek on
New Year's Day 1888,
and here the Hatfield
supporters were tried in
September 1889. The
courthouse where the
trials were held is at the
left edge of the picture.
(*Courtesy Paul B. Mays,*
Pikeville, Ky.)

24.
Andy Hatcher riverboat,
1894. This riverboat
plied the Levisa Fork of
the Big Sandy all the
way to Pikeville, which
was the end of the line.
From the time of the
Civil War, riverboat
traffic linked Pikeville
with the rest of the
country and made it a
different kind of place
than the Tug Valley.
(*Courtesy Henry P.
Scalf Collection, Photo-
graphic Archives, Alice
Lloyd College, Pippa
Passes, Ky.*)

25.
Colonel John R. Dils,
Jr., 1887. This sketch
was published in Wil-
liam Ely's book, accom-
panying the "Autobiog-
raphy of Col. Dils."
Next to O. C. Bowles,
Dils may have been
the wealthiest resident
of Pike County. Dils

had been a prominent
Unionist during the
Civil War and was later
the legal guardian of
both Perry Cline and
Frank Phillips. Just as
in Logan County Devil
Anse Hatfield headed
the Confederate back-
ers, so Dils was re-
nowned in Pike County

for his leadership in the
Union cause. Although
Dils was not actively
involved in the feud
violence of the 1880s, it
is likely that he pro-
vided strong political
support for Cline and
Phillips. (*From Ely*, Big
Sandy Valley)

26.
Residence of Col. John R. Dils, Jr., 1887. This house demonstrates that at least some residents of Pikeville aspired to a wealth and opulence unknown in the more remote regions of the Tug Valley. Contrast this with the log house (fig. 12) typical of the Tug Valley. (*From Ely*, Big Sandy Valley)

27.
J. Lee Ferguson. This sketch of Perry Cline's friend and ally was published in 1887, before the feud attained its subsequent notoriety. At the very time this sketch was being published, Ferguson was accompanying Cline to Frankfort to persuade the new governor of Kentucky to revive prosecution of the Hatfields. Ferguson was a member of the new commercial elite who supported Cline's vendetta against Devil Anse Hatfield. (*From Ely*, Big Sandy Valley)

28.
Rebecca Scott Cline, ca. 1890. Rebecca was Perry Cline's sister-in-law and named one of her sons after him. This portrait demonstrates the Pikeville elite's emulation of the Victorian middle class in their quest for upward mobility. The dress, furnishings, and hairstyle all present a striking contrast to Tug Valley women such as Roseanna McCoy and Levicy Hatfield. (*Courtesy Paul B. Mays, Pikeville, Ky.*)

29.
Pauline Cecil Bowles (1839–1905). The wife of O. C. Bowles of Pikeville, Kentucky, Mrs. Bowles, like Rebecca Scott Cline, demonstrates the middle-class social standing of the Pikeville commercial elite. Her husband was a well-known politician and merchant; he owned several of the riverboats that linked Pikeville to the outside world. He also lobbied the Kentucky legislature to invest in the economic development of the region. (*Courtesy Pike County Historical Society, Pikeville, Ky.*)

The Conflict and Its Consequences

The Hatfield-McCoy feud was one manifestation of the emerging conflict between traditional Appalachians and their town-dwelling neighbors. This conflict had two unfortunate consequences; the first was the actual bloodshed of the feud itself and the grim scene in 1890 as one of the feudists was hanged in the last such public ritual in Pike County. The second was the feud publicity's contribution to the enduring hillbilly stereotype that has played no small role in the subsequent justification of the economic and cultural exploitation of Appalachia. This series of illustrations focuses on the feud's aftermath.

30.
Mineral buyers in the 1880s. Sometimes the men in the carriages offered to buy the land outright, or sometimes simply the timber and mineral rights. The buyers could be outsiders representing eastern coal and railroad companies, or they could be local merchants—like John C. Mayo in Pike County and J. A. Nighbert in Logan County—who hoped to obtain the land cheaply before local farmers became aware of the potential value of their land. County deed books show that such buyouts began soon after 1880. Although many of his neighbors sold out early, Devil Anse resisted until the feud forced him to move away from the Tug Valley. He began selling his Grapevine Creek lands in 1888, ten days after the battle of Grapevine Creek. (*Courtesy Photographic Archives, Alice Lloyd College, Pippa Passes, Ky.*)

31.
"Bad" Frank Phillips. A friend of Perry Cline, Phillips was chosen to act for the state of Kentucky when prosecution of the Hatfields was revived in 1887. Phillips and his posses captured the nine Hatfield supporters who were later tried in Pikeville. Although Phillips assumed the role of a disruptive bully, he was actually one of the wealthiest men in Pike County. At the height of the feud, he and Nancy McCoy Hatfield, Johnse's wife, began living together. They were married in 1895. *(Courtesy West Virginia Department of Culture and History, Charleston)*

32.
The jail in Pikeville, Kentucky, where the nine Hatfield prisoners were held from the time of their capture in January 1888 until their trials in September 1889. This sketch was published in the *Louisville Courier-Journal* on 18 February 1890. For a time, Perry Cline was the deputy jailor of Pike County. (*Courtesy Louisville Courier-Journal*)

33.
Ellison Mounts, 1890.
Ellison, reputedly the illegitimate son of Ellison Hatfield, was said to be somewhat "slow" or "dimwitted." He was persuaded to accompany Cap and Johnse and other Hatfield supporters when they burned the McCoy home on New Year's Day 1888. Although Sarah McCoy insisted that Cap Hatfield shot her daughter Alifair, it was Ellison Mounts who was convicted of that crime. He was the only Hatfield prisoner to be hanged. The others all received life sentences. (*Courtesy Paul B. Mays, Pikeville, Ky.*)

34.
The hanging of Ellison
Mounts, 18 February
1890. No one had been
hanged in Pike County
in forty years and no
one would be ever
again. Thousands of
people came to witness
the hanging. It is not
known which, if any, of
the figures on the gal-
lows is Ellison Mounts.
(*Courtesy Paul B. Mays,
Pikeville, Ky.*)

35.
Devil Anse Hatfield,
probably ca. 1910

36.
Devil Anse's funeral,
1921

37.
Dedication of statue
marking Devil Anse's
grave, ca. 1925

These three photo-
graphs show that in
later life Devil Anse
came to identify with
the wealthier, urban
segment of Logan
County society. His
new image is exempli-
fied in the gentlemanly
portrait, the frame
house typical of town
dwellers, and the Italian
marble statue which he
and his family thought
appropriate in an other-
wise unadorned and re-
mote cemetery. (*Cour-
tesy West Virginia
Department of Culture
and History, Charleston*)

38.
An eastern Kentucky
coal town in the 1930s.
This easily could be
Grapevine Creek or any
place in the Tug Valley
after the railroad began
shipping coal in the
1890s. (*Courtesy Photo-
graphic Archives, Alice
Lloyd College, Pippa
Passes, Ky.*)

39.
Sid Hatfield, the folk
hero of Tug Valley min-
ers during the coal
mine wars of 1920–21.
Sid was defending his
class (the miners), not
his family, showing how
much things had
changed since the feud
thirty years before.
(*Courtesy Robert Y.*
Spence, Logan, W.Va.)

All these drawings were published in 1889 in T. C. Crawford's book. The artist had accompanied Crawford on his travels through Logan County. Although the sketches were done from life, they reflect the stereotyped perceptions of the northeastern middle class toward Appalachians, and they contributed heavily to the creation of the Hatfield-McCoy legend. (*From Crawford*, An American Vendetta)

44.
Cap Hatfield

42.
Roseanna's Midnight
Ride to Save Her Lover

40.
Devil Anse

41.
Mountain Girl

43.
Execution of the
Three M'Coy Boys

47.
"Who and What Are
You, Stranger?"

45.
The Shooting of
Jeff McCoy

46.
The House-Burning
Tragedy

48.
Home of Elias Hatfield

49.
"Devil Ance's
Family Circle"

These two photographs were taken in 1897, some eight years after the feud was over. The Hatfields were already legendary, and an itinerant photographer requested that they brandish their guns for two contrived pictures which, through the years, became the most famous images of the Hatfield feudists. They undoubtedly contributed enormously to the feud mythology already begun by authors such as T. C. Crawford. (*Courtesy West Virginia Department of Culture and History, Charleston*)

50.
The family of Devil Anse Hatfield, 1897. *Standing (left to right):* Rosada or Rose Lee, daughter; Detroit (Troy); Betty Hatfield Caldwell, daughter; Elias Hatfield; Tom Chafin, nephew; Joe Hatfield; Ock Damron, a hired hand; Shephard Hatfield, son of Cap (he died the next year); Coleman, son of Cap; Levicy Emma, daughter of Cap; Bill Borden, store clerk. *Middle row, seated (left to right):* Mary Hensley-Simpkins-Howe, daughter of Devil Anse, with her child Vici Simpkins; Devil Anse Hatfield; Levicy Hatfield, wife of Devil Anse; Nancy Elizabeth, wife of Cap, with her child Robert Elliot on lap; Louise, daughter of Cap; Cap Hatfield, holding long rifle. *Front, seated on ground (left to right):* Tennyson (Tennis), son of Devil Anse; Vicy, daughter of Johnse Hatfield; Willis, son of Devil Anse; and Yellow Watch, their coon dog.

51.
Back row, standing (left to right): Ock Damron, a hired hand; Elias Hatfield; Detroit or "Troy" Hatfield; Joe Hatfield; Cap Hatfield; Bill Borden, a friend who arranged for the picture. *Front, sitting (left to right)*: Tennis Hatfield; Devil Anse Hatfield; Willis Hat-field. *In background*: Levicy Hatfield, wife of Devil Anse (*sitting*) and Mary, daughter of Devil Anse (*standing*).

PART TWO
The Politics of Feuding

Interim, 1882–1888

. . . .

The brutal stabbing of his brother by Ranel McCoy's sons in 1882 brought home to Devil Anse in dramatic fashion the hostility toward him in the community. He must already have recognized that his political and economic gains of the 1870s were beginning to erode; creditors and rivals in the timber business were becoming bolder and more insistent in bringing suits to court. More menacing, however, were changes in the government and political power structure of Logan County. Fundamental jurisdictional changes in the judicial system and county government, mandated at the state level, altered the political dynamics of local government and reduced Devil Anse's political influence.

These political alterations were combined with a new economic orientation. Although the full impact of industrialization would not be felt in Logan County until the latter half of the 1890s, in the 1880s the groundwork was being laid. Local merchants and large landholders found that eastern corporations were interested in developing timber and coal resources by building a railroad through the region; agents of such companies appeared on the scene early in the decade. Recognizing the potential for profit, local boosters welcomed these outsiders and acted as promoters of economic modernization, often at the expense of their own neighbors. The resulting conflict between subsistence farmers, as well as small-scale independent entrepreneurs like Devil Anse, and the local allies of distant corporations defined the political conflicts of the decade. The exploitation of the mountains, then, was not a simple struggle between outsiders and natives but a complex set of struggles at the local level over control of Appalachia's vast resources. Parallel developments on the state level that led to the virtual colonization of West Virginia have been carefully traced by historian John A. Williams.[1] Of greater concern here are the changing patterns of political economy in Logan County and their impact on Devil Anse Hatfield and, ultimately, the feud.

Before 1870, even though Devil Anse was admired as a war hero, his political activity was limited by the state laws disenfranchising former Confederates. Although these restrictions were circumvented in many cases, political participation had been effectively dampened.[2] This could explain why election and county court records are extremely spotty for the period. In 1870, however, ratification of an amendment to the constitution removed these restrictions and once again allowed former Confederates to exercise voting privileges. The passage of this amendment—known as the Flick Amendment—accompanied the return to power on the state level of Democrats—southern sympathizers who had opposed secession from Virginia during the Civil War. The rapidity with which former secessionists regained power after the war demonstrates the weakness of the Republican minority that had engineered the creation of West Virginia. Most of the Republican founders resided around Wheeling in the northern, most industrialized region of the state, and they had hoped that an alliance with the North would foster industrialization.[3] To further this identification with the North, the Republican founders adopted a constitution with a governmental structure modeled on that of New England, making boards of supervisors and townships the local governmental unit, instead of counties. Despite initial success, however, their control was always shaky, particularly in central and southern West Virginia. Logan County, for example, simply ignored state government and refused to send delegates to the statehood and constitutional conventions. Always tenuous, Republican hegemony collapsed completely in 1872 when the Democrats won passage of a new constitution that rejected the township structure and returned to the traditional southern county court system. Although these state-level politics were not yet relevant to Logan Countians, Democratic control heralded an era when Logan politicians would not be further harassed for their Confederate loyalties.[4]

The period from 1870 to 1881 was a kind of heyday for Devil

Anse and his supporters. Officially allowed to vote and participate in politics, as they had not been before 1870, they were as yet unchallenged by the external forces that later shaped the political and economic life of the county. Devil Anse became a powerful local entrepreneur with political clout that most community residents did not care to challenge directly. Anse himself served as deputy sheriff, his brothers were constables and judges, and several of his closest allies and friends, such as Dr. Elliot Rutherford, were influential county officials.

The diminution of Anse's influence in Logan County began in 1881, just a year and a half before the election-day stabbing of Ellison. In February of that year the West Virginia legislature restructured the entire county court system. As noted earlier, the county court had been a comprehensive and autonomous institution, combining three functions—judicial, legislative, and administrative. The structure was responsive to local needs and the justices, or commissioners as they were called after the constitution of 1872, were drawn from all geographic districts and social classes. The president of the court was elected by county voters every four years. When tax levies were discussed, a majority of the justices for the entire county (seven in Logan) were required to be present.[5] Court records indicate that Valentine Hatfield, who was elected a justice of the peace in Magnolia district for almost fifteen consecutive years, frequently served on the county court, on occasion even as president. Because the county court was the center of political, economic, and social decision making for the community, and because court days brought people together from all over the region, judges were at the very heart of the social and economic structure. They were not only adjudicators but town officials with power to lay out roads, levy taxes, probate wills, and license ministers and taverns. Thus the court, representing the assembled elder statesmen of the county, was much more than an official body—it was a symbol of the total community integration experienced by county residents.

The new structure mandated in 1881 by the legislature brought about nearly revolutionary changes in the local political structure.[6] Judicial powers were removed from the county court and thus from the web of kinship and personal relations. Justices of the peace still heard minor cases at the district level, but the next level of appeal above the justices was no longer the county court but the circuit court. Circuit courts were not new, but they had previously been closely bound to the county court system. For example, the last circuit court judge before the reorganization went into effect was Evermont Ward, who had been born in Logan and was a county court justice as well as the circuit judge. Judge Ward was held in great esteem by the citizens of Logan County even though he had been born out of wedlock and "never attended a day of school."[7] Because circuit courts in the new system were presided over by a single justice who was elected from a judicial district containing several counties (the 9th Judicial District, which encompassed Logan, contained nine counties), there was only a small chance that the circuit judge would be a resident of Logan County.[8] Indeed, the first two circuit judges under the modified system were both from Huntington—a city built by Collis P. Huntington, the financier, as a terminus for his railroad.[9] The changes meant a significant loss of autonomy and of the community sense that most decisions were being made at the local level. More than autonomy was at stake, however; urban judges were likely to have little sensitivity to issues concerning rural mountaineers. Unlike district justices of the peace, the new circuit judges were usually educated, professional lawyers sympathetic to the values of the urban middle class. An example is T. H. Harvey, who became circuit judge in 1888. Notorious as a "law and order" judge, Harvey began, declared the *Logan Banner*, "to mete out justice with a vigor lacking in the past." The newspaper especially applauded his intention to stamp out boisterous, rowdy behavior, whiskey drinking, and sabbath breaking—activities not necessarily considered criminal in mountaineer culture.[10] Harvey was also a land speculator with investments in Logan economic development that tended to influence his decisions in favor of speculators and developers.[11] Judicial decisions reflected not only the economic interests of outside developers, but their cultural preferences as well.

The county court, though without its judicial function, still existed in a stripped-down version as a legislative and fiscal body. It continued to make important economic policy decisions about such matters as roads, taxes, education, and poor relief, but the decisions were now made by three officials, called commissioners, who were elected from the pool of local justices. In Logan County this change brought a very different group to power. Previous court

justices had been primarily farmers of widely varying economic resources, sprinkled through all six judicial districts of the county.
Most, like Valentine Hatfield, were economic and social equals of
their neighbors. They had virtually no education in the law and not
much interest in events beyond the district and county level. Their
chief virtues were their availability to district residents when legal
matters arose and their intimate knowledge of all the families in
the district. Although district justices were accorded a measure of
deference, they did not constitute a distinct power structure.[12]
The three commissioners elected in 1881 represented the coming
to power of a local political elite—an elite separated from the majority of farmers by residence patterns, wealth, education, and cosmopolitan outlook. None of the group elected in 1881—R. D. Bal-
lard, M. B. Lawson, and J. A. Nighbert—had served on the court
before. They and the others who followed them in the 1880s did
own farms, but they were primarily merchants, lawyers, and land
speculators and thus represented a powerful, but minority, commercial class.[13]

The tone of the new county court was set by its first president,
James Andrew Nighbert. Of German origin, Nighbert had come to
Logan Courthouse in 1844 at the age of twelve. Both Nighbert and
his father were merchants and soon allied themselves with the
Lawsons, who were, in the early years of the settlement, the largest
landholders in the Tug Valley.[14] By 1858, when James was twenty-
six years old, Dun and Bradstreet reported that the young man was
"well sustained by a heavy capitalist [Lawson]; his father is well off;
he is the only child," and his business was "good and reliable."[15]
During the Civil War he served as a major in the First Virginia
Confederate Regiment until the creation of West Virginia, at which
time he was elected to the new state's legislature.[16] At the end of
the war he returned to Logan, resumed his mercantile business, and
actively promoted economic development. In the mid-1870s, Dun
and Bradstreet reported that his "is a strong firm and they stand
high in every respect."[17] By the 1880s Nighbert had become the
largest individual landowner in the county.[18]

Soon after coming to power, Nighbert and his fellow commissioners demonstrated their intention to dignify the court and its proceedings. Funds were authorized to spruce up the courthouse and
surrounding square, and the clerk began referring to the officers of

the court as "gentlemen commissioners."[19] These tangible signs of differentiation between the commissioners and the general population indicated the desire of this new elite to end what many observers have denigrated as a rustic, crude, and haphazard atmosphere surrounding court days. The actual effect was to increase social polarization. This new breed of local politicians, set apart economically and socially from the surrounding farmers, perceived themselves as purveyors of social and economic progress to "backward" Logan.

The differences between the Tug Valley region of the county and the Guyandotte Valley where Logan Courthouse was located had always existed, but now they became acute. Where political power had been reasonably equally distributed, now the Logan area became a commercial as well as a political center. Even members of the court whose homes were in the Tug Valley, such as M. B. Lawson, represented mercantile interests rather than farming. Lawson was a land speculator and the son of George Lawson, a merchant on Mates Creek and one of Devil Anse's creditors. Unlike Valentine Hatfield, his predecessor on the court, Lawson was likely to feel more rapport with Logan merchants like Nighbert than with the farmers of his own district. Because power was now vested in the hands of the commercial elite, the Tug Valley slipped from the orbit of political power.[20]

Although some members of this new elite—Nighbert and Lawson, for example—were anxious to lend money to and profit from local timbering operations such as Devil Anse's, they were really interested in bigger things. They hoped to attract investment by eastern timber, railroad, and coal capitalists. By representing corporate interests, these local leaders hoped Logan's economic development would put them at the top of the local social and economic structure.[21] This shift from a local to a national economic focus only became realistic in the 1880s when the plans of outside industrialists began to coincide with the hopes of local developers. With such development a real possibility, the Logan elite intensified the effort to consolidate its leadership; monopoly over the county court made it easier to institute policies that would attract outside investors.

Logan's economic modernization was further advanced by H. C. Ragland. Ragland, a business partner and close friend of Nighbert's, promoted Logan's development by starting its first newspaper, the *Logan Banner*, in 1889. A relative newcomer, Ragland had arrived in the county in 1874 and began his career as a lawyer. During the eighties he became a leading politician, serving in the West Virginia House of Delegates and operating a real-estate business that invested extensively in property with timber and coal potential. Together, Nighbert and Ragland were at the head of a clique of Logan promoters whose economic activities and cooperation with outside investors were designed to bring profit to themselves as well as development to Logan. Their political activities served to bring about favorable conditions for development at the local and state level.[22] The newspaper, of course, was intended to convince investors that Logan was a progressive town, but it also aimed at persuading uninterested or resistant local farmers that railroads, large-scale timbering, and coal mining would be beneficial to *all* the residents of the county, not just outside investors and the local elite.

Although the newspaper did not begin publication until 1889, it provides insight into the perspective Ragland and Nighbert brought to Logan County throughout the 1880s. In a typical editorial, for example, Ragland fervently advocated a railroad for the progress it could bring to the region. "Ere we can realize it we will hear the snort of the Iron Horse, and see wealth and prosperity staring us in the face."[23] Statements like this one were intended to counteract the opposition of rural farmers to public aid for the railroads. Ragland was obviously upset when, in 1889, the voters of neighboring Cabell County defeated a proposal that would have authorized the county to subscribe to railroad stock. Fearing that Logan Countians would also resist subsidization, he stridently insisted that such opposition was shortsighted.[24] Ragland consistently advocated cooperation with investors from outside the region. When their agents were in town buying timber and coal lands or pursuing court cases against recalcitrant local farmers, Ragland and the *Banner* gave them a warm welcome and proudly reported just how much profit these outsiders were making.[25] Benefits, he insisted, would accrue to everyone. "There is no occasion," declared the *Banner*, "for any man in the county to be idle, who wants to work for good wages."[26] It did not seem to occur to Ragland that, for the local farmers, losing the independence of land ownership and self-sufficiency was a threat both to economic survival and self-esteem. But his position reflected the attitudes of many politicians at the state level as well. John Williams has traced the links between Ragland and the influential state politician, Johnson N. Camden. Camden allied himself with eastern railroad and coal interests and was instrumental both in bringing about the industrial development of West Virginia and in altering the state political system so that it became subservient to those capitalist entrepreneurs.[27] In this way remote Logan County was beginning to feel the impact not only of industrialization but also of the growing partnership on the state and national level between business and politics.

The effect of this alteration in the political system on Devil Anse's commercial activities was quickly apparent. Along with the erosion of his family's power in the court, Devil Anse also lost influence over the single most important office in the county—that of the sheriff. During the 1870s a succession of his close friends, Elliot Rutherford, Harrison Blair, and G. W. Taylor, had occupied that office.[28] All were not only friends but associates in the timber operation who, because they were educated, could provide essential help in making contracts, deeds, and law briefs. They also lived in the southern tier of the county near the Mates Creek Hatfields, insuring that their sympathies lay with the residents of the Tug Valley. With their help Anse had successfully pursued his lawsuits against Perry Cline, Moses Mounts, and John Smith. In 1879, however, a new Logan County sheriff was elected, one who had no connections with Devil Anse. Charles MacDonald was from a family that belonged to the new order in the town of Logan.[29] His election barred Anse completely from influence with the most important political office in Logan County. However, the election of MacDonald was only the capstone; Anse's difficulties had begun when one of his friends and business partners, former sheriff G. W. Taylor, abandoned him and joined the new elite.

G. W. Taylor is a mysterious figure in both the community and the feud. Census records indicate that he grew up in Pike County and first went into business near the mouth of Pond Creek; Dun and Bradstreet records identify the business as a general store. From 1867 to 1873, remarks of the Dun and Bradstreet informant were tediously negative: "Not worth anything."[30] One longer evaluation concluded that "his store is not prompt—he has to be sued to collect and we regard him as doubtful." When his business failed, Taylor moved across the Tug River into Logan County and by 1874 was elected sheriff, probably with the help of Devil Anse Hatfield.[31] Yet in 1872, when Hatfield began his suit against Perry Cline for trespass, he named G. W. Taylor as one of the defendants. One must suspect that Taylor was cleverly playing both ends against the middle. Considering his history, it is likely that Taylor had dishonest intentions from the beginning, first influencing the twenty-three-year-old Cline to cut timber on Anse Hatfield's land, then encouraging Anse to file suit against Cline. Soon Taylor was assisting with the timbering along Grapevine Creek and, in his role as sheriff, discouraging court cases against Devil Anse.[32]

By 1878 this collaboration ended dramatically. Taylor emerged in his true colors. Representing the Singer Manufacturing Company of New Jersey, which at that time was the only outside corporation running a timber operation in the region, Taylor filed suits against not only Devil Anse, but many Logan County residents.[33] He had joined the local elite who hoped to prosper by representing outside corporations. Taylor appears to have used Devil Anse's influence when it furthered his career but turned against him as soon as it was obvious that the real power would soon be in the hands of companies like Singer. Taylor filed a debt suit against Devil Anse in Logan County Court and won. But apparently he could not collect from Anse, and in 1881 he appealed once again to the court, this time obtaining an order for Anse to pay the judgment. Devil Anse responded by filing an explanation as to why he hadn't complied and petitioning for an injunction against the order.

Devil Anse's official "answer" in the case of *Taylor* v. *Hatfield* reveals a maze of complicated relations between the two men, but the essential point was that the two had a number of private financial arrangements and understandings, some of which were verbal and contradicted written contracts. What is clear in all this is that G. W. Taylor, like John Smith in the earlier case, had been careful to put in writing those agreements beneficial to himself while making verbally those agreements beneficial to Devil Anse. When the case came to court, Anse was faced with the difficult task of convincing the court that the verbal agreements did indeed exist. In his long explanation Devil Anse expressed his "great surprise" at the turn of events and pled that he would suffer "irreparable danger and loss" if

Taylor were allowed to practice this "fraud." Despite the fact that the agreements were merely verbal, Anse argued, "it would be inequitable and unjust" for Taylor to get way with abrogating them.[34] This case was heard in 1881, however. The county court had just been reorganized and could not adjudicate such cases. The new circuit court judge used a technicality to deny Anse's petition for an injunction and ordered that he pay Taylor. From this time on, Devil Anse never won a case in circuit court; the court's official judgment lien docket index shows that, between 1881 and 1900, nineteen cases were brought against Devil Anse. He lost all of them.[35]

Anse also clashed with the commissioners of the new county court. In August 1880 he applied to the county court for permission to "erect a dam across the Tug Fork of Sandy River," in order to build a "water grist and saw mill."[36] In accordance with normal procedure, a team of commissioners was appointed to study the matter and prepare the equivalent of a modern environmental impact statement concerning flooding, crop destruction, and effects on neighboring farmlands. The justices demonstrated their positive attitude toward Anse's proposal when they chose Samuel Simpkins, William Ferrell, Elliot Rutherford, Joseph Murphy, and Uriah McCoy as commissioners; all were Anse's close friends and associates.[37] But when the committee was ready to report in October 1880 the county court was undergoing reorganization. When the new county commissioners came to power, they summarily "dismissed" the petition.[38]

In yet another set of actions beginning in 1882, the commissioners threatened the very title to land owned by Anse's brothers Elias and Valentine. The Mates Creek and Beech Creek land owned by the Hatfield brothers had originally been surveyed and purchased before the Civil War. The Hatfields had been living on and farming these lands since then. The 1872–73 session of the legislature passed a statute known as the School Land Law, which was designed to make it possible for the state to reclaim lands that had been granted as early as the 1780s, but on which no improvements had been made nor any taxes paid. The law was aimed at the large speculative grants made early in the nineteenth century, but it also affected small landholders like the Hatfields who had neglected to pay taxes or to record their deeds.[39] At that point, in the mid-1870s, the Hatfields were secure in their position in the county; their land was not in reality being threatened. They simply repurchased it for a small charge and assumed that the title had been cleared.[40]

Around 1882, however, another School Land Law was passed by the legislature, offering the commissioners a second chance to reclaim lands for the state.[41] This time Valentine and Elias Hatfield (along with Elliot Rutherford and others) seriously were threatened with the possibility of losing their land. The School Lands commissioner claimed that in the 1875 public auction Valentine and Elias had not paid a sufficient price for the land and that the sale had never been confirmed by the county court. In a clearly hostile action, the commissioners were attempting to take away, on a technicality, lands that had been in the Hatfield family for two generations. One suspects that the commissioners were being so zealous in their duty to the state because they were aware that the prospect of economic development would raise the value of the land. If the state claimed the land as forfeit, it could easily be bought by speculators such as Nighbert and Ragland for profitable resale later.[42] Both the challenged Hatfields managed to keep their land by hiring lawyers, fighting the maneuver in court, and finally paying the difference between what they had paid in 1875 and the amount the court thought the land was worth.[43] Devil Anse and his family were hanging onto their lands and their timber business but they must have felt increasingly disturbed about the obstacles placed in their path. Clearly nervous because he had not officially recorded his deed to the five thousand acres of "Cline land," thus making it vulnerable to forfeiture, Devil Anse finally did so in August 1882.[44]

Thus, the stabbing of Ellison Hatfield on 7 August 1882 occurred just at a point when Anse was becoming most fully aware that his economic gains and political power were severely threatened. The erosion of influence may help explain why Anse and his brothers were no longer confident of obtaining a fair hearing in the legal machinery of either Pike or Logan County. They felt assaulted from every side.

Devil Anse's timber business, too, suffered from his inability to get a fair hearing in the circuit court. An unbiased decision had been difficult enough to obtain in the 1870s when he sued John Smith for payment for his timber, but by the mid-1880s it had become impossible. An example is Anse's case against a business partner, Ralph Steele. This case, like the Smith case, was rooted in

Anse's apparently naive trust in his partners, compounded by his own illiteracy. In early 1883 Anse had formed a timbering partnership with three men, one of whom was Ralph Steele. After the timber had been cut and hauled to the river, Steele was designated to act as the firm's agent to market twenty-one rafts in Catlettsburg, Kentucky. Steele sold the rafts for a total of $5,200, but when he returned home he reported to his three partners that the rafts had brought only a total of $3,700. He pocketed the balance. Anse said later that he was "confiding in the honesty of . . . [Steele] and believing that his representations were true." It was not until 1886 that Anse "ascertained . . . the true amount for which the timber sold."[45] Just after the bill of complaint was filed, however, Ralph Steele died; apparently Anse realized his chances in circuit court were nil, because he dropped the case. He never recovered the $1,500.[46]

By 1886, then, Anse, his family, and his business were feeling the impact of the alteration in Logan's political economy. With the new elite in power in Logan Courthouse, Anse, like most other residents of the Tug valley region, no longer had recognition, status, or influence in county affairs. Equally frustrating was the difficulty in mustering any support for resistance to the new order. Most of Anse's neighbors in the southern tier of the county (the part that would become Mingo County in 1895) were not yet acutely affected by the fact that the new commissioners were merchants, lived in the northern tier, and were interested in attracting lumber and coal corporations to the region. They were farmers who only rarely had legal business other than the filing of a family land transaction in Logan Courthouse. If Devil Anse hoped to stem the growing power of the new elite, he would have to do it himself. Finally he did just that, resorting to a show of force.

In 1886 there was an election in Logan town to choose a representative to the state senate. One of the candidates was John B. Floyd, the son of a former Confederate general whom Anse greatly admired. Floyd had grown up on Marrowbone Creek in the Magnolia district where Devil Anse lived, and apparently the two had become friends.[47] The other candidate was S. S. Altizer, a Logan merchant closely associated with the Nighbert-Ragland group. He was vociferously supported by circuit clerk William Stratton's son Dave, who it seems had been unofficially charged with organizing support for Altizer. In a story related by an undisclosed source to novelist John Spivak nearly forty years later, when election day arrived Anse rode into Logan with "a hundred horsemen," sufficiently intimidating enough voters that Floyd won the election. Stratton, according to this story, was furious, telling Anse to "go to Hell!"[48]

Although the tale may be suspect because of some known errors of detail, its general thrust does have the ring of truth. Devil Anse's pattern seems to have been one of attempting to observe legal, peaceful procedures as long as they matched, even partially, his sense of justice and fair play. After that, as demonstrated by the execution of the McCoy boys, Devil Anse was not averse to the use of force. It is unlikely, however, that he could have mustered a hundred men to threaten voters in Logan; Devil Anse, mounted and in the company of ten or twelve men would probably have been sufficient. Another indication of the story's accuracy is that immediately following this event Dave Stratton became an active supporter of Perry Cline and the McCoys in the feud.[49] As we shall see, he was to play an important role in the battle of Grapevine Creek.

In contrast to his economic and political dominance in Logan County during the 1870s, in the 1880s Devil Anse was struggling to preserve some semblance of influence in the county power structure. From an offensive he had been forced into a defensive position. Unfortunately for Devil Anse, this pattern was replicated in the economic arena. The timber industry in which he had taken the initiative and made such striking gains was on the brink of spectacular growth and prosperity, but it was a prosperity that would elude local producers. In the 1880s small-scale family operations like Devil Anse's made money because there was little competition from large companies and outside capital. During the decade, however, these companies sent in agents and began to buy up land and timber rights in Logan, Pike, and surrounding counties. By the early 1890s timber companies such as the Yellow Poplar and Little Kanawha, owned by capitalists in New York, Boston, and Philadelphia, hired loggers and went into full operation, edging out the local producers.[50] Aware that the Norfolk and Western Railroad was about to build an extension through either the Tug or the Guyandotte Valley, these companies knew that timbering would soon become a highly profitable investment.

What the arrival of the railroad meant to Logan County went far beyond timber, of course. For years people had been aware of the rich coal resources in the region; the impediment to development of the coal industry on a large scale had been the lack of transportation out of the mountains. With the coming of the railroad, not only could the timber industry expand, but coal mines suddenly appeared like mushrooms after a night's rain. As Ronald Eller points out in his study of Appalachian economic history, the railroad, coal, and timber industries were closely intertwined; agents for railroad companies often purchased timber and mineral rights to the land along with the railroad right-of-way.[51] As early as 1873 several railroad companies had been formed to explore the possibilities of laying tracks through the region. By the early 1880s, the Big Sandy Railroad Company was actually negotiating for a right-of-way. Although this particular company was not successful, it was obviously only a matter of time before a railroad was built.[52] In 1883 John Dickinson Sergeant, representing New York and Philadelphia capitalists, appeared in Logan and began buying land and timber and mineral rights. Sergeant bought thousands of acres from farmers in the Tug Valley, but not from Anse, who was still determined to operate his business independently.[53]

This same pattern—that of transforming land into a capitalist monopoly *before* the actual onslaught of industrialization—has been explored for several eastern Kentucky counties by Alan Banks. "The monopolization of land and resources," writes Banks, "was weakening the material basis upon which the farmers and independent commodity producers operated and was simultaneously strengthening the inflow of outside capital." It is clear that considerably before mountaineers actually became wage laborers building railroads or mining coal, they were losing the already small amounts of land available to them for farming and hunting. This land shrinkage, coupled with the rapidly increasing population, contributed to the problem of a "rootless" and troublesome class.[54]

Unfortunately, Anse's competition was not limited to outside corporations. That would have been formidable enough, but local competition presented a more immediate threat. Members of the new political elite in Logan Courthouse, many of whom were already Anse's enemies, were quick to take advantage of rising land values. They hoped to buy land or mineral rights cheaply, before farmers in remote districts discovered the potential value of the land. They could then sell to outside capitalists at a profit. In this manner local speculators, who often could obtain deeds when outside agents could not because their neighbors trusted them, became an important mechanism for the economic colonization of West Virginia and eastern Kentucky. Pike County's John Mayo, who grew up in neighboring Floyd County, went away to college, and later returned to buy up thousands of acres of land for resale to capitalists, is the most famous example of this phenomenon.[55] In Logan County, several families played similar roles in the economic transformation. In his history of Logan County, written in 1927, G. W. Swain identifies those families as the Altizers, the Nighberts, and the MacDonalds, all of whom, as we have seen, were powerful opponents of Devil Anse in the political arena.[56]

J. A. Nighbert was particularly active. In addition to buying up lands from the school lands commissioner, he also was an official representative for Cole and Crane, one of the first big lumber companies to operate in the region.[57] Nighbert, in fact, became so important in Logan's political power structure as well as its economic development that when he died in 1898 his friend H. C. Ragland proposed changing the name of Logan Courthouse to "Nighbert."[58] Apparently, many residents were not so enthusiastic about Nighbert's activities, because the proposed change was defeated.[59] This is not surprising, perhaps, when one recognizes that Nighbert and his political cronies, with all the advantages of large landholdings, education, and commercial connections, were using their influential positions in county government to increase their own wealth while opposing small operations like Devil Anse's. As we have seen, it became more and more difficult for Anse to keep from being cheated by business partners or merchants when he could not count on redress from the county court. For Devil Anse, the disadvantages of illiteracy, lack of capital,and local opposition were finally beginning to outweigh his sheer energy, aggressiveness, and determination.

Ironically, Devil Anse's greatest problems surfaced when it became obvious that the railroad was likely to be routed right through the Tug Valley and across his Grapevine lands. In 1886 F. J. Kimball, president of the Norfolk and Western, decided that his company would build an "Ohio Extension," to connect Virginia with the Ohio River. This commitment came after the failure of other, smaller companies to construct the essential link. This decision meant that land values in the whole region would rise, particularly in either of the two most likely routes—the Guyandotte Valley, where Logan Courthouse was located, or the Tug Valley.[60] Excitement and speculation ran rampant in 1887–88 among Logan developers such as Ragland and Nighbert. It was during this period that Ragland and Nighbert began making plans to publish the *Logan Banner*.[61] The uncertainty finally came to an end when the company made its final decision in February 1889.[62] That the chosen route was along the Tug River was a blow to Logan Courthouse boosters. Ragland and Nighbert had hoped, of course, that the route would lie through the Guyandotte Valley and the town of Logan. But they had not been idly waiting for the final decision; the Logan elite, since the first announcement in 1886, had been scrambling to purchase land in *both* valleys. It was not long before these tactics paid off; in 1889, Ragland reported in the *Banner* that "several large firms from Pennsylvania, Kentucky and Virginia are buying all the lands that can be had and are paying a good price."[63] That same year Ragland, in what may have been an attempt to keep Tug farmers from realizing the potential value of their land, was reporting in the *Banner* that the route was still in doubt when, in fact, the Norfolk and Western engineers were already surveying in the Tug Valley.[64] Considering the attitude of Logan Courthouse residents toward the remote Tug Valley, they must have been irritated that it was there that land values were sure to rise most rapidly. Tug lands, worth about $1.25 to $2.50 an acre in 1885, were selling for $15.00 an acre by 1890.[65]

In 1887, as speculators breathlessly awaited the final decision on the route, Anse's creditors—merchants Nighbert, Altizer, Lawson, and Taylor, in concert—brought cases against him in circuit court, hoping to attach his potentially extremely valuable five thousand acres of land. Of the six cases brought against him, Anse lost them all and was suddenly faced with a debt of $850.[66] In addition, in December 1887 J. A. Nighbert began pressuring Anse for repayment of a debt incurred nine years before. To pay all these debts, Anse mortgaged his property on Grapevine Creek to Logan merchants J. B. Wilkinson and H. C. Ragland. The mortgages stipulated that if Anse did not repay the debt by June 1888, Wilkinson and Ragland could foreclose on his property and sell it.[67] Clearly, none of these creditors would be willing to grant Anse any leeway. If he defaulted, the Grapevine lands would be theirs.

With Devil Anse's economic and political position in such jeopardy, it is understandable why he would wish to avoid any revival of feuding. His sons Johnse and Cap, however, did not comprehend the seriousness of the situation. Between 1882 and 1886 there were only a few scattered incidents which some writers have attempted to connect with the feud. Most of these involved Johnse or Cap, both of whom had tendencies to cause more problems for Devil Anse than they helped solve. Johnse had a reputation as a good-natured, if rebellious and irresponsible, playboy, while Cap was serious and hardworking but overly sensitive to slights and quick to resort to violence. In the late 1880s they unwittingly stirred up the old feud and added to their father's accumulating economic problems.

The difficulty arose from Johnse's marital situation. After Roseanna had left him, Johnse married sixteen-year-old Nancy McCoy, a daughter of the murdered Civil War Unionist, Harmon McCoy. As was customary in mountain families, Anse provided his son with a plot of land. On the newly valuable Grapevine Creek land, Johnse built a home for Nancy and himself. But Johnse was an inveterate "ladies man"; he continued to exasperate Nancy as well as Devil Anse by disappearing from home for long stretches at a time. Nancy complained bitterly and soon was spending time with her relatives, particularly her sister Mary, on the Kentucky side of the Tug Fork.[68] From these family connections, Cap and Johnse Hatfield learned that Old Ranel had not given up his pursuit of retaliation for the murder of his three sons; he apparently made many long, arduous trips to the town of Pikeville, hoping to persuade Perry Cline to take legal action against Devil Anse. Although Cline was not yet in a position to act, Cap and Johnse seemed afraid that Old Ranel's persistence would have some effect. Feud legend asserts that they tried several times to intimidate Old Ranel and his family. First, attempting to ambush the old man, they mistook John and Hense Scott for their prey and wounded Hense. Next, according to Truda McCoy, Cap, Johnse, and eight or nine others surrounded the McCoy home in a threatening manner. None of the men in the family were home, but Aunt Sally, Roseanna, and Sam's wife Martha managed to scare the invaders off.[69] What Devil Anse thought of these escapades is not recorded but, given his past and future efforts at suppressing the feud, it seems safe to conclude that he was more annoyed and angry at his own children than at the McCoys.

In the fall of 1886, Cap provoked another incident that was more serious in nature and consequence. Cap and his hired farmhand, Tom Wallace, decided to punish Mary McCoy Daniels and her daughter for transmitting information about Hatfield activities to the McCoys. Mary was the sister of Johnse's wife Nancy; apparently Cap and Tom thought information was being transmitted from Nancy to Mary to Old Ranel. As punishment they whipped both the women with cows' tails, admonishing them not to "gossip" further. Feud legend is not clear on this incident, though, and it could be argued that it had no relation to the feud at all. One author has pointed out that Wallace had been living with Mary Daniels's daughter, that she had rejected him, and that the rejection may have been as much a motivation for the whipping as the gossip story.[70] Truda McCoy, muddying the waters still further, insists that it was Mary Daniels's mother who was whipped.[71]

Whatever motivated the incident, the consequences helped reawaken the feud. Jeff McCoy, a brother of Mary Daniels and Nancy, took it upon himself to avenge the whippings. Although Jeff was known as one of Pike County's "dangerous" men, he had not previously been involved in the feud. In fact he, like his sister Nancy, had remained on good terms with Devil Anse, Cap, and Johnse throughout the first phase—good evidence that he did not connect his father's murder with the later trouble. But now, angry and ready for a fight, Jeff went to Cap's home and threatened his wife. At that point, Tom Wallace appeared and the two exchanged shots. Jeff then fled. Although he was quick to anger, Cap did not entirely ignore legalities; he filed a complaint with the district justice of the peace. With arrest warrant in hand, he and Wallace captured Jeff near the Tug River. When their prisoner bolted and attempted to swim to Kentucky and safety, someone, either Cap or Tom, fired shots that killed the fugitive.[72]

This was an incident Devil Anse could not ignore. What he said to Cap we can only imagine; what he said to Perry Cline is recorded. On 26 December Devil Anse had an unidentified individual write a letter to his old enemy in Pikeville. The fact that this letter was addressed to Cline rather than to Ranel McCoy indicates that

Anse was well aware that without Cline's support Old Ranel was powerless. "We are very sorry," Anse wrote to Cline, "that the trouble occured [sic] but under somewhat aggravated circumstances it happened. But I know and solemnly affirm that if such could have been prevented by me I would have stoped [sic] the Trouble. But it has gone and cannot be stop." If he was frustrated and angry with Cap, the tone of this letter to Cline was apologetic, suggesting Anse's anxiety over the incident. It also clearly indicates that Anse was taking responsibility for the shooting, even though he argued in the letter that it was actually Tom Wallace, not Cap, who shot Jeff. He included a statement from William Ferrell, a witness, declaring that Cap had not fired any shots. "I hope," said Anse, "that if there is any ambition Relative to this affare that it will be quieted by a fair statement of the case." The choice of the word "ambition" is a revealing one. Anse must have been aware that Cline stood to make both a reputation and money by reviving the old indictments against the Hatfields. This, added to the possibility of Cline's recovery of his five-thousand-acre inheritance now that its value was sure to skyrocket, made for an explosive situation. Aware of the potential for renewed conflict, Anse concluded that "neither one of the Hatfields has any animosity against them [the McCoys] and am very sorry that such has occured and sincerely Trust that their [sic] will be no more Trouble in regard to the matter." He signed the letter, "Your Friend, Ans Hatfield."[73]

By December 1886, when this incident presaged a revival of violent feuding, Devil Anse had good reason to feel threatened on several fronts. Competition in the timber business was increasing and the political power structure in Logan County was heavily weighted against him. At the very time that Cap was stirring up the feud again, Anse apparently felt so threatened that, for the first time, he used force to win an election for one of his friends. It is not surprising that he desperately hoped to prevent further trouble in the guise of feuding. What he didn't know, of course, was that the same social and political changes which had transformed Logan County into a hostile environment were also at work in Pike County. Perry Cline, entirely unmoved by Devil Anse's pleas for peace, effectively marshaled those forces against him.

6

The Feud Recast

• •

Like Devil Anse Hatfield and Old Ranel McCoy, Perry Cline had
grown up in the Magnolia district of Logan County. In the 1870
census he is listed as the nearest neighbor of Devil Anse; at about
that same time he was employed briefly by Hatfield's timber business. Shortly thereafter, as we have seen, Devil Anse sued Cline,
forcing the young man to leave the valley. Cline's choice of Pikeville rather than Logan Courthouse as his refuge is a revealing one.
The two towns were each located about twenty-five miles, south
and north respectively, from the Tug River Valley. Both were county
seats and centers of regional trade for the surrounding countryside.
At first glance, for a young man who had grown up in Logan County
to migrate to Pikeville seems somewhat unusual. Cline's choice
reveals the contours of his social network as well as the important
differences between Pikeville and Logan.

Perry Cline's father Jacob had been, before his death in 1858, one
of the wealthiest men in the Tug Valley. Owning over six thousand
acres on both sides of the Tug River near the mouth of Peter Creek,
he was also one of the few residents of the valley to own slaves.[1]
Before moving to the Logan side of the river, he established several
of his children on his extensive lands on the Kentucky side. One of
these was a daughter, Martha or "Patty," who married Harmon Mc-
Coy. Harmon, who was unable to count on his own father for land,
was fortunate to marry into the wealthy Cline family, thereby sharing in Jacob's property and status. But Jacob Cline's largest landholdings were on the West Virginia side of the river and these, along

with his slaves, he willed to his youngest sons, Jacob, Jr., age eleven, and Perry, age nine.[2]

The 1860 federal census shows the orphaned Perry living with his brother and sister in his father's home near the Tug. When the Civil War broke out a year later, Perry was only twelve, too young to fight on either side. From age nine to age eighteen, the young Perry was an orphan without an official, court-appointed guardian; this was an unusual situation considering that one of the county court's basic responsibilities was to arrange for the care and guardianship of orphans. The most obvious explanation for the lack of court action in Cline's case was the war, which entirely disrupted the functioning of county government. At the war's end, when the county courts of both Pike and Logan resumed, it was not to Logan County Court that Perry Cline turned, but to Pike County Court. Because Cline resided in Logan County, he must have had a strong reason for resolving his family affairs in Pike County. That reason becomes apparent with his choice of a guardian. (Cline had the right to choose his own guardian since he was over the age of fourteen.) Cline's choice, made in 1868 when he was eighteen, and recorded in the minutes of the Pike County Court, was John R. Dils.[3] The connection to Dils was enormously significant in the shaping of both the young Cline's future and the Hatfield-McCoy feud.

John R. Dils was one of the wealthiest, most prominent men in Pikeville, Pike County, or indeed the entire region. He arrived in Kentucky from northern Virginia in the 1840s and settled not in the Tug Valley but in Pikeville. Dils was convinced that although the tiny village, consisting of only twenty or thirty families, could barely be called a town, it had a promising future. After a stint at schoolteaching, Dils and a partner opened up a dry goods merchandising business. According to Dils's own autobiography, he was poor and without resources but soon remedied this situation by marrying a daughter of one of Pike County's wealthy residents. At the outbreak of the war, Dils eschewed neutrality and became the most vociferous supporter of the Union in the county. Arrested by the Confederate home guards, he was confined to Libby Prison in Richmond for a year. Embittered by the experience, he returned to Pikeville to form his own Union regiment, the Thirty-ninth Kentucky. Although most of his recruits came from the southern tier of

Pike County and surrounding areas, a handful of Tug Valley residents, including Harmon McCoy, joined. At the war's end, Dils came home to Pikeville and became one of its most prominent citizens.[4] With profits from the dry goods business he began investing in land. Starting in 1865 he purchased nearly fifteen thousand acres of what the county termed "unoccupied and vacant" lands.[5] The price was low—only 2.5 cents an acre—but nevertheless Dils was one of the few residents who could afford more than fifty or a hundred acres.

Dils also, through his business, became involved in the Tug Valley. He formed a partnership with John Smith, the merchant Anse was suing for breach of contract. Although Dils apparently did not have any direct dealings with Devil Anse, he knew the people of the Tug Valley well; in fact, he often sued them for debt in Logan Courthouse. He must have been aware of Anse's litigation against John Smith as well as the damage suit against Perry Cline. In fact, one of Dils's pieces of property was directly across the river from Cline's Grapevine Creek home.[6] Thus, at an early date, the young man had formed close ties with an individual who had good reason to dislike Devil Anse and was powerful enough to help in Cline's eventual quest for vengeance.

The appointment of Dils as Perry Cline's guardian was indicative more of a formality than of any real change in living arrangements. The year after the court appointment, Cline married Martha Adkins, daughter of a Pike County family, and brought her home to Grapevine Creek.[7] In the 1870 census the couple was listed as having a child one year old and as still being next-door neighbors of Devil Anse.[8] But Cline's obvious intention to settle on his father's extensive lands on Grapevine Creek was thwarted by Devil Anse's lawsuit. As we have seen, almost immediately after the lawsuit was filed, Cline conceded defeat and moved his family to Pikeville. Although bitterly resentful of his expulsion from the Tug Valley, Cline had connections and resources unavailable to many young men. Dils's support eased his path toward a business and professional career as well as providing an introduction to the economic, political, and social leadership of the county, including county judge Tobias Wagner, county attorney J. Lee Ferguson, and state representative Orlando C. Bowles. These county leaders were zealous advocates of economic development—the Pikeville equivalents of

J. A. Nighbert, S. S. Altizer, and H. C. Ragland in Logan Courthouse—and were invaluable personal contacts for the young man. But there were other reasons for Cline's choice of Pikeville over Logan.

Unlike Logan, where prospects for development did not become apparent until late in the 1880s, Pikeville's natural advantages made earlier development feasible. In the era before railoads, when communication and transportation out of the mountains depended upon rivers, Pikeville enjoyed an obvious superiority. Although Logan was located on the Guyandotte, that river was similar to the Tug in that it was not navigable by anything larger than pushboats. Merchants in Logan—such as Lawson and Nighbert—were faced with long, arduous overland journeys in order to procure goods; until the coming of the railroad in the 1890s, economic development was necessarily severely limited. Pikeville, however, was located on the Levisa Fork of the Big Sandy, a river navigable by large vessels. Steamboats already plied the river from the Ohio to Pikeville, a distance of 105 miles.[9]

As early as 1870, Pikeville's leaders—Dils and Bowles—agitated for funds to make the river accessible to even larger boats by dredging and building dams. Bowles, a representative from Pike and Letcher counties to the Kentucky house of representatives, was also the owner of several of the steamboats in use on the river. Lobbying in his own interest as well as that of Pikeville, he had by 1870 persuaded the state to award some $62,000 worth of contracts to improve navigation on both the Levisa Fork and Big Sandy.[10] Although the grandiose dreams of making Pikeville into a significant urban center were never realized—only one dam was built and very little dredging was done before the railroad era made river transportation obsolete—a few energetic developers such as Dils and Bowles made the future of Pikeville look extremely promising. Compared to Logan, Pikeville in the 1870s was booming.

Another indication that Pikeville was "progressive" was the religious revival that occurred in 1880. In the antebellum period, remote mountain areas like the Tug Valley rejected the modernizing impulses accompanying the widespread popularity of evangelical Protestantism. The Primitive Baptists held onto their traditional fatalistic values long after the majority of Americans embraced both the national market economy and evangelical Christianity.

Between 1850 and 1880, however, most mountain regions were affected, if unevenly, by trade, markets, and railroads. This economic change was accompanied by the gradual, and also uneven, appearance of more flexible religious beliefs. Just as the Northeast a half century before had Charles Grandison Finney, who articulated these changes, the Appalachians produced a similar revivalist.[11] The "mountain evangelist" was a former Presbyterian minister, George Owen Barnes. Barnes grew up in the mountains in Garrard County, Kentucky. His father was a conservative Presbyterian minister of strict Calvinist views. After a career as a missionary in India, Barnes experienced a conversion, rejecting the judgmental harshness of predestinarian Calvinism and adopting ideas close to liberal and evangelical Protestants in mainstream America. He— like the most popular spokesman for the "gospel of love" in middle-class America, Henry Ward Beecher—preached that God's love was not stern and unbending, but unconditional and forgiving. In the early 1880s Barnes began a preaching career in the southern Appalachians, in the course of which he converted 27,000 people.[12]

Barnes's were just the sort of modern religious values that leading citizens in mountain towns hoped to encourage. They wanted rural farmers to become more open in their economic and social thinking, and the more cosmopolitan worldview encompassed by liberal, evangelical religion would aid that cause. Not surprisingly, it was Col. John R. Dils who invited the evangelist to Pike County. During the preacher's two-week stay, he converted four hundred people, suggesting that the population in Pikeville and surrounding areas were susceptible to the set of values he preached. It is also apparent that the "country folk" were not quite so ready; they stayed away from the revival meetings. Many of these country folk were residents of the Tug Valley, where evangelicalism still represented the evils of a commercial and money-hungry world that had no place in their scheme of things. The Pikeville district of Pike County may have been ready for progress, but the Tug Valley was not.[13]

But for all Pikeville's natural advantages and social progressivism, it was Cline's personal contacts that made his career so remarkably successful. Almost as soon as he arrived in the town in 1874, the young man was appointed deputy sheriff, and by the next year he was elected sheriff.[14] This position was an extremely powerful and lucrative one in the southern county system. The sheriff received fees for all his activities, which included collecting taxes, making arrests, and serving warrants. For a young man with no resources, just starting out, the office was a real plum.[15] Cline was not content with just being sheriff, though; in 1876 he applied for a tavern license, and in 1880 for a license to sell drugs.[16] Apparently he was not greatly successful at any of these ventures, because Dun and Bradstreet evaluated his business as "promising" but not entirely "safe."[17] By 1884, however, Cline had found his niche: he was admitted to the Pike County bar.[18] Once established, the ambitious young man quickly became involved in politics by running for the state legislature. By 1886 his contacts and influence reached beyond the local level. When Simon Buckner ran for governor in 1887, Cline actively campaigned for him. Two feud historians assert that Buckner owed Cline a favor for his political support, and that is why Buckner's election in the fall of 1887 catapulted the Pike County politician into a position of influence and power of which he could only have dreamed a few years before.[19]

What was good for the young lawyer, however, boded ill for his old enemy, Devil Anse Hatfield. By 1887 Perry Cline had achieved a position of power that would allow him to strike back for the loss of his inheritance. Cline's awareness of this potential seems apparent from the interest he suddenly showed in the feud. The shooting of Jeff McCoy in December 1886 came at an opportune moment— precisely when Cline's power was in the ascendant. It is unlikely that Cline was angered solely by the shooting itself, although Jeff McCoy was his nephew. Jeff as well as his brothers, Bud and Lark, were known in the valley as troublemakers—"bad" or "dangerous" young men who were constantly engaging in drunken brawls. Worse, Jeff was reputed to have recently murdered someone in Pike County and thus was a fugitive in both counties.[20]

Most community residents probably thought of Jeff and his brothers as examples of the irresponsible character of Daniel McCoy now being replicated in his children and grandchildren. If anything, these were the kind of people from whom Perry Cline hoped to disassociate himself in his quest for upward mobility. Yet Jeff's shooting provided the leverage he needed in his appeal to county and state officials for prosecution of Devil Anse. Significantly, Cline made no move to pursue indictments against Cap Hatfield and Tom Wallace for Jeff's killing, but instead he proceeded to argue for revival of the five-year-old indictments against Devil Anse for the killing of the McCoy brothers. Whether his motives were revenge, real sympathy for Randolph McCoy and his family, or the hope of reclaiming some of his land we cannot know. But Cline must have known by 1887 that there was an excellent chance that the route of the Norfolk and Western Railroad would run through or close to the land he had lost, dramatically inflating its value. It is clear, however, that Cline, despite his recent acquisition of influence, needed more than a personal desire for revenge or justice to win the support of county and state officials. The new governor may have owed him a favor for his support in the election campaign, but more persuasive arguments were required to resurrect a five-year-old feud in the Tug Valley.

Fortunately for Cline, the time was auspicious. Forces outside his control—the impetus for economic development and the high visibility of other feuds in the Kentucky mountains—predisposed local and state officials to listen to his arguments. In the late 1880s, the possibilities for economic development in both Pike and Logan counties seemed nothing short of spectacular. The boom that had seemed so slow in coming in the 1870s finally arrived. Funds had been granted by the state to improve slack water transportation on the Levisa Fork of the Big Sandy, even as steamboat traffic rapidly increased. The timber industry was on the verge of an unprecedented boom. A visitor to Pike County in 1883 noticed that "the exports from the mountains are considerable, especially along the Big Sandy, which is navigated by steamboats. Railroads are now penetrating the remote places and the mineral resources . . . will soon be developed."[21] In 1888 Western Kentucky newspapers, which had never before shown much interest in the eastern mountain region, finally became aware of the economic importance of the rich resources of timber and coal in that region. The *Louisville Courier-Journal* reported "the Surprising Fact shown that the Lumber trade Leads All Others in the City," and "no doubt the opening of the vast and rich lumber tracts in Eastern Kentucky has largely contributed to this end."[22] As early as 1881, investors were surveying the region for possible coal deposits and rail routes.[23] By 1886–87, state and local officials like Perry Cline realized that properties with timber and coal potential were about to undergo a dramatic increase in value, especially if outside capitalist investment could be attracted.

If the late 1880s brought general recognition that the Appalachians would soon be the focus of intensive development efforts, that decade also witnessed competition between regions to attract that development. Local boosters such as Nighbert and Ragland in Logan Courthouse and Cline and Dils in Pikeville vied with each other to secure investments from eastern capitalists. In that race, Pike County seemed a front-runner, especially when the results of a geological survey authorized by the legislature were published in 1887. This report was aimed not only at informing the legislature of the potential for development but also at attracting investment; it argued that "capitalists will not furnish money to build railways and open mines on generalities . . . but demand . . . facts." The "facts" provided by this geological survey focused attention on Pike County, where "a thick bed of the highest quality coking coal," sixteen hundred square miles in area, had been discovered. The quality of the coking coal and its value in the smelting of iron, the report stated, were such that its "importance . . . and bearing upon the future industrial development of the State, cannot be overestimated."[24] This information, coupled with the knowledge that the Norfolk and Western Railroad was about to construct its Ohio Extension, made Pike County the center of attention for investors as well as state and local officials. Thus, at the same time that the attention of Kentucky legislators and the governor was focused on the crucial role Pike County could play in the state's economic development, the governor was hearing Perry Cline's tale of chaotic violence in the same region.

Cline's story of the Hatfield "desperadoes" had special resonance for other reasons as well. Not only had mountaineers gained a reputation for violence, but they also seemed resistant to development. Local boosters and state officials were under pressure to demonstrate that mountaineers were peaceful and welcomed industrialization. This was not always easy to do, as evidence of local opposition to development was uncomfortably apparent. In 1887 Pike County, for example, ten local residents were sued by a railroad company because they refused to sell a right-of-way under an agreement that had been made at the state level. Pike County Court officials, dismayed by this resistance to their hopes for progress, held special and "important" meetings to determine what action should be taken.[25] The officials included Dils and Cline as well as their friends, the county judge and prosecutor, and they were, of course, all professionals or merchants whose economic well-being was linked to successful development. Like Nighbert and Ragland in Logan County, they saw their task as that of persuading unenlightened farmers to cooperate. In the case of the right-of-way, however, persuasion was ineffective, and the court simply condemned land and required that it be sold to the railroad. Although the resistance could usually be overcome by the alliance between capitalists and local promoters, its presence remained disturbing.

In Kentucky, the disfavor with which officials regarded the mountaineers' reluctance to cooperate with developers was exacerbated by the state's reputation for violent feuding. Although the mountain regions of several other states were also identified with feuding, Kentucky seemed to draw the most publicity. One Appalachian historian has pointed out that "of the dozen or so major feuds, most were associated in some way with the state of Kentucky."[26] In the mid-1880s, although as yet few outside the Tug Valley had heard of the Hatfields and McCoys, numerous Kentucky feuds were splashed across the pages of newspapers from New York to California. The Kentucky legislature felt enough pressure to convene special hearings on violence in mountain counties, and the new governor felt compelled to mention in a major public address the need to curtail feud violence. During the summer of 1887, the same year that Perry Cline approached the governor with tales of the murderous Hatfields, the Martin-Tolliver feud in Rowan County became national news.[27] What bothered state officials more than the actual violence was the negative effect such publicity might have on the economic modernization of the mountains. The *New York Times* made the connection between the suppression of feuding and economic development explicit when, in July 1887, it carried an article entitled, "Tolliver-Logan Vendetta Affects Business." Although the governor had always been reluctant to use state troops to quell local disturbances, in the case of Rowan County he finally agreed, so threatening had the situation become.[28] Thus, Kentucky boosters, from newspaper editors to the state legislators to the Governor, publicly wrung their collective hands and searched for some way to assure capitalists that Appalachian Kentucky was safe for investment.

It was at this volatile moment that Perry Cline interjected the Hatfields and McCoys. The argument for renewing the prosecution against Devil Anse was strengthened by the fact that Cline was not alone; he was accompanied to Frankfort by the county prosecuting attorney, J. Lee Ferguson, and the soon-to-be-notorious Frank Phillips.[29] The trio also claimed the support of county judge Tobias Wagner and merchant John R. Dils. In other words, all the "best" citizens (i.e., developers) of Pike County were expressing their concern that violence instigated by the Hatfields not only threatened the safety of Pike citizens but also would prevent progress. The governor was assured that he was not simply aiding one side of a family vendetta; at the same time he could demonstrate that the state of Kentucky would no longer tolerate lawlessness and disorder. The deciding argument, however, may have been that these feudists—the "worst marauders ever," in the words of Perry Cline— were *not* Kentuckians but West Virginians! The publicity engendered by a crackdown on the Hatfields would put Kentucky in a favorable light, for a change, as champion of law and order while deflecting the stigma of feuding onto West Virginia. Subsequent events and the "war" between Kentucky and West Virginia newspapers over which state was to blame for the Hatfield-McCoy feud proved the strategy a viable one.

By the end of the summer of 1887, Cline was successful in his suit. The governor authorized the town of Pikeville to hire a special deputy to handle the case and sent an official extradition request to the governor of West Virginia.[30] He also issued a proclamation offering rewards for the Hatfields, thus insuring that private detectives and bounty hunters would enter the region, provoking more violence.[31] Ironically, it was this decision that led to national notoriety for the Hatfield-McCoy feud. The combination of Cline's personal grievance against Devil Anse, the interests of Pikeville merchants, and the desire of the governor to make eastern Kentucky "safe" for development brought about a revival of feuding in the Tug Valley. Cline and the governor literally recreated the feud in order to suppress it.

In a strange twist of fate, Old Ranel McCoy, who, in the feud's first phase, had never been able to garner more than a handful of supporters against Devil Anse, was now backed by the full judicial authority of the state of Kentucky. Consider the irony of the situation. Old Ranel, in his opposition to Devil Anse, had been acting out diffuse fears of the ruthlessness, ambition, and competition associated with a market economy. Although Ranel himself had violated codes of acceptable social behavior, he was in fact in the vanguard of resistance to economic change. When, through Perry Cline's mediation, Ranel won the sanction and support of the governor and state of Kentucky, he allied himself with more powerful forces of capitalist transformation than Devil Anse ever could have mustered. Thus Perry Cline and the forces he represented seized upon the existence of internal community tensions, exemplified by the feud, to accomplish their own ends. Old Ranel, quite unwittingly, had switched sides. From his initial role as resistor to Devil Anse's modernizing activities, he had now become a standard-bearer in the forces of capitalist development.

Conversely, Devil Anse was forced into the opposite position— that of a defender of local independence, autonomy, and traditional values. Up until this point there was nothing to indicate that, given the opportunity, Anse would not have joined with Logan development advocates, perhaps becoming an agent for a timber company, and gone down in local history as a harbinger of progress. But the new merchant class in Logan had consistently opposed him, and now the entire state of Kentucky was plotting his destruction. No choice had been left open to Devil Anse; he had to defend his hard-won status and independence.

In Logan County, Devil Anse and his followers were well aware of Cline's visits to the governor of Kentucky in Frankfort. Outraged, not only by this attempt to revive the feud, but also by Cline's efforts to enlist powerful external help, the Hatfields responded with threats. Two weeks before the governor issued his proclamation offering rewards for the Hatfields, Devil Anse and his friends composed another letter to Perry Cline. This time the tone was far from conciliatory; Cline was not addressed as "Perry" nor did Devil Anse sign it, "Your friend, Ans." This letter issued a stern warning to the Pikeville lawyer. Dated 29 August 1887 and posted from the "Logan County Court House," it was signed by the "President and Secretary" of the "Logan County Regulators."[32]

The use of the term "regulators" was significant for the course of the feud; it indicated that a dramatic transformation had taken place since the election-day killings of 1882. Cline's enlistment of the powers of the state effectively abrogated the local structure of authority. From the perspective of the Hatfield group, this alliance with powerful external authority was unfair and removed the feud from the realm of family or even community conflict. Therefore, the formation of a local, organized group willing to use force against the interlopers was clearly justified. Because the customary avenues of redress were blocked by external intervention, Devil Anse resorted to a time-honored remedy known as "regulation." This term had a long history in both England and America, where it had been invoked frequently in the seventeenth and eighteenth centuries by those engaged in popular protest movements. By the late nineteenth century, however, the term "regulation" had become obsolete in most of the United States, where it was replaced by "vigilantism," a term usually associated with frontier movements. On the frontier, in fact, such extralegal groups as the one Devil Anse now formed referred to themselves as "vigilantes."[33] The fact that Devil Anse and his supporters called themselves regulators rather than vigilantes indicates their links with an older tradition, one that had been especially strong in both North and South in the latter half of the eighteenth century. In fact, in the years before the American Revolution, regulators from the Stamp Act protesters to the Committees of Safety perceived themselves as upholding justice and the rights of the people against oppressive and often distant governments. After the Revolution the tradition persisted, most notably in the protests of western Massachusetts farmers against the inequitable state taxation policies which culminated in Shays' Rebellion and also in urban and rural mob protests against the economic hardships of the 1830s and 1840s.[34]

In choosing the term "regulators," then, the Hatfields demonstrated their conviction that the feud was no longer a family conflict confined to the Tug Valley community. The intervention of Cline and the state of Kentucky seemed to demand not a family but a community response, because it was the fundamental autonomy and integrity of the local authority system which was now being challenged. This constituted an entirely different situation than the one which had prevailed during the first phase of the feud, when Devil Anse's extralegal response to the McCoys' attack on his brother had stretched and strained the traditional system of justice but had not completely fractured it. The resiliance of that system, despite the shocking impact of the pawpaw bush killings, was due to the local awareness that the boys were indeed guilty but that formal justice was frustrated by the state boundary line that arbitrarily divided their community. Although Devil Anse's solution was outside the letter of the law, his neighbors still concluded that it was justice. This new threat of force by the state, however, was a complete negation of traditional authority and produced just what might have been expected—the abandonment of normal legal channels by the Hatfields. Yet by employing the term "regulators," the Hatfields were claiming to *preserve* the very system of local justice now being threatened. Far from showing contempt for the legal system, the feudists sought to defend the law *as they knew it.*

Although other extralegal movements in the South during the same period identified themselves as vigilante groups, the impetus for their existence and their objectives were very similar to those of the Logan County Regulators. All saw themselves not as innovators, but as protectors of a way of life threatened by outside intervention. Several studies make the case that southern vigilantism in the 1880s and 1890s was related to the steady, though uneven, penetration of market capitalism into the region. As William Holmes and David Thelen have shown for Georgia and Missouri, collective violence was an attempt to resist the loss of local autonomy and independence, whether in the economic or social arena.[35] Now it has become apparent that the Hatfield-McCoy feud, too, contained the elements of such a struggle.

The Logan County Regulators formally addressed their letter "To Perry A. Cline" and began, "My name is Nat Hatfield." By adopting the single collective identity of Nat Hatfield, the group established their unity as representatives of a single-minded community. "I am not a single individual but a good many, and we do not live on Tug River, but we live all over this county." Because almost everyone associated Devil Anse with the Tug Valley, the regulators explicitly rejected this narrow construction of their membership and geographic location. "We live all over this county," they insisted. If Perry Cline could claim the entire state of Kentucky as his ally, the Hatfields could at least claim all of Logan County. This was more wishful thinking than reality, of course. As we have seen, the northern region of Logan County, with its new elite, had been vigorously opposing Devil Anse's economic and political influence for half a decade. But it may not have been far-fetched to hope Logan's leaders would be so incensed by Kentucky's intervention in their affairs that they would support the Hatfields.

After identifying themselves, the regulators came right to the point. "We have been told by men from your county that you and your men are fixing to invade this county for the purpose of taking the Hatfield boys, and now, sir, we, forty-nine in number at present, do notify you that if you come into this county to take or bother any of the Hatfields, we will follow you to hell or take your hide, and if any of the Hatfields are killed or bothered in any way, we will charge it up to you, and your hide will pay the penalty." The identification here of a specific number of "Hatfield boys"—forty-nine— was apparently meant to impress Cline with the strength of Devil Anse's active supporters, but it also reveals just how few Logan Countians were involved. In the 1880s Logan County had about 1,800 households. Forty-nine regulators would represent less than 3 percent of those families. The forty-nine, then, offered official notification that Cline would be held responsible for actions which might be taken by others; whatever the official representatives of the state of Kentucky might do, promised the regulators, Perry Cline personally "will pay the penalty."

This attempt to personalize legal issues highlights the unfamiliar predicament in which the Hatfields found themselves. They were unsure of how to cope with the threat of a distant and unapproachable authority. Although at a later date the Hatfields petitioned the governor of West Virginia for protection against extradition, the very novelty and scope of such inexorable and impersonal forces was overwhelming. Despite the inroads of the timber market, the culture of the mountaineers was still traditional, couched in the personal and familiar. Laws and forces separate from particular people or a social context were almost incomprehensible. Thus, the face-to-face traditions of the culture, coupled with fear of alien power, produced a response that was official and legalistic, yet at the same time entirely personal. If Perry Cline could marshal such forces, reasoned the Hatfields, he could also stop them. From the perspective of the regulators, Cline, not the law, was the key to Hatfield survival.

Yet the tone of the letter also indicates an underlying sense that one man might not be the whole problem. The extent of the threats to Cline constitute a kind of bravado that the Hatfields suspected might not work at all. The second paragraph began with what is almost a plea for a truce. "We are not bothering you and neither are the Hatfields, and as long as you keep your hands off Logan County men, we will not do anything, but," threatened the Hatfields, "if you don't keep your hands off our men, there is not one of you will be left in six months." Finally the writers of the letter, in a further attempt to frighten Cline, became graphic in their threats. "We have a habit of making one horse lawyers keep their boots on and we have plenty of good strong rope left, and our hangman tied a knot for you and laid it quietly away until we see what you do. We have no particular pleasure in hanging dogs, but we know you and have counted the miles and marked the tree."[36]

As the regulators undoubtedly realized when they dispatched this letter to Pikeville, Cline, having won the support of the governor, was not going to be easily intimidated. Indeed, this proved to be the case. Two weeks later Governor Buckner issued his proclamation offering rewards for the Hatfields, followed by an extradition request sent to the governor of West Virginia. Cline's success, however, did not mean that he was immune to Hatfield threats. Observers in Pikeville noticed that the young lawyer, who had also been appointed deputy jailor, moved about the streets only when surrounded by several armed guards. Cline was apparently afraid that Devil Anse and his followers might actually be so foolish as to ride into Pikeville, where they could be arrested and thrown into jail without the legal formalities of extradition. With armed protection, though, he proceeded to make plans for the capture of Devil Anse, with or without extradition. In October, at Cline's behest, the county court appointed a special deputy charged with forming a posse to pursue the Hatfields.[37] The deputy was chosen carefully; Cline wanted someone who had no fear of anything, someone with a reputation for cruelty and tenaciousness, someone who would show no mercy whatever to his prey. This deputy was to become one of the most colorful and flamboyant figures in the feud. He was known as "Bad" Frank Phillips.

In 1887 Frank Phillips was a young man of twenty-five with an unsavory reputation. He had grown up in the Johns Creek district of Pike County just south of the ridge that divided the Tug Fork Valley from the region surrounding Pikeville. Because of the intervening ridge, Johns Creek was not really a part of the Tug community in which Devil Anse, Ranel McCoy and Perry Cline had grown up. Born in 1862, just after the outbreak of the Civil War, Phillips never knew his father, who was a casuality of the war. Phillips's father, like Harmon McCoy, had sided with the Union, joining the Thirty-ninth Kentucky Infantry Regiment headed by Col. John Dils. Relatives characterized Frank's father as reckless in courting danger, a trait which led to his unnecessary death.[38] The 1860 census had showed him to be a substantial landholder supporting a wife, three children, and two servants.[39] After the death of their father, Frank and his siblings were taken in by their grandfather, Jesse Phillips, who was one of the wealthiest residents of Pike County, owning $3,300 worth of real and personal property.[40] The arrangement did not prove to be permanent, however. Whether the five young children were too much for sixty-year-old Jesse and his wife isn't clear, but by 1868 Jesse had resigned as guardian of all the children; he was replaced by the same individual who had become Perry Cline's guardian, John R. Dils. Clearly, Dils was an important influence on the lives of two of Devil Anse's most implacable enemies.[41]

It is unclear what motivation Dils had for offering himself as guardian for these as well as other orphaned children; county court records name about ten children for whom Dils acted as guardian between 1865 and 1880. All except Perry Cline were orphans of Pike County Union soldiers. Possibly Dils, as head of a Kentucky Union regiment, felt some responsibility toward the children. A second, perhaps complementary, explanation is that guardians such as Dils were paid by the county court for their service in taking care of orphans. The pay was not much but, during the time of the guardianship, the guardian had access to the financial assets belonging to the children. There was always the temptation to misuse these funds, and some evidence suggests that Dils's eagerness to take on the task of guardian was self-serving. In 1868, the same year that Dils became the guardian of both Perry Cline and Frank Phillips, he was "dismissed" by the county court as guardian of the "infant heirs of Squire Ratliffe." Relatives of the children produced evidence that Dils was mishandling the children's assets. The court, "after hearing evidence," ordered that in addition to dismissal Dils must "hand over all the funds he may have in his hands as guardian of said heirs."[42]

If it is true that Dils's motivation was exploitation, Phillips may have endured some stressful experiences; in 1874, at the age of twelve, Phillips left Dils's supervision. From then until he was appointed special deputy in the Hatfield case, there is scant record of his activities. He is absent from the federal census schedules and local tax records, and we know only that by 1887 he had been married twice and was separated from his second wife and four children.[43] If anything describes Phillips at this point in his life, it might be the old cliché "at loose ends." His public exhibitions of drunkenness, reckless fighting, and crude pursuit of women had earned him the epithet of dangerous or bad. A later newspaper article described him as "a handsome little fellow, with piercing black eyes, ruddy cheeks, and a pleasant expression, but a mighty unpleasant man."[44]

If such antics were rare in mountain communities, we might attribute Phillips's antisocial behavior to an unpleasant and difficult childhood. Loss of his father in a war, followed by forced residence with an avaricous guardian, could be enough to disturb any young man. However, as we have seen, the type represented by Phillips was becoming increasingly common in mountain communities. Boisterous, rowdy, lacking in deference to their elders, resorting to weapons as part of fights and street play, these young men were avoided and ostracized by most community residents.

When Bad Frank Phillips, along with the state of Kentucky, entered the fray, the nature of the feud was altered completely. Phillips, with all the reckless courage and defiance of authority characteristic of "dangerous" men, took on the pursuit of Devil Anse Hatfield as some great game. Devil Anse's reputation as the most accomplished hunter, the sharpest shot, and the most fearless fighter in the valley was a challenge Phillips could not resist. For Phillips, the challenge and excitement were enough. He was unconcerned with the history of the feud, or his friend Perry Cline's personal interest in it, or, for that matter, whether justice was done. Nor did he care about the issues of economic development that so motivated the governor of Kentucky and local leaders like John R. Dils in Pikeville and J. A. Nighbert in Logan. Phillips was out to match wits and brawn with Devil Anse Hatfield, using means fair or foul.[45] Perry Cline had chosen well; Bad Frank Phillips was the perfect instrument to carry out the larger, if somewhat different, goals of Perry Cline and the state of Kentucky.

At first both Cline and Phillips seemed to believe that the governor's request for extradition of the Hatfields would produce results quickly. In this they were soon disillusioned. The governor of West Virginia, E. Willis Wilson, responded slowly to the first requisition from Kentucky. Claiming that the paperwork was not complete, he requested more affadavits. On 13 October Governor Buckner supplied the affadavits but, once again, there was no immediate response from Wilson. The delay was caused by the tactics of Devil Anse and his supporters. The Hatfield leader had enlisted the aid of an old friend, John B. Floyd, now assistant secretary of state in Wilson's cabinet. Floyd did not let his old friend and supporter down.[46] He instructed Anse to have those named in the 1882 indictment assemble affadavits and depositions proclaiming their innocence and to get Logan neighbors to sign petitions attesting to the good character of the Hatfields. With these in hand, Floyd argued to Governor Wilson that extradition should be resisted. Citing the history of provocation on the part of the McCoys, specifically the slaying of Bill Staton and the brutal stabbing of Ellison Hatfield, Floyd argued that, essentially, justice had been done and the feud was long since over. Sending the Hatfields into Kentucky for trial, he insisted, was tantamount to signing their death warrants. Undoubtedly he also informed Wilson of Perry Cline's old animosity toward Devil Anse and his present role in persuading the governor of Kentucky to revive the feud.

All this gave the governor a lot to think about. Wilson was an old-fashioned politician who had won the governor's office in 1884 because of bitter divisions in both the Democratic and Republican parties. The largest factions of both parties were supporting economic development such as railroads and coal mining and were willing to support legislation that would favor easy profits for outside corporations. Wilson, however, represented a small group of "agrarian Democrats" whose political program resembled that of the Populists. This wing of the party proposed to advocate the interests of farmers by demanding that corporations pay significant taxes and be subjected to strict regulation by the state. Wilson went so far as to argue that railroads should be public utilities owned by the state instead of private, profit-making companies.[47]

Wilson and his faction of the Democratic party were a minority in West Virginia politics, but they exerted disproportionate power in the 1880s because of the bitter contention between the Democrats and Republicans who represented the interests of the industrialists. Serving as governor from 1884 until 1890, Wilson was the last governor of West Virginia vigorously to challenge exploitation of the state by railroads, timber, and coal companies. The politicians, Democrats or Republicans, who came to dominate the state after 1890 were consistently allied with outside capitalists whose goals were rapid industrialization and profits. Their response to feudists, vigilantes, or labor organizers was uniform: violent suppression. All were seen as obstacles to the economic transformation of the mountains. Fortunately for Anse Hatfield, the requisition for his arrest and extradition came while E. Willis Wilson was still governor. If it had come two years later, it is highly likely that the "industrialists' handpicked" governor, A. B. Fleming, would have dispatched the Hatfields off to Kentucky without a further thought.[48]

Because Wilson's sympathies were populist, he seemed receptive to the argument that the Hatfields were being treated unfairly. Therefore, although Wilson did not refuse Governor Buckner's request, he delayed compliance until more information became available. Of course, as Governor Wilson considered what action to take concerning the Hatfields, he was probably not thinking in terms of the abstract issues of economic and social change; he had simply been persuaded by Floyd that Devil Anse was not the bloodthirsty outlaw portrayed by Cline. While he weighed the problem, several events occurred which added convincing evidence to Floyd's arguments.

During the second week in November, Wilson received a personal letter from Perry Cline. Apparently Cline had become impatient with the delays in the legal process. When no word had come from

West Virginia's governor in three weeks and he had heard that Devil Anse had influential connections, Cline decided to expedite matters. Inquiring as to the status of the case, Cline claimed that he had some inside information. If the Hatfields had sent a petition in their defense, he told the governor, it was only because "they have and can make the people sign any kind of petition they want." "I was *rased* [sic] near them men and know them," he told Wilson, "they are the worst band of *meroders* [sic] ever existed in the mountains, and have been in arms since the war; they will not live as citizens ought to." In a long liturgy alleging Hatfield crimes such as murder, Ku Kluxing, and selling liquor, Cline referred to his own grievance against Devil Anse. "These men," he wrote, "has made good citizens leave their homes and forsake all they had, and refuse to let any person tend their lands." After fifteen years and considerable success in Pikeville, Cline was still furious about the loss of his land to Devil Anse Hatfield. Despite his bitterness, he assured Governor Wilson that the Hatfields' claim that Pike County wanted Devil Anse only to murder him was "false as anything can be." No harm would be done to the Hatfields "except to see they get the law. Appealing to the governor to act quickly, Cline closed with "I deem it of great importance."[49]

When Governor Wilson did not respond to this appeal, Cline and Phillips restrained themselves no longer. On 12 December, armed with bench warrants for the arrest of twenty Hatfields, they organized a posse and crossed the Tug into West Virginia. Although their action was illegal because the Kentuckians were not observing extradition procedures, the posse returned that evening with one prisoner, the only "Hatfield" they could find. That prisoner, ironically, was Selkirk McCoy—the same Selkirk who had been the McCoy "traitor" in the hog trial ten years before.[50] Flushed with success, Phillips planned more raids into West Virginia even as he composed his own personal appeal to Governor Wilson. Hoping to succeed where Cline had failed, Phillips enclosed fifteen dollars for legal fees and self-importantly instructed the governor to send official warrants to "Frank Phillips, the agent appointed by the Governor of Kentucky."[51]

If Phillips was much impressed with his own success at capturing a Hatfield, as well as with his position as deputy sheriff and agent of the governor, many Pike Countians were dismayed. It was bad enough that so-called dangerous men made the streets of Pikeville unsafe for law-abiding residents, but that they should be given official sanction by the county court was an insult. Apparently some Pike County residents, especially those living in the Tug Valley who knew the history of the feud and of Cline's private quarrel with Devil Anse, objected to the intervention of Cline and the governor, and most of all to the employment of Frank Phillips as deputy sheriff. A few days after the raid that captured Selkirk McCoy, Pike County sheriff Basil Hatfield, a distant cousin of Devil Anse although not a supporter, requested the removal of Phillips as deputy sheriff.[52] Basil Hatfield knew the history of the feud; not only had he grown up in the Tug Valley, but he was a deacon of the church and an elderly, respected member of the community.[53] Confronted with this opposition, Phillips's sponsors—Cline, prosecuting attorney J. Lee Ferguson, and county judge Tobias Wagner—found it difficult to deny that Phillips's behavior on his raids into West Virginia, as well as his generally antisocial demeanor, made it absurd for him to be designated as a deputy sheriff. Phillips was dismissed.[54] Although, theoretically, community opinion had triumphed, it made not a whit of difference to Phillips or Perry Cline. Now without official standing, they continued their raids into West Virginia.[55]

Whether the Hatfields knew of Phillips's dismissal or not, Devil Anse and his supporters had good reason for anxiety. That a Pike County posse led by Cline and Phillips would actually raid West Virginia and take a captive back to Pikeville was completely unexpected. The rules of the game had changed dramatically. Local opinion, community protocol, even Devil Anse's social prestige and reputation, counted for very little. No matter that everyone in the vicinity understood that Devil Anse had won Cline's land legally or that the McCoys had instigated a feud that nobody wanted and that was long since over. The law as it was being applied from Frankfort was not the law of the Tug Valley. The state of Kentucky had taken action that essentially destroyed the operation of the local system of social authority. The issue now revolved around just which side would be able to enforce its own version of the law—the developers or the local residents of the Tug community. The developers claimed to have reason and rationality and justice on their side, while local residents could only fall back on an intuitive sense of what was both "right" and customary. Although the developers liked to portray the conflict as the law versus lawlessness, this was far from being the real issue. The fundamental question was which side had the power to impose its will, and the answer must have been almost as apparent to Devil Anse as to the governor of Kentucky. The Hatfields' awareness of their own impotence produced a frantic and desperate debate over the options available to them.

That the situation was the subject of many discussions in Devil Anse's home near the Tug River there can be no doubt, but because no written records survive, it isn't known who proposed what, which solutions were rejected outright, which ones debated and dismissed. All we can be sure of is the action finally taken by members of the Hatfield group. The first was an attempt to bribe Perry Cline—an indication of just what Devil Anse thought of Cline's principles. A messenger was sent to Pikeville to offer Cline money for calling off the Hatfield hunt. Surprisingly, it seemed to work; Cline accepted $225 and agreed "to use all his influence with the Governor of Kentucky to take no further steps for the arrest of the . . . parties."[56] If the Hatfields were jubilant at first, they soon realized that they had been double-crossed. Cline and Phillips continued to press for extradition and, worse, to cross the border into West Virginia attempting to capture Hatfields.

The situation must have caused considerable panic among the Hatfields. It was probably Devil Anse who had suggested the bribery attempt; it bears his stamp of practicality while avoiding violence. But after its failure, some members of the regulators argued for more violent solutions. Old Jim Vance, always identified by legend as one of the most ruthless feudists, was in the forefront of this line of thought. But apparently it was Anse's most troublesome son who came up with a specific suggestion. Why not, suggested Cap, get to the root of the matter? Why not kill Old Ranel McCoy and his family? They, after all, were the ones who had started all the trouble and who would have to testify against the twenty Hatfields who had been indicted for the execution of the McCoy boys. Without the McCoys, Perry Cline would not have a case.[57] This argument, of course, was specious. The McCoys had not witnessed the killings, and only Aunt Sally and Tolbert's wife had seen the boys in captivity. The very spurious nature of the argument shows the panic, fear, and anger gripping the Hatfields. Frustration at suddenly having to engage in conflict without customary guidelines led them to a patently irrational, to say nothing of ineffective, solution. It came from sheer desperation and an impatience to *do something*.

Whether Cap had the agreement of his father or the majority of the Hatfields is unknown. It seems unlikely, however, because when he rounded up a group of men to accompany him on this raid, only eight out of an identifiable thirty-seven members of the Hatfield "boys" went along. Devil Anse was not among them. Feud legend claims that Anse would have gone had he not been ill, but such behavior would have been out of character. If Anse had instigated the raid, he would have led it. Anse's grandson, in his reminiscences, insists that Anse argued against the whole idea from the beginning. Other absentees formed a significant group: Anse's brothers Valentine and Elias declined involvement, as did the three Mayhorn brothers, two of whom were Valentine's sons-in-law. One must suspect that Devil Anse and most of his group were not willing to take such drastic action or even to sanction it—possibly they didn't even know when or where it was to occur. Jim Vance and Cap led the group. The rest consisted of Johnse Hatfield, two sons of the murdered Ellison, and three others, all of whom had reputations as violent men: Tom "Guerrilla" Chambers, Charlie Gillespie, and French Ellis. Although Charlie Gillespie later claimed that his role was minimal because he was not told what was really going on until they reached the McCoy home, it was Ellison Mounts who was the most unwitting victim on the Hatfield side of this raid. Mounts was rumored to be the illegitimate son of Ellison Hatfield; he was also known to be "slow" or dimwitted. He probably did not understand the implications of the action the group was about to take. Including him in the raid seems a desperate attempt to shore up the group's numbers.[58]

In the early morning hours of 1 January 1888, the group crossed the river into Pike County, rode up the Hatfield Branch of Blackberry Creek and over the ridge to the home of Old Ranel McCoy. Cap apparently relinquished leadership to his uncle, Old Jim Vance, who instructed the rest not to fire until he gave the word. The group, however, was undisciplined and a nervous Johnse fired at the house before the signal. Before Randolph and his sons managed to organize resistance, Vance set the house on fire. In the ensuing melee two of Ranel's children, twenty-six-year-old Calvin and thirty-year-old Alifair, were killed as they ran out of the house. A younger daughter, Fannie, later claimed that it was Cap who shot Alifair, not the unfortunate Ellison Mounts who was later executed for that crime. Aunt Sally, attempting to reach her dying daughter, was clubbed and beaten by Jim Vance. Old Ranel escaped by hiding in the pigpen.[59] Altogether it was a bloody, ignominious affair and the Hatfield group, as they retreated down the mountain, knew that a terrible blunder had been made. Even the dimwitted Ellison Mounts realized what a mistake the raid had been. "Well, we killed the boy and girl, and I am sorry of it," he told Charlie Gillespie as they returned to the West Virginia side of the Tug. "We have made a bad job of it. . . . [T]here will be trouble over this."[60] Mounts's fears could not have been more accurate.

7

The Battle for Grapevine Creek

• •

It was a sad sight indeed that January 1st of 1888 when Old Ranel McCoy, in a wagon laden with the beaten, half-frozen body of Aunt Sally and his two dead children, Alifair and Calvin, straggled into Pikeville. Ranel went right to the home of Perry Cline where Rose-anna was living and taking care of the Cline children. Cline took the family in and Roseanna was given the task of nursing her mother back to health.[1] Barely had the family settled in and buried Calvin and Alifair when Perry Cline and J. Lee Ferguson were composing dispatches to state senators and newspapers. Both were anxious to inform Kentucky officials and the public of the latest atrocities committed by the Hatfields. The first newspaper notice of the feud was a letter from Ferguson published in a local paper, the *Big Sandy News*, in nearby Louisa, Kentucky, on 5 January. However, the story that first reached a broader readership was an 8 January article in the *Louisville Courier-Journal*. Picked up by papers all over the country, this was the story that first shaped the public impression of the feud. Headlines like "A Terrible Tragedy Perpetrated in Pike County by Desperadoes," and "A Murderous Gang," revealed the Pikeville origins of the article, from the pen of either Cline or Ferguson.

A letter has been received by Senator A. H. Stewart from a friend in Pikeville, Kentucky, giving an account of a terrible tragedy in Pike County on January 1. It appears that in 1882 parties led by a man named Hatfield abducted three boys named McCoy, and conveyed them to West Virginia. A reward was offered for the arrest of the Hatfield party, and one of the gang was captured, who is now in the Pike County jail. On Sunday last others of the same party went to the residence of Randolph McCoy, in Pike County, and killed his wife, mother of the three boys mentioned and his son; also set fire to the house, which with its contents, was entirely consumed. . . . The Pikeville jail is strongly guarded, but fears were entertained at the hour of writing that an attempt would be made to release the member of the gang confined there.[2]

According to this widely disseminated version of the feud, Devil Anse kidnapped the boys for no apparent reason and then followed up with a gratuitous house burning. It was typical of newspaper accounts of feud events that would appear over the course of the next several months. Although Cline intended to paint the Hatfields as deviants—desperadoes and outlaws—he only succeeded in enhancing the emerging stereotypical view of *all* mountaineers as irresponsible, ignorant, and violent. But for the moment, buoyed by the public outrage created by this kind of sensational publicity, Cline and Frank Phillips renewed their efforts at locating Hatfields on the West Virginia side of the Tug. Despite Phillips's dismissal as a Pike deputy sheriff, he continued to insist that he was an "agent" of the governor, with the full authority of the state of Kentucky. In the name of the state, the raids into West Virginia were continued.

On the same day that the initial feud story appeared in the *Louisville Courier-Journal*, Phillips, on just such a raid, encountered Old Jim Vance, his wife, and Cap Hatfield. Vance and Cap were not expecting a fight, but merely walking a mountain trail from Vance's home to Cap's. Outnumbered ten to one, they put up a fight, but to no avail. After Vance was hit by a bullet, Cap and Mary Vance barely made their escape. As the wounded Uncle Jim lay bleeding on the ground, a triumphant Phillips moved up to point-blank range and shot him to death. This was Phillips's first success since the capture of Selkirk McCoy the month before, and it encouraged the cocky young deputy to step up his pursuit of Hatfields, especially Devil Anse himself; over the next ten days he conducted a half-dozen more raids and succeeded in capturing Hatfield supporters Andy Varney, L. D. McCoy (Selkirk's son), Tom Chambers, Moses Christian, and Sam, Dock, and Plyant Mayhorn.[3] Devil Anse, however, continued to elude Phillips.

Then, in a surprising move, Valentine Hatfield, Devil Anse's older brother, decided to surrender to Phillips and Cline and stand trial in Pikeville. In a letter to Phillips, Valentine said that he would allow himself to be arrested but would rather not be "taken" until a few weeks before the trial would be held. Phillips, paying no attention to the last stipulation, rushed to Valentine's home to arrest him. Thus Valentine, by his own choice, joined the other eight Hatfields ensconced in the Pikeville jail.[4] Apparently, his position as local magistrate weighed heavily on Valentine, convincing him that his younger brothers, Smith and Patterson, were right in rejecting the extralegal violence that had begun with the killing of the three McCoy brothers and escalated to the use of terrorist tactics in the McCoy house burning. But the most astonishing aspect of Valentine's surrender is what it reveals about his unshaken confidence in the legal system. Valentine was convinced that even in hostile Pikeville he could clear his name and disassociate himself from the group who had burned the McCoy home.[5] Even with all the adverse publicity and excitement on both sides of the river, even with Perry Cline's obvious intent to revenge the loss of his inheritance, Valentine Hatfield believed that his side of the case would be seriously considered. It is a startling reminder of the mountaineers' faith in the ultimate prevalence of justice.

Although Devil Anse demonstrated no such faith, he still preferred to act within the bounds of legal authority. Impressive evidence that Devil Anse did not impulsively resort to violence was his failure to respond to these raids into West Virginia in the ways predicted by Perry Cline. No massive Hatfield forces rode into Pikeville attempting to release the prisoners, threaten peaceful residents, or burn the town.[6] On the contrary, now that Phillips and Cline had committed murder in West Virginia, Devil Anse thought he might have enough bargaining power to end the whole feud. Through his intermediary, John B. Floyd, Anse pointed out to Governor Wilson that there was now as much evidence against the McCoys as against the Hatfields.[7]

While the governor was considering these new developments, Anse approached the Logan County Court. Despite their hostility toward Anse Hatfield, Logan officials were now angry at the "invasion" of their county, and they prepared to defend the Tug boundary. With evidence in hand that Phillips and his men had killed Jim Vance in Logan County, the court issued warrants for the arrest of the twenty men in the posse.[8] They also directed Constable John R. Thompson to raise a posse to patrol the Tug boundary. Instructed not to cross the river, the men were only to hold themselves in readiness to arrest Phillips and the others who had taken part in Jim Vance's murder if they should once again cross into West Virginia. The stage was set for a violent conflict between the two groups. It came on 19 January, ten days after the killing of Jim Vance, when Phillips, this time with eighteen men, made another raid.

On the banks of Grapevine Creek the two posses met and engaged in the last skirmish of the feud, the "battle of Grapevine Creek." One has to wonder if Devil Anse, as he realized a fight was about to begin, thought it ironic that this first real pitched battle between the two sides took place at the very place where the feud began. It was undoubtedly his lawsuit against Perry Cline for the possession of Grapevine Creek, begun some sixteen years before, that had brought about this confrontation. What began as a dispute between neighbors over timber rights ended as a symbol of conflicting historical forces, with ramifications far beyond the two families or even the two states involved.

The conflict was no longer rooted in the internal dynamics of the community; instead, the feudists were now enmeshed in a raw struggle for economic and political power. Despite the fact that Cline had been successful in labeling the Hatfields as "feudists," "outlaws," and "desperadoes" and his own group as a legally constituted posse, this was only a useful fiction. Cline's supporters, despite their claims, had no official authority for their raids into West Virginia.[9] The conflict was not one of law versus lawlessness, but a power struggle between the local authority system and external forces. In such a contest, whether the localists won any one skirmish made no difference; they were doomed in the long run to failure. The superior resources available to the modernizers guaranteed their eventual triumph.

In the actual fight of 19 January, however, neither side made any substantive gains. Phillips captured no more Hatfields, and the

Hatfields failed to put a stop to the raids. Two casualties resulted from this skirmish on Grapevine Creek, one wounded and one killed. On the Cline-McCoy side, Bud McCoy was wounded in the shoulder. Bud was another young man with a reputation similar to that of Frank Phillips—he was known in the community as dangerous. The son of Unionist Harmon McCoy and brother of Johnse's wife, Nancy, he had not been involved in the first phase of the feud. After Cap Hatfield shot his brother, Jeff McCoy, however, he vowed revenge and was an eager participant in Phillips's posses. The only death that resulted from the battle was that of young Bill Dempsey, a resident of Logan Courthouse who had been deputized by Constable John Thompson. Before that day he had not been involved in the feud. Dempsey was first wounded, then cold-bloodedly shot to death by Frank Phillips as he begged for mercy, pleading that he was only acting as a sheriff's deputy, that he had nothing to do with the Hatfield gang.[10] That the two casualties of the only major battle of the feud were men who had taken no part in the first phase is symbolic of the fact that the second phase was a substantially different conflict than the first. Different people had become involved and a different set of social dynamics were at work.

Though the nature of the feud had been radically altered, it was not Devil Anse's group which had changed. Except for Bill Dempsey and Constable Thompson, most of Anse's supporters at Grapevine Creek were veterans of the feud's first phase. Of the forty-nine supporters claimed by the Hatfields in the feud's second phase, thirty-seven have been identified. Indeed, thirty-seven is probably a more accurate count, because the Hatfields may have exaggerated their numbers; the knowledgeable John B. Floyd estimated that there were only about thirty to forty men in the Hatfield "gang." (See Appendix 1 for a list of Hatfield supporters in the feud's second phase, along with their ages, residences, and property values.) Although nine, or one-third, were new recruits in the second phase, three of those were sons of Devil Anse or his brothers, Elias and Ellison, who had come of age since the first phase, and the other two were Old Jim Vance, Anse's uncle, and French Ellis, who had married a niece. Thus, only four were really brand-new to the feud.[11] (Although Jim Vance was killed ten days before the battle of Grapevine Creek and so obviously could not have participated in it, this analysis of second-phase feudists includes all those who participated *at any point* during the second stage.) Apart from these four, Anse's followers were identical to the first-phase group. Yet there was a subtle difference. In the first phase less than half his supporters were related to Anse, whereas 84 percent were either employed in the timbering crew or had bought land from him. In the second phase, the number of those related to him rose to nineteen, or 50 percent of the total, while the number of those with economic connections declined slightly, to 81 percent. The solidarity of Anse's group, while still bound by economic relationships, was more firmly rooted in family ties than it had been in the first phase.

For the McCoy-Cline group, just the reverse was true. In the initial phase, Old Ranel, his five sons, and his two nephews were the *only* McCoy feudists, but by the second phase the McCoys numbered forty men, only about a third of whom were in any way related to Old Ranel.[12] The very fact that so few of Ranel's relatives would join his vendetta indicates their strong disapproval of his behavior, even when it was aimed at one of the least-liked members of the community, Devil Anse Hatfield.

If Old Ranel's relatives made up only a small portion of the posses recruited by Cline, who were the others? If not relatives, could they have been neighbors and friends who resided in the Tug Valley? Residency patterns revealed in Table 4 demonstrate that Tug Valley inhabitants were almost as reluctant to become involved in the new feud as they had been in the old. Only twelve of Ranel's supporters, or 30 percent, actually lived in the Tug Valley; of these, five were carryovers from the first phase while seven were new to the conflict. Even these seven lived, not near Old Ranel in the Blackberry Creek district, but in Peter Creek district. Three were sons of Unionist Harmon McCoy and brothers of Johnse's wife, Nancy, and thus nephews of Perry Cline. They, along with four neighbors from Peter Creek, chose to join the Phillips posse.[13] Did they join out of loyalty to Old Ranel, and if so, then why had they not been participants in the earlier hostilities? Or did they join merely for the excitement and adventure? Several of these young men already had reputations as dangerous men. Yet even if we assume that all seven, either because of their residence in the Tug Valley or their relationship to Old Ranel, were motivated by the original feud, the total of new feudists with origins in the Tug Valley still amounts to only

TABLE 4

Residence Patterns of Second-Phase Feudists

Place	Hatfield	McCoy-Cline
Logan Courthouse	2 (5%)	1 (3%)
Tug Valley (W.Va.)	35 (95%)	2 (5%)
Tug Valley (Ky.)	0 (0%)	10 (24%)
Pikeville region	0 (0%)	27 (68%)
Total	37 (100%)	40 (100%)

Sources: U.S. census, population and agricultural schedules for Logan and Pike counties, 1870–80, NA.

twelve out of forty, or less than one-third (see Appendix 2). This clearly was no indigenous uprising against the Hatfields—remember that thirty to forty of Devil Anse's Tug Valley neighbors rallied to his support. As John B. Floyd observed, "while the McCoys are among the Kentucky men [Phillips-Cline posse], they constitute but a small portion of the gang."[14]

Apparently Floyd knew what historians have since overlooked: in the feud's second phase, a new contingent of men had taken over the anti-Hatfield role of the McCoys. Twenty-eight out of the forty, or 70 percent of the group identified as "McCoys," were completely new to the conflict. Not only were they unrelated to the McCoys, but they did not even reside in the Tug Valley. With one exception, all lived in the districts of Pike County surrounding Pikeville, separated from the Tug Valley by the mountain ridge that divided the two regions. Like Frank Phillips, they knew Devil Anse only by reputation. The one exception to this pattern—Dave Stratton—is a notable one. Stratton resided not in Pike County but in Logan Courthouse. A son of circuit clerk William Stratton, Dave belonged to a group of Anse's political adversaries in Logan. Following the defeat of their candidate in the 1886 election, Stratton offered his assistance to the Cline-McCoy group.[15] It seems that Stratton had his own grudge against Devil Anse not connected to the original feud; he merely seized the opportunity offered by Cline and Phillips to wreak his own private revenge. But what of the remaining twenty-seven? Since they were not part of the old feud, how and why did they get involved in 1888? (See Appendix 3 for a list of Cline's supporters, with their ages, district of residence, and property values.)

The question of how they became involved seems easily answered upon examination of their geographic distribution. Twelve, or almost half, lived in the district where Pikeville was located. Seven of these actually lived in the town of Pikeville, where they would have been neighbors of Cline, Dils, and Ferguson. Cline's personal influence in persuading them to join the posse is apparent. Eight, or another third, came from the Johns Creek district, where they would have been neighbors of Frank Phillips. Like Cline, Phillips aggressively prodded his neighbors to join in the pursuit of the Hatfields. The remaining four new recruits resided in districts immediately adjacent to Pikeville. Face-to-face communication, then, was responsible for the network of individuals who chose to join the posses. But this becomes clear only when one understands that the leader of the feud's second phase was Perry Cline rather than Randolph McCoy. In neither phase of the feud was Old Ranel able to recruit more than a handful of his own family and friends. It took Cline's broader influence to attract new participants. Yet for all his effort, it is surprising that Cline could attract less than thirty recruits. If the mountaineers really had some predisposition to violence, here was a chance to engage in violent action legally sanctioned by the county. But only a few took advantage of the opportunity.

If the question of *how* members of the group were recruited is relatively uncomplicated, the reasons *why* they chose to join are another matter. One explanation might be that these were young men, boisterous and rowdy, ever ready for excitement and adventure. Some crime historians cite the propensity of young, energetic men for violent activity. A quick perusal of the ages and family statuses of Cline's supporters belies this explanation. Almost two-thirds of the Cline group were over the age of twenty-five, and twenty or 71 percent were married heads of households. Table 5 compares the age distribution of the McCoy-Cline group to that of the Hatfields. Although Phillips and a few others had bad reputations, the group as a whole was not made up of antisocial, brawling young men. More representative were respected farmers like Ran-

The Politics of Feuding

TABLE 5

Age Distribution of Feudists

Age	Hatfield (37)	Cline (28)	McCoy-Cline (40)
Under 25	5 (14%)	8 (29%)	9 (22.5%)
25–35	16 (43%)	6 (21%)	13 (32.5%)
35–45	5 (14%)	9 (32%)	11 (27.5%)
Over 45	6 (16%)	2 (7%)	4 (10%)
Unknown	5 (14%)	3 (11%)	3 (7.5%)
Average age	35	35	33

Sources: U.S. census, population schedules for Logan and Pike counties, 1850–80, 1900, NA.

som and Moses Maynard, aged thirty-seven and forty-one respectively, who had families. Indeed, all of the anti-Hatfield group had extensive ties to the community; their families can be traced back to the settlement period of the 1820s and 1830s. In age distribution and family status they were not unlike Devil Anse's supporters. In neither group were the members primarily young or lacking the stabilizing influences of family and community roots.

The supporters Cline attracted were not, however, simply ordinary farmers. Many were among the wealthiest individuals in Pike County; even Frank Phillips was no pauper, but held property valued at $1,600. By Pike County standards this made him very well-to-do, indeed. Unlike Phillips, whose reputation was unsavory despite his wealth, many others held positions of social and political prominence in the village. Two of Cline's most enthusiastic supporters were the county judge, Tobias Wagner, and the county prosecutor, J. Lee Ferguson. Ferguson had accompanied Cline and Phillips to Frankfort to win the governor's backing and, for reasons that are not altogether clear, he seemed just as anxious as Perry Cline to capture and imprison Devil Anse. Besides these political leaders, four members of the Sowards family—large landholders and merchants in the Pikeville region—also joined in the Hatfield hunt. In

TABLE 6
Wealth Distribution of Feudists

Wealth	Hatfields	Clines	McCoy-Cline
Under $200	9 (24%)	9 (32%)	17 (42%)
$201–$999	19 (51%)	4 (14%)	8 (20%)
Over $1,000	4 (11%)	11 (39%)	11 (28%)
Unknown	5 (14%)	4 (14%)	4 (10%)
Totals	37 (100%)	28 (99%)	40 (100%)

Note: Figures are based on *family* (not individual) assets. Names of feudists in each group are listed in Appendixes 1–3.
Sources: U.S. census, population and agricultural schedules for Logan and Pike counties, 1850–80, NA; land tax books, 1880–90, LCC; Pike County tax books, 1880–90, UKL.

all, eleven or a stunning 40 percent of Cline's new recruits were wealthy, each possessing property valued at more than $1,000. They represented, in fact, most of the elite of Pikeville. But impressive as this group was in terms of its political and economic influence in Pikeville, it is likely that Cline had even more influential support from John R. Dils. Dils is not formally included in my list of Cline supporters (see Appendix 3) because there is no direct evidence of his *active* involvement in the feud; however, his role as guardian for both Cline and Phillips and his consistent support of Cline on various issues in county court sessions suggest that he must have played a crucial role in the revival of the Hatfield indictments. If he was involved, Dils would have been by far the wealthiest and most influential of Cline's supporters. As Table 6 shows, anyone holding property valued at more than $1,000 was considered well-to-do, but John Dils's property value in the 1880s was listed at close to $40,000. If anything, then, the official roster of Cline's supporters in the second phase understates the political and economic power behind the Cline-McCoy group.

The participation of this commercial and economic elite made Cline's group quite different from the Hatfields, who, although once powerful, now held only minor offices and were rapidly losing

The Politics of Feuding

TABLE 7

Personal Property Distribution of Feudists

Value	Hatfields	Clines	McCoy-Cline
Under $500	28 (76%)	18 (64%)	29 (72%)
$501–$999	3 (8%)	3 (11%)	4 (10%)
Over $1,000	1 (3%)	3 (11%)	3 (8%)
Unknown	5 (13%)	4 (14%)	4 (10%)
Totals	37 (100%)	28 (100%)	40 (100%)

Note: Figures are based on *family* (not individual) assets. Names of feudists in each group are listed in Appendixes 1–3.
Sources: U.S. census, population and agricultural schedules for Logan and Pike counties, 1850–80, NA; land tax books, 1880–90, LCC; Pike County tax books, 1880–90, UKL.

their political influence to the modernizers and developers in Logan County. Although Devil Anse and three of his brothers were large landholders with property valued at more than $1,000, they constituted only 11 percent of the group. Most of the Hatfields (51 percent) were neither wealthy nor poor, but solidly in the middle of the economic structure; they were average farmers whose primary assets were small tracts of land. Since all resided in the Tug Valley, none of the Hatfields lived in or near a regional commercial center as did Cline's supporters. Moreover, members of the Cline group, reflecting their status as commercial farmers or merchants, held considerably more of their property in personal estate (movable property such as business merchandise and luxury possessions) than the Hatfields did. Cline himself was taxed for a gold watch, a piano, and a carriage. Among his supporters, three were taxed for more than $1,000 in personal property, whereas among the Hatfields, only Anse's brother Elias had a similar amount.

As important as the elite leaders were to Cline's prosecution of the Hatfields, they formed a slight minority in the total number of his supporters. Many of those came from among the poorest men residing around Pikeville. Nine, or one-third, of the group were from families that owned property valued at less than $200. Lindo

Hardin, Joe Ramsey, Sam Miller, and Ed Stewart were all in this category of younger men who had neither land nor much hope for acquiring any from their impoverished families. By contrast, only nine, or 24 percent, of Anse's supporters came from the poorest families in the valley.

The significant difference between the two groups, then, was in the percentage who occupied the middle of the economic structure. Twenty or 71 percent of Cline's supporters were either very well-to-do or very poor; only about 14 percent occupied the middle social strata. In contrast, only thirteen or 35 percent of Hatfield's supporters were either very poor or very wealthy, whereas 51 percent represented the middle of the economic scale in the Tug Valley. Despite their timbering business, the Hatfields' interests were rooted in subsistence farming and small-scale timbering, while the Cline group's prosperity depended upon increased commerce and industrial development—a difference creating a basic divergence in economic outlook. The interests of the Cline group would be advanced by development and investment; the results would be increased profits for the wealthy 40 percent of the group and, for the poorest third, wage-labor opportunities in the timber, railroad, and coal industries. From the Hatfield perspective, however, massive development and control of the land by outside corporations threatened to deprive them of their land and destroy small-scale, independent timbering operations. Therefore, the economic interests of the two groups were in very real competition.

Nevertheless, a difference in economic outlook does not fully explain the willingness of Cline's supporters to take violent action against Devil Anse. Only Cline himself, Stratton, and possibly Dils had personal grievances or stood to benefit directly from the destruction of Devil Anse's business. In the absence of a direct economic or personal interest, what motivated the majority of the group? One contemporary observer, the ubiquitous John B. Floyd, had an answer; after the battle of Grapevine Creek, he told the *Wheeling Intelligencer* that the hostilities were rooted in the Civil War.[16] As we have seen, scholars have rejected this theory, but they have done so on the grounds that most Hatfields and McCoys fought on the same side—that of the Confederacy. What these scholars failed to recognize was that the driving force behind the McCoys in this second incarnation of the feud was not Old Ranel, but Perry Cline and his influential supporters in Pikeville. With this new perspective, it is time to reconsider the Civil War theory.

It is very possible that Perry Cline himself was a Unionist, as were his sister and his brother-in-law Harmon McCoy; we have already noted that after the war Cline chose as his guardian John Dils, the most prominent Unionist in the entire region. All the other youngsters for whom Dils acted as guardian were the children of Union soldiers. In fact, just as Devil Anse was known as the leader of a notorious band of southern rebels in the Tug Valley, John R. Dils was widely recognized as the leader of Pikeville's Unionists. That the latter was not an insignificant group is suggested by an 1868 county voting list showing that 46 percent of the registered voters in the Pikeville region were Republicans.[17] Because of Dils's highly visible role as a Unionist and a Republican, it is difficult to avoid the conclusion that, although Cline himself was raised in the Tug Valley, his family's social network was strongly intertwined with Pikeville's Unionists.

The Unionists in Pikeville had good reason to harbor an enduring fear and resentment of Devil Anse Hatfield. Because the guerrilla band he led had ranged so widely in and around Pike and Logan counties, it seems extremely likely that these Union loyalists had been threatened or harrassed or even had property confiscated by the Confederates. Unlike the Tug Valley, where Anse and his Logan Wildcats were heroes who protected the community, a good portion of those living around Pikeville regarded Devil Anse as a feared and dangerous enemy.

Thus, the Tug Valley and Pikeville regions of Pike County had been at odds since the Civil War; this new "war" in the guise of a feud could be interpreted as an extension of that struggle, as it was from the Unionist families of the Pikeville region that Cline drew many of his anti-Hatfield supporters. No less than ten had fathers— Harmon McCoy, Lewis Sowards, William H. Sowards, Samuel King, Henry C. Sowards, and Billy Phillips—who had served in Dils's Union regiment.[18] Another five were sons of men who were registered Republicans in 1868.[19] Two of Cline's strongest supporters, Tobias Wagner and J. Lee Ferguson, were well-known Republicans in the 1880s.[20] In all, eighteen, or 45 percent, of the combined McCoy-Cline group were from Unionist/Republican families or were themselves Republicans. (See Appendix 4 for the political affiliation of McCoy-Cline supporters.) This evidence suggests that the chance to "get even" with Devil Anse may well have motivated others besides Perry Cline.

But the feud was more than just an opportunity to even an old score; since the war, economic and cultural differences between Pikeville and the Tug Valley had become more and more pronounced. During the war, Confederate supporters seemed intent on preserving the autonomy and independence of their communities from the encroachment of outside economic, political, and religious influences. Unionists, on the other hand, as early as the 1860s advocated economic development and greater integration into the national economy. In Pikeville local boosters had been working for economic development since the war. With Pikeville the center of Republicanism and enthusiasm for economic modernization and the Tug Valley the center of resistance, it is not surprising that old war animosities combined with new hopes for regional development persuaded Pikeville area residents to perceive Devil Anse, not only as an old enemy, but as a dangerous obstacle to future prosperity.

This political and economic clash was exacerbated by cultural differences, which had also become more apparent since the war. Pikeville merchants and politicians adopted and fostered the development of evangelical religious values. But it was only the towns and their immediately surrounding areas that were receptive to the new religious beliefs—the Tug Valley was not. It is significant that the same people who promoted middle-class values associated with evangelical religion were also the most vigorous in renewing a long-dormant feud. In their minds economic development was inextricably linked to the rational cultural values prevalent in the rest of the country. This suggests that the posse's effort to suppress Devil Anse Hatfield was not simply, or even primarily, an economic power struggle; it was also a cultural struggle. Bringing Devil Anse to "justice" would demonstrate to investors, to the world, and to the posse members themselves that they stood for the "progress" of civilization.[21]

None of these differences can fully explain the feud's second phase; they can only illuminate the social and cultural context within which the feud erupted. The broad patterns of conflict were not unique to the Tug Valley but were widespread in Appalachia throughout the late nineteenth century. However, in Pike and Logan counties in 1888 they were manifested in a specific set of violent episodes known as the Hatfield-McCoy feud. The second stage of the feud reveals the way in which these broader historical forces had overwhelmed the original conflict, at the same time creating the misapprehension that Appalachian culture itself was the culprit.

Nevertheless, the conflict was not simply a confrontation between traditionalists and modernizers. In fact, each side contained adherents of both positions. As we have seen, Devil Anse himself actually had a foot in each world, while the Cline-Phillips posses contained individuals who represented a variety of forces (sometimes at odds with each other). Perry Cline, although he was carrying out a personal quarrel, was only able to do so because he mustered the support of local Pikeville developers as well as officials at the state level. They, unlike Cline and perhaps Stratton, had no personal grudge against Hatfield, but they were convinced that prosecution of the feudists would increase the chances of an immediate infusion of capital from outside the region. Their motivation was more than economic, however. They were part of the new merchant professional class in Pikeville that had already espoused the cultural values associated with the American middle class. Progress, education, and evangelical religion, they believed, would all be furthered when people like Devil Anse were suppressed. To this new elite, Devil Anse represented parochialism, stubborn independence, backwardness, and ultimately resistance to progress. Their participation in the attack on him was more a rejection of mountain culture than a personal vendetta. Ironically, Devil Anse had come to stand for the ignorant obstructionist instead of the ambitious entrepreneur he really was. His defeat was necessary less for economic gain than for the inevitable march into Appalachia of what they had come to think of as civilization.

Another group within the McCoy-Cline faction consisted of younger, landless men. Many like Jake, Lark, and Jeff McCoy were known as Pike County's "dangerous" men. On the surface it seems that they joined the posse for adventure, but at the root of their daredevil spirits lay the lack of economic or social opportunity. One means of personal redemption was to earn a tough, fearless reputation, but another was to aid the cause of bringing development, and thus jobs, to Pike County. Perhaps the motivation for most was some combination of the two. It is ironic that the same frustrations that led Devil Anse's supporters to rally to his defense moved the young men of Pikeville to join in the "war" against him. The determining factor in which side they joined had more to do with an accident of geography than anything else. Their families, sixty years before, had settled around Pikeville rather than in the Magnolia district of Logan County from whence Devil Anse drew his supporters, and so they sought to prove their manhood by fighting against him rather than for him.

Yet another small contingent of the posse, led by Old Ranel's son James, represented the old feud, the one begun ten years before. James McCoy, according to a McCoy family historian, was fighting old battles. He hoped to avenge the death of his brothers and his sister. Ironically, he symbolized the goals of the old feud, when opposing Devil Anse meant opposing the callous and roughshod manner with which Anse bested his neighbors. James and his faction unwittingly had joined forces with developers whose victory promised economic modernization on a scale incomprehensible to Old Ranel and his family. But James didn't realize that; he thought he was fighting for his family's honor.

The difference between Frank Phillips and James McCoy is apparent in their attitudes toward the enemy. During their raids into West Virginia, first when Phillips was about to shoot wounded Jim Vance and later at Grapevine Creek when Bill Dempsey pled for mercy, James McCoy intervened. There was no reason, he argued, to murder wounded opponents. Phillips responded by insulting James and rudely pushing him aside; for one brief moment onlookers thought that McCoy and Phillips were ready to fight each other, but McCoy finally backed down.[22] It must have been painfully obvious that Frank Phillips, not the McCoys, was in charge of the Hatfield hunt. James McCoy had discovered that his allies had recast both the nature and purpose of the feud. Instead of the state simply backing the McCoys' search for justice, the McCoys had become pawns in a larger struggle for economic and cultural control of the Tug Valley. It was a struggle eventually lost by both the Hatfields and McCoys.

When the battle of Grapevine Creek was over, Phillips and his posse returned to Pikeville jubilant. They had proven their mettle in a pitched battle with Devil Anse Hatfield and his boys. It was like returning victorious from a war. In her book on the McCoys, Truda McCoy recounts that members of the posse regaled everyone again and again with tales of the fight: how Ed Stewart had turned yellow, hid under some bushes, and finally run for home; how Jim McCoy, Ranel's son, tried to persuade Phillips and Dave Stratton not to kill Bill Dempsey; and how Cap Hatfield had been in such a hurry to escape that he shed his overcoat in flight. Sam McCoy, another of Ranel's sons, picked up the overcoat and wore it home, where admiring young women gathered around begging Sam for a button from Cap's coat "as a souvenir." Sam's wife, Martha, jealous of the girls' attention to Sam, "made the overcoat disappear."[23] The men who had fought the Hatfields had become local heroes.

Perry Cline, too, felt his efforts had been rewarded. Although Devil Anse had not been captured, there were nine Hatfield supporters locked in the Pikeville jail awaiting trial. Before long he heard another piece of news that must have given him more than a little pleasure. Immediately after the "battle" Devil Anse's political and business enemies in Logan County took advantage of his vulnerability and went after his land. Debt cases that had been long pending in the court were brought quickly to trial and judgments issued. On 28 January 1888, nine days after the battle, a series of old court judgments were officially entered in the docket book, indicating a concerted effort to collect them all at once.[24] Anse found that he owed hundreds of dollars, payable immediately. Lacking cash, he needed to sell land quickly. Beginning on 30 January 1888, in a series of transactions, Anse sold his Grapevine lands to J. D. Sergeant, a coal agent for a group of Philadelphia capitalists.[25] As part of the bargain, Sergeant paid off Anse's debts; the judgment docket book of the county court lists debt after debt, "paid by J. D. Sergeant."[26] Devil Anse had been forced into what many of his neighbors had been doing voluntarily since 1883. He sold his land to outside capitalists. True, the sale brought him a profit, but one not nearly as high as it could have been in just a few short years when the railroad was completed. Although Cline had not regained his lost inheritance, he could take some satisfaction in his revenge. The pressure he had brought to bear with the threat of arrest and prosecution by the Pike County authorities had finally defeated Devil Anse's entrepreneurial ambitions. Cline's feelings of triumph

were probably reflected in his friend J. Lee Ferguson's gleeful statement to the press that Devil Anse had been forced to sell for $7,000
when the land was really worth $15,000.[27] By 1890 the same land
would be worth $75,000.[28]

Despite the arrest of his nine supporters and the loss of his land
and entrepreneurial ambitions, Devil Anse—contrary to the predictions of Pike officials—made no attempt to ride into Pikeville to
exact vengeance, but instead turned his attention to moving his
family away from the Tug Valley. Twenty miles north, just outside
the town of Logan, he purchased a tract of land on Main Island
Creek and, high up a mountain ridge from which he could observe
all approaches, he built a new home guarded by a barricaded fort.[29]
There, in virtual seclusion, Devil Anse awaited the outcome of the
legal proceedings and the fate of his nine supporters in Pikeville
jail.

The battle of Grapevine Creek marked not only the end of the
feud but also the end of an era in the Tug Valley—an era that, despite subtle intrusions of a market economy, was still dominated by
traditional institutions and values. Historians agree that the year
1888 was the most important turning point in the history of the
Tug Valley, but it was neither the battle nor Devil Anse's move
away from the valley that made that year memorable. It was the
year, explained one historian, that "a company of railroad surveyors
first broke a path along the Tug."[30] With the appearance of those
surveyors only a few months after the battle of Grapevine Creek,
the valley was initiated into a new industrial order, which dramatically altered the character of the valley as well as its relations with
the surrounding region.

Before 1888, the Tug Valley had been considered, by the relatively
more cosmopolitan residents of Pikeville and Logan Courthouse, as
the remote and primitive backyard of their respective counties.
Both these villages were county seats, regional trading centers, and
communication hubs linking the surrounding areas to the outside
world. It was in each of these villages that the local elite concentrated their efforts to attract investment and forge economic links
with the national economy. Yet a single decision by a corporation
based hundreds of miles away thwarted their efforts and altered the
direction of economic development in the region. By deciding to
build the Norfork and Western Railroad along the Tug Fork of the

Big Sandy, the president of that company bypassed the budding commercial centers of Pikeville and Logan Courthouse and decreed that the Tug Valley would become the fastest-growing area in land values, new towns, and population—would, in fact, undergo an economic boom while Logan and Pikeville languished.[31] The disparity was not overcome until 1905, when Logan Courthouse and Pikeville each acquired their own railroads and thereby the inevitable timber and coal companies.[32]

As soon as Devil Anse moved away from his old home, his creditors and enemies moved in. While Devil Anse hunted bears a few miles from the town of Logan, the Tug Valley was developed into what is now proudly advertized as the "heart of the million dollar coalfield." No sooner had Anse sold his land to J. D. Sergeant and moved away from the valley than the Logan and Pikeville elite moved quickly to gain control of land in the Tug Valley. Between 1890 and 1892 land in the Tug Valley increased in value by more than 400 percent.[33] Where there had been not a single town or village, two suddenly appeared. At the mouth of Pond Creek, a few miles from the Hatfield enclave on Mates Creek, Williamson was laid out by a group of investors that included T. H. Harvey.[34] Harvey was Logan's "law and order" circuit court judge, who prosecuted liquor and sabbath-breaking violations with such "vigor."[35] A newspaper, the *Sandy New Era*, was planned for the town and was capitalized by, among others, several of the Logan elite.[36] In much the same way, the town of Matewan was created by investors who were friends and political allies of *Banner* editor H. C. Ragland. Located in the heart of Hatfield-McCoy country at the mouth of Mates Creek, the town swallowed up the house where Ellison Hatfield had been taken to die and the old schoolhouse where the three McCoys had been held prisoner. The town was named not for Mates Creek but for Mattewan, New York, the hometown of one of the railroad engineers. Local residents eventually triumphed though, at least in the matter of a name, by deleting one "t" and changing the pronunciation.[37]

Between 1888 and 1892 the tracks of the Norfolk and Western were laid amid spectacularly rising land values and a rush by local elites to found instant towns—to the bewilderment of local residents who still assumed that the major threats to their well-being came from bounty-hungry detectives. Suddenly their lands were being seized for the railroad right-of-way and hundreds of strangers—engineers, surveyors, speculators and construction workers—flooded the valley. This industrial invasion of the Tug brought more than bewilderment and social disruption; it increased violence and lawlessness. In a letter to the Norfolk and Western's English investors, the president of the company wrote that the most difficult section to construct was the one through the Tug Valley. "There has been so much lawlessness and shooting that we have found it almost impossible to get good men to work," he claimed.[38]

This violence was not due to feuding. H. C. Ragland, although a staunch supporter of railroads and modernization, was quick to point out that railroad construction, not feuding, was responsible for the increased crime in the Tug Valley. To prove it he broke down Logan County misdemeanor indictments for the year 1891 geographically: 74 percent of the indictments for carrying concealed weapons and 84 percent of those for selling illegal whiskey originated in the Tug Valley, on what Ragland called the "Sandy side" of the county where railroad construction was underway.[39] Murder and assaults were also more frequent in the Tug Valley than in the Guyandotte Valley. This high rate of crime Ragland attributed both to the violent tendencies of the immigrant railroad workers and to high levels of whiskey consumption. Much of the crime committed in the Tug Valley involved railroad workers and not mountaineers. But the mountaineers, concluded Ragland, were not blameless; they, too, carried weapons and engaged in the production and sale of whiskey. It was said, he lamented in one editorial, that "on the Sandy side of this county, both men and women, are peddling out whiskey even to children."[40] Despite the *Banner's* unwavering contention that the railroad would ultimately bring prosperity, progress, and civilization to all, it was open in admitting that, for the moment, social chaos was the result.

Ragland and the local elite in Logan Courthouse, however, were unshaken in their faith in the benefits of economic modernization. They considered the increasing crime and disorder to be not an economic or social problem, but a cultural one. The traditional culture of the mountaineers, they concluded, was unsuited to the new economic order and required reshaping. Although Ragland did not have much hope for civilizing the black and immigrant workers—he treated them with contempt—he thought of the rural mountaineers as primitive but good people whose slothful and degenerate habits could be altered by some combination of coercion, education, and exposure to evangelical religion.[41]

It was to this end that he and J. A. Nighbert, in the spring of 1889, began publication of the *Logan Banner*. As we have seen, the *Banner* took on the task of persuading the local farmers that the railroad, and even the buying up of Logan lands by eastern capitalists, would eventually benefit everyone. Beyond that immediate task, from the day it began the *Banner* waged an unrelenting campaign against the unselfconscious and boisterous culture of the mountaineers. Ragland intended the paper to serve as a kind of "how to" manual for Logan citizens, both regenerate and unregenerate. For example, he advocated that the courts should be more vigorous in prosecuting rowdiness and drunkenness and that businessmen should take the lead by refusing to employ men who carried guns and by lending financial and moral support to the founding of evangelical churches.[42]

All these efforts were aimed at rooting out what Ragland perceived as the cause of crime and violence: alcohol. Consistently condemning whiskey consumption as the single most culpable mountain cultural trait, he stridently insisted on its total eradication.[43] Not that Ragland completely ignored other issues—he editorialized repeatedly against such things as the proliferation of firearms and their indiscriminate use, the rowdiness rampant on court days, and the reluctance of young men to get and hold wage-labor jobs. But Ragland was firmly convinced that at the root of all these objectionable behaviors lay alcohol and the lack of self-control it produced.

Whether mountaineers were actually drinking more at that time than they had in the past is questionable. Whiskey had been part of their culture in the same way that rum had been an integral part of colonial American culture from Virginia to New England and was still a part of Catholic immigrant culture. The temperance crusade that began in 1830s New England had never reached Appalachia, which simply continued a cultural tradition once dominant in all regions. Yet it is possible that in the 1880s actual consumption of whiskey increased, aggravated by declining economic prospects for landholding and agriculture. The appearance of a whole class of young men categorized as "dangerous" because of drunken brawling seems to support this analysis.

Whether drinking was actually increasing or not, the crusade embarked upon by the *Banner* was out of proportion to the problem. Absolutely opposed to all drinking, anywhere, at any time, Ragland was not simply calling for a return to the moderation of the past. Whiskey was detected not only behind violence and crime, but also behind the mountaineers' "irrational" resistance to wage labor and the new order. Ragland and the *Banner* were blaming whiskey for behavior that might have been exaggerated by social tension but that was rooted in traditional mountain culture. In fact, this crusade aimed at a fundamental alteration of mountain culture; whiskey was only the symbol. Whiskey consumption became the one behavior that separated the middle class from the lower class. It symbolized the conflict between the values of self-discipline and self-control cherished by a newly created middle class and the more boisterous and easy-going style of the mountaineers. In this regard the crusade can be seen as almost a rerun of the struggle played out earlier in the century in the Northeast. The importance of the contests in that earlier period and in the Logan County of the 1890s was that they delineated the difference between new middle class and lower class. Temperance became a badge of middle-class respectability and at the same time served as a mechanism to control the working class.[44]

The divisiveness caused by the antiwhiskey campaign was exaggerated by the fact that such social differentiation was new to Logan and Pike counties. Class had not previously been a useful category for describing social relations. Although there assuredly was a hierarchy of wealth and status recognized by everyone, most male heads of families considered themselves independent farmers and based their social organization on kinship and geographic proximity rather than professional or class identification.[45] The industrialization of the region brought sudden alterations in this social structure. It created a society based on three classes: (1) a group of absentee speculators and corporations who made the economic decisions and received the profits from the region's natural resources; (2) a small, emerging middle class, which we have been calling the local elite—large landholders, merchants, lawyers, and other professionals who depended on the absentee elite for economic prosperity and cultural models; and (3) the majority of mountain dwellers— whether small farmers or, increasingly, wage laborers in the timber and coal industries.

Although local elites were in the minority, they had a better chance of winning the battle for social control and cultural hegemony than the working classes. Backed by the financial and moral power of the absentee owners, they also had secured control of local institutions. We have already seen how the alterations in the judicial system and county government in the 1880s benefited the merchant and professional classes. This advantage was reinforced by the evangelical clergy and the printed word—such as newspapers like the *Banner*. By focusing on whiskey as the cultural cause of lower-class poverty, ignorance, lawlessness, and violence, the local elite deflected attention from a very real set of economic and social damages being inflicted not only on traditional mountaineers but on black and immigrant workers.[46] In the case of the mountaineers, landownership and size of farms had been gradually declining for three generations; by 1900, they plummeted. In that year only 30 percent of heads of families owned their own farms, down from 45 percent in 1880, and the average size among those who did own farms was 110 acres, or one-third of what it had been only twenty years before.[47] Tug Valley residents were becoming wage laborers, and the consequences reached far beyond the economic level. Landownership had always been a symbol of independence and manhood; it was essential to self-esteem and social status. When mountaineers went to work as laborers on railroad construction crews, they were forced to work or perhaps compete with black and immigrant workers brought in by the company. The bosses felt that mountaineers deserved no more status or respect than their imported workers, and they frequently treated both with disdain. For young mountaineers, accustomed to independence and nurtured in the sheltered environment of familiar friends and kin, such treatment was a rude shock, perhaps enough of one to cause the excessive drinking and bravado that came to be defined as lower-class. The middle class, however, saw the problem not as social or economic, but personal, and the solution was simple—temperance first, followed by education and religion. Just as the feud was blamed on some inherent moral failing in the mountaineers, social disruption caused by economic transformation was blamed on their inferior culture. Cultural enlightenment, claimed the modernizers, would cure the problem, and the intensity of campaigns against whiskey like Ragland's attested to the sincerity of their conviction.

As the Raglands, Nighberts, Clines, and Dilses seized the initiative in helping eastern capitalists to industrialize the Tug Valley and Devil Anse retreated to his mountain fortress, the changes overtaking the valley were epitomized by Grapevine Creek. Indeed, the tiny creek symbolizes both the struggle over capitalist transformation and its outcome. One might say that the battle *of* Grapevine Creek was more accurately the battle *for* Grapevine Creek— one in a series of contests for hegemony over Appalachia's rich resources. After the fighting was over, the hollow through which the creek ran became one of the richest coal-producing hollows in the Tug Valley. A feeder railroad line ran along its narrow bottom and the water ran red with sludge from the mine, which produced fabulous profits for the developers, but only ugliness and poverty for the people who lived there.

On Trial

If the battle of Grapevine Creek ended the actual events of the feud, it also signaled a new incarnation in the newspapers and the courts. For it was in both arenas that the Hatfields would be tried. The courts accomplished the limited objective of finding Valentine Hatfield and the other eight Hatfield supporters guilty of the deaths of four of Randolph McCoy's children, but the newspapers found the Hatfields, the McCoys, and Appalachian culture generally guilty of lawlessness, violence, and willful resistance to "progress."

The feud first appeared in regional and national newspapers in the weeks following the Hatfield attack on the McCoy home, but it did not become front-page news until after the battle of Grapevine Creek. The first dispatches describing the burning of the McCoy home by Hatfield "desperadoes" reflected the bias of Perry Cline and his anti-Hatfield group in Pikeville, and the majority of newspaper stories in papers all over the country continued that interpretation in the following weeks when feud publicity was at its height. Although articles appeared in a variety of newspapers, there were actually only a few sources which were widely repeated. One of the most prolific writers on the feud was a reporter in Catlettsburg, Kentucky, a regional trading center and the nearest railroad terminus to the Tug Valley region. This unknown reporter must have been a friend of Perry Cline or some other member of the the Pikeville group, because he consistently portrayed their interpretation of events; defenders of the Hatfields soon dubbed him the "Catlettsburg Liar."[1] For example, in an article describing the Grapevine

Creek episode that appeared in the *Cincinnati Enquirer*, the *Louis-ville Courier-Journal*, and the *New York Times*, among others, this writer began by calling the conflict a "war of extermination" be-tween the Hatfields and McCoys. The McCoys were described as a "posse" pursuing the Hatfield "gang" which has "warned" the peo-ple of Pike County that it proposed to "kill them and burn their property." In this account, there is no doubt as to the identity of the villains. Although both sides tended to excessive violence, accord-ing to the Catlettsburg writer, the Phillips-McCoy-Cline contin-gent were attempting to carry out justice, whereas the Hatfields were "desperadoes," "murderers," and "outlaws."[2]

It was not only the sensational quality of the story that brought so much press coverage in the next few weeks. The feud caused an unprecedented judicial controversy between the states of West Vir-ginia and Kentucky that went all the way to the Supreme Court of the United States. Early in January 1888 Governor E. Willis Wilson of West Virginia had continued to delay his decision in regard to extradition. Finally, on 21 January, he wrote to Governor S. B. Buck-ner of Kentucky, reviewing the case. Despite his own doubts about extraditing the Hatfields on five-year-old indictments, he told Buck-ner, he had ordered the warrants issued. But recently he had learned that Cline had solicited a bribe. Extradition was being used, he indignantly told Buckner, "not to secure the ends of public justice, but to extort money from the accused." Wilson enclosed three de-positions purporting to prove that Cline had accepted money to call off the Hatfield hunt, and he concluded that "neither Cline nor Phillips . . . are proper persons to intrust with [due] process of either Kentucky or West Virginia." On the basis of this new information he had decided to refuse the extradition request.[3]

A few days later Wilson heard of the battle of Grapevine Creek and the capture of eight more Hatfield supporters, including justice of the peace Valentine Hatfield and his three sons-in-law. Furious at the audacity of Cline and Phillips, Wilson sent the Kentucky gover-nor a telegram, angrily pointing out that Bill Dempsey had been killed "while acting as a deputy in assisting the officers of the law in arresting Frank Phillips and three of the McCoys, on a warrant for the murder of James Vance."[4] Meanwhile Logan Countians, fear-ful of the violence caused by these raids, held a "mass meeting" and resolved to ask the governor for protection, while in Pikeville Judge

Tobias Wagner and J. Lee Ferguson undertook a journey to Frankfort to request similar help from Governor Buckner. Apprehensive of an impending crisis, Wilson telegrammed Buckner that he planned to send in "troops to assist the civil authorities" and suggested that Kentucky do likewise. At the same time Wilson appointed a personal emissary to visit the troubled region and hoped that Buckner would do so as well.[5] At this point, relations between the two governors were cool but still not actively hostile. Both seemed to believe the exaggerated reports in the newspapers that, whatever the origins of the feud, it had somehow gotten completely out of hand and would take the military intervention of two states to bring it under control. This fear was considerably alleviated when both governors' personal agents made their reports.

Wilson's agent, Col. W. L. Mahon, returned first on 30 January with good news. He reported that "while the whole surrounding country has been in a state of excitement and tumult bordering on a genuine war, that peace has again been restored, and the belligerent parties on both sides have disbanded, and no further trouble is anticipated." Relieved, Wilson immediately telegrammed Buckner that there was no need for military intervention and he had "countermanded" his previous order.[6] What he didn't express to Buckner was his escalating anger as he heard from Mahon that the Hatfields were not the aggressors in the feud. "I visited all the Hatfields," declared Mahon, "and found them to be good, law-abiding citizens, who have the respect and confidence of everyone in the neighborhood." It was, he reported, Phillips and Cline who were causing the trouble. Without proper warrants, they had "kidnapped" nine citizens of West Virginia.[7] This confirmed for Wilson what his assistant secretary of state, John Floyd, had been telling him all along. "I never regarded them [Hatfields] in the light of criminals or desperadoes," said Floyd, "and they are not so regarded by the people of Logan County." The reason, he said, that the case had lain dormant for five years was that "the authorities of Pike County regarded the McCoys as the aggressors." It was only because Perry Cline decided "he would stir up the thing again and make some money out of it, knowing that the Hatfields owned some good property," that the feud had become active once again.[8] If Wilson had been wavering before, he now resolved to fight back in the courts.

At about the same time Buckner's investigator, Sam Hill, returned from Pike County. His report concurred with Mahon's that the violence had abated, and Buckner, too, canceled plans to send in the militia. While the reports of the two emmissaries may have concurred on the abatement of violence, however, they agreed on little else. The Kentucky investigator corrected some of the worst exaggerations about Hatfield "gang" violence, but he disagreed with his West Virginia counterpart's assessment on the issue of culpability. "The assertion that Anderson Hatfield and his sons, Johnson and Cap, are reputable, law-abiding people, is not sustained," wrote Hill, "for the stories of their lawlessness and brutality, vouched for by credible persons, would fill a volume; while, on the other hand, old man McCoy and his boys are represented as law-abiding, honest people by reputable men who have known them long and intimately." However, Hill had obtained this information not in the Tug Valley home of the Hatfields and McCoys but in Pikeville, where he spent three days talking to people whom he termed "the most reliable sources."[9] It is not difficult to imagine who those sources might have been.

With the intervention of the two governors and the contradictory reports of the two investigators, publicity about the feud began to assume a distinctly partisan character. Kentucky papers led by the *Louisville Courier-Journal* vehemently claimed that the McCoys were the victims of the Hatfield "outlaws"; it printed the West Virginia investigator's report of the "law-abiding" Hatfields with the sarcastic title "Innocents at Home," intending to undermine its credibility. This interpretation was also the most popular with other papers across the country. The *Pittsburg Times*, for example, carried stories with such titles as "West Virginia Barbarians," "Crimes of the Hatfields," and "West Virginia's Bad Characters." The *New York World* called it "West Virginia's Vendetta."[10]

West Virginia fought back in the *Wheeling Intelligencer*. Although its first stories had accepted the Pikeville bias (it labeled the raid on the McCoy cabin "A Terrible Story"), by the end of January the editors had noticed that "with one or two exceptions, all the press dispatches relating to the matter which have appeared, have been sent from Kentucky towns. They contain a decided coloring in favor of the McCoy faction, and are evidently calculated to make it appear that the Hatfields are the aggressors."[11] The *Intelligencer* was frequently the voice of a minority of industrialists in West Virginia and was just as prepared as its counterpart in Louisville to denounce the violent culture of the remote mountaineers, but when it became apparent that the Kentucky papers were denouncing not feud violence in general but *West Virginia* lawlessness and violence, the *Intelligencer*'s editors bridled. In a front-page story the paper asserted that "the truth of the matter is that it is a Kentucky feud, and is the result of a difficulty which occurred at a local election between rival factions in Pike County, Kentucky, some years ago." Furthermore, "the reports of the depredations by both gangs show that the crimes have nearly all been committed in Kentucky." However, the paper was careful to insist that if half the reports of violence were true, the result should be the "summary hanging of the whole lot."[12]

As the newspapers recast the feud into a state-against-state conflict, the governor of West Virginia took steps that would emphasize the same divisions in the courts. On 8 February 1888 Wilson had his secretary of state send an official requisition to Governor Buckner for the extradition of Frank Phillips and twenty-three members of his posse for the killing of Jim Vance and Bill Dempsey.[13] Next, he petitioned the U.S. district court in Louisville for writs of habeas corpus on the nine Hatfield supporters imprisoned in the Pikeville jail. Arguing that Kentucky had acted illegally in authorizing its agent (Frank Phillips) to abduct the Hatfields from West Virginia's territory rather than following due process of law, he insisted that Kentucky should be required to return the prisoners. Two days later Wilson's hand-picked representative, Huntington lawyer Eustace Gibson, was in Louisville arguing West Virginia's case.[14] In contending that one state had no right to invade another, Gibson managed to slip in a jibe at Kentucky more worthy of the newspaper sparring than the dignity of the courtroom. Vividly describing the mountain warfare of eastern Kentucky, he reminded the court that such notoriety for feuding had never been associated with West Virginia.[15] Although this point was reported by newspapers in Cincinnati and Huntington, West Virginia, it was completely ignored by the *Louisville Courier-Journal*.

When the judge found the writs admissable and ordered the nine prisoners brought to Louisville for a court hearing, the *Courier-Journal* responded with furious indignation. "For years the press and the officers of the state have been earnestly endeavoring to make the law a terror to evildoers, and now for the first time in the history of any civilized community the power of a 'sovereign state' is invoked to give protection, license, and immunity for the past and assurances for the future to a band of white savages whose brutalities, whose inhuman tortures have not been paralleled in Kentucky since Boone and his followers drove the Indians to other hunting grounds."[16] The *Courier-Journal*, so consistently an advocate of liberalism and reform, apparently saw no contradiction between those principles and its conviction of the feudists before any trial had been held; perhaps its middle-class editors assumed that the "white savages" were beyond the pale of justice.

With the judge's order that the Hatfield prisoners be brought to Louisville, the stage was set for the final act of the feud drama. This act, however, was played out far from the mountain environment in which the conflict had begun. Valentine Hatfield and the eight others were brought into a city that was an economic and cultural center for western Kentucky, a city whose leading newspaper, the *Courier-Journal*, was nationally reknowned for its advocacy of liberal political values and progressive attitudes. The mountaineers and their culture were brought into direct confrontation with a culture and legal system touted as far superior to their own. Governor Wilson of West Virginia considered the case so important that he made plans to appear personally at U.S. district court along with his major source of information for the case, Assistant Secretary of State John Floyd. Governor Buckner of Kentucky chose not to appear but was represented by former governor Procter Knott. As the day approached when the famous feudists would arrive in the city, excitement mounted.

In Pikeville, deputy jailor Perry Cline and prosecuting attorney J. Lee Ferguson prepared for their own moment of glory. Although a federal marshal had been dispatched to escort the Hatfields to Louisville, Cline and Ferguson were anxious to perform that function themselves. Ignoring the marshal, they carefully chose five of their supporters to "guard" the Hatfields on the long journey; it was not that any resistance was expected, but the guards would receive all the adulation due to heroes who had subdued the "savage" Hatfields. Old Ranel McCoy was also asked to accompany the group and share in this triumph. Although Cline claimed that the situation was dangerous because at any moment Devil Anse might attempt a daring rescue, the reality was that Valentine and the eight other prisoners had been convinced that they had very little to fear from the courts, either in Pikeville or in Louisville. They had been in jail in Pikeville for almost a month, and Perry Cline himself had been acting as a lawyer for Valentine and his three sons-in-law, Plyant, Sam, and Dock Mayhorn. Valentine told reporters in Louisville that he had not really been locked up, that he had been allowed the freedom of the village, even to the point of frequently visiting Perry Cline's home and having conversations with Aunt Sally McCoy about the feud. The judge in Pikeville had not even asked for bail, Valentine said, though Colonel Dils had offered to pay it if necessary. If Valentine had wanted to escape, it seems likely that he could have done so. Apparently he now trusted Cline and expected that a trial in Pikeville would absolve him from guilt. Whatever Cline told him about the proceedings in the U.S. district court, Valentine agreed to go peacefully, and his judgment was deferred to by the others.[17]

Cline began the journey early, before the U.S. marshal had time to make the trip to Pikeville. The first leg was by steamboat from Pikeville down the Levisa Fork of the Big Sandy River to Catlettsburg, where the travelers embarked by train for Louisville. A *Courier-Journal* reporter was enterprising enough to get on the train at Catlettsburg and had a chance to talk to the Hatfields before they were paraded in front of the people of Louisville. Valentine seemed eager for the chance to proclaim his innocence and give his own version of the feud's history. The reporter, perhaps expecting some wild and wooly frontiersman, found a man of almost sixty, short in stature, with iron-gray hair and greenish-gray eyes that avoided direct contact. He "bears the appearance of a quiet, inoffensive citizen," declared the surprised journalist. Valentine and the rest of the prisoners, commented the reporter, "seemed confident that they will be released after they have been given a fair hearing."[18]

When the train arrived in Louisville, there was a large crowd milling about, anxious to get a look at the Hatfield gang. Although federal marshals were now officially in charge of the prisoners, Cline refused to surrender custody until they were inside the jail, carefully orchestrating their transfer from train to prison. It was done, said the *Courier-Journal*, "in something like military order." A line was formed with the prisoners marching two by two, flanked by two guards for each two sets of prisoners. In this formation the march proceeded several blocks to the jail, accompanied by a crowd of "small boys." Despite Cline's elaborate precautions there was "no exhibition of bravado or ruffianism" on the part of the prisoners. Quite the contrary, reported the *Courier-Journal*, they all maintained an "air of indifference." Considering the *Courier-Journal's* usual hostility toward the Hatfields and mountaineers generally, it is surprising that its description of the feudists was so sympathetic. "Their appearance," commented the paper in its front-page coverage the next day, "was very unlike that of the mountaineers who are frequently guests of the United States while attending court here for making moonshine whiskey. Nearly half of the crowd wore white shirts, and three of them had collars about their unshaven necks. Soft felt hats covered all their heads and there were nine mustaches among the nine prisoners." This description was accompanied by an artist's sketches of all nine Hatfields and of Randolph McCoy as well. Louisville residents were left to contemplate the oddity of a group of quiet, decorous, sober, and orderly feudists, while the reporters turned their attention to the captors.

If Valentine Hatfield had been the spokesman for the prisoners, J. Lee Ferguson acted in that capacity for the guards. Apparently Perry Cline was too busy directing the march through Louisville's streets to converse with reporters, but the loquacious Ferguson proved an eager informant, delighted with the opportunity to gloat over his own and Cline's triumph. With a sarcastic laugh, Ferguson waved aside Valentine's claims of innocence, but he did admit that the "worst" of the gang had evaded capture. Perhaps hoping to counteract the impression made by the nine Hatfields as more or less normal citizens, Ferguson confidingly told the reporter that "Valentine Hatfield had recently confessed to him that he had five living wives and thirty-three living children." The old man, according to Ferguson, "has peculiar ideas of polygamy, and does not marry his wives according to the law, but takes them and apportions his time out between them."

Going on to justify the abduction of the prisoners from West Virginia, Ferguson claimed that the "prosperity" of Pike County and Pikeville had been "greatly damaged" by the Hatfield raids. The "invasion" of West Virginia, he insisted, had been necessary because the "law could not reach the ruffians and assassins who were destroying the McCoys and all others who incurred their enmity." But beyond justifying the kidnapping, Ferguson was anxious to show that he and Cline had won a victory over Devil Anse himself, even though the feud leader had eluded capture. "Until a short time ago," crowed Ferguson, Anderson Hatfield was a man of "considerable means" who owned five thousand acres of land in West Virginia. (It was less than two weeks since Devil Anse and members of his family had sold their lands on the Tug River to eastern capitalists, but Ferguson was well aware of the details.) Hatfield "recently" sold this land, declared Ferguson triumphantly, for $7,000 in cash, "though it was worth fully $15,000." The reporter, presumably somewhat at a loss to know what to make of this information or why Ferguson was so anxious to discuss it, failed to elicit further information on the subject. What he couldn't know was that he had just been exposed to the roots of the feud in the bitter legal conflict between Perry Cline and Anderson Hatfield over five thousand acres of valuable timber and coal lands.[19]

When the story was picked up the next day by the *New York Times*, such subtleties were also lost. It was Ferguson's assessment of the "savage" nature of the Hatfields that was unqualifiedly accepted. On its editorial page the *Times* lamented that "the latest vendetta in the backwoods of Kentucky shows the purely savage character of the population more strongly than almost any previous instance." Not only did the *Times* condemn the "savage" nature of the entire mountain population, but it swallowed completely Ferguson's assertions of Valentine Hatfield's immoral character. By the very fact that Hatfield "admits the possession of five living wives," argued the editorial, "it is evident that a strong course of common schools, churches, soap and water, and other civilizing influences is required before these simple children of nature will forbear to kill a man whenever they take a dislike to him."[20] The *Times*, like the *Courier-Journal*, had already passed judgment, not only on Valentine Hatfield, but on Appalachian culture.

The first full hearing on the writs of habeas corpus was held on 27 February before Judge John Watson Barr. The courtroom was crowded with spectators hoping to get a look at the famous "desperadoes" and perhaps witness some typical mountain ruffianism. In this they were once again disappointed; the nine filed into the courtroom, sat down in the double row of chairs reserved for them, and spent most of the day, reported the *Courier-Journal*, "looking straight ahead with the same air of indifference that Indians in a romance wear." Most of the session was occupied in technical arguments between the lawyers over admission of various kinds of evidence. The only break in the monotony seemed to come from observing the governor of West Virginia who, accompanied by his assistant secretary of state, John B. Floyd, had arrived with stacks of official-looking books and papers. Wilson sat immediately behind West Virginia's two lawyers and "often conversed earnestly with them." The *Courier-Journal* described him as "a small, rather slender man who has the thin and wrinkled face of one who habitually suffers from ill-health." Unlike the stoic Hatfield group, Wilson was quite animated, gesturing to the lawyers and biting nervously on his "bushy red mustache." The *Courier-Journal* concluded that he was a man of "unusual ability."[21]

West Virginia's case rested on the claim that because Frank Phillips had been acting as an official representative of Kentucky when he entered West Virginia and forcibly brought the Hatfields back to Pikeville, it was therefore the state of Kentucky that had injured West Virginia by "invading" its territory and depriving its citizens of "due process of law." Phillips had been fully aware of the correspondence between the two governors and the extradition proceedings then in progress. Why, asked West Virginia's lawyer, had the Congress established formal extradition procedures if the representatives of one state could simply enter another for the purpose of arresting individuals who had allegedly committed crimes in their state?

Kentucky's lawyers did not argue with the fact that Phillips and others had forcibly abducted the prisoners from West Virginia, but they disagreed that Phillips had been an official representative of the state of Kentucky; he was simply a private citizen, they declared. Even if Phillips had acted in an official capacity, it made no difference. The state, the lawyers insisted, had nothing to do with the manner in which the prisoners got into Kentucky. Once they were there in the Pikeville jail, law enforcement officials had every right to arrest them for crimes committed in Kentucky. Further, argued the Kentucky lawyers, if this really was an issue between two states, then it could not be resolved in a district court; only the U.S. Supreme Court had jurisdiction over disputes between states.

In the end, it was the jurisdictional argument that prevailed. On 3 March Judge Barr, after commenting that the case was without precedent and taking several days to consult with Constitutional authorities, handed down his decision. The case was, he said, based on a controversy between two states and therefore it was not within the jurisdiction of his court. The nine prisoners would be returned to jail in Pikeville to stand trial. The judge did, however, grant West Virginia's appeal to the U.S. circuit court in Louisville.[22] On 5 April the higher court concurred by agreeing with the district court decision that the case was not within the jurisdiction of either court and upheld Kentucky's right to keep the prisoners in jail. But another appeal was granted, this time to the U.S. Supreme Court. Kentuckians and the *Courier-Journal* regarded this as a victory, and the newspaper entitled its coverage of the case "Kentucky Again Wins."[23]

The Hatfields were in Louisville for about a month altogether, during which time they appeared only two days in court. The delay in their return to Pikeville was caused by Perry Cline's financial difficulties. Apparently both West Virginia and the federal government refused to pay for the cost of transporting and keeping the Hatfields in Louisville; it looked as though Cline might have to foot the bill himself. Hurriedly, he made a trip to Frankfort in an effort to persuade Governor Buckner and the state of Kentucky to pay his expenses.[24]

By the time Cline was back in Louisville, ready to shepherd his charges back to Pikeville, it was clear that the prisoners had formed some negative opinions of "civilized" culture and justice and were eager to return to the mountains, even if that meant Pikeville rather than the Tug Valley. In some ways they had adjusted quite well. After an initial period when they all refrained from conversing with other prisoners and kept entirely to themselves, they began to socialize and seemed especially pleased when the other inmates read to them—an entirely new activity. They also attended Sunday services, singing with deep, rich voices and holding the hymnbooks in front of them despite the fact that they could read neither words nor music.[25] Still, they showed considerable discomfort both with confinement and with the rhythms of civilization; they awakened at dawn every morning and noisily proceeded to rise and dress, to the annoyance of the other prisoners. Inactivity did not seem to lessen their appetites, and the other inmates found themselves always last in line for meals.[26]

After four weeks, however, the Hatfields were annoyed and impatient with the tedium of sitting and waiting. One of the group, Andy Varney, during the court hearing apprised the judge and onlookers of his discontent. As the court was adjourning, Varney called, "Judge!" As everyone turned to stare at him, Varney continued, "I wanna go back to Pike." When the startled judge asked why, Varney explained, "Cause, the court thar are gonna be aholden for a week, an' I wanna go back and show I ain't guilty." When the judge patiently attempted to explain that his presence in Louisville was due to a writ of habeas corpus filed on his behalf, Varney was unconvinced. "It warn't on my account I were brought here," he pleaded, "I didn't know nothin' 'bout it till I got here."[27]

Valentine Hatfield, too, made it clear to the *Louisville Courier-Journal* reporter who visited him just before his departure that he was very glad to be returning to Pike County. As always, he was eager to converse with the reporter and had several points to make about the case and his stay in Louisville. For one thing, Valentine asserted, they would not be so confined in Pikeville where they would be released on bond and allowed the freedom of the town. Once the trial was held, the old man predicted, they would be acquitted because "we have overwhelming evidence to prove our innocence." When the reporter followed up with a question about who had committed the crimes, Valentine responded without hesitation. "Well, my brother Anderson and his three sons, Robert, Johnson and 'Cap' Hatfield and four or five others. They are all bad men."[28] However, before the journalist could ask further questions about this startling accusation, Valentine moved on to the point he had really been waiting to make—one that had been bothering him for the four weeks he had been in Louisville. "I wish you would contradict the statement that I have seven wives," he pleaded, "I have never had but one, and, I don't want any more." Disturbed by the image presented of him in the newspapers, Valentine went on to make an astute assessment of what had been happening in Louisville in regard to both the feud itself and the manner in which the press was making judgments about mountaineer culture. "Well," he complained, "we have been tried, convicted, and sentenced by the press before they knew the facts of our case." If the reporter would visit the Tug Valley, insisted Valentine, "you will find us all different people from the general ideas entertained of us."[29] Having seen civilization, Valentine understood why his chances were better in hostile Pikeville than in supposedly impartial Louisville.

With the Hatfields back in Pikeville, assiduously guarded by jailor Cline, Kentucky and West Virginia lawyers prepared to take their cases to the Supreme Court of the United States. Both arrived in Washington on 13 April and the hearing began on 23 April. After each attorney had presented essentially the same arguments as he had in Louisville, Chief Justice Stephen Field read the majority opinion. In invoking writs of habeas corpus to obtain the release of nine prisoners from the custody of Kentucky officials, stated the opinion, Governor Wilson had assumed that it was the duty of the United States "to secure the inviolability of the territory of the State from the lawless invasion of persons from other states." This assumption was in error, continued the opinion, because states possessed only limited sovereignty, not absolute sovereignty. If Kentucky were a foreign state, then West Virginia or the United States could make such demands, resort to reprisals, or "take such other measure as they might deem necessary for redress for the past and security for the future."[30] However, because states possessed only limited sovereignty and the federal government provided no means for redress in such cases, the only recourse for a state in such a situation would be to issue warrants for any crimes committed by the abductors and proceed with extradition. But there was no method by which the state could retrieve its citizens directly through a writ of habeas corpus once such citizens were physically under arrest in the state where the crime had been committed. Thus, concluded the court, it would uphold the action of the Louisville circuit court in denying the writs of habeas corpus. Despite the violation of extradition procedures in the capture of the nine prisoners, the Supreme Court ruled that Kentucky had the right to hold them in custody for subsequent trial.

Two of the nine justices dissented from this majority opinion—one, Justice Bradley, quite vigorously. He said that Governor Wilson had taken appropriate action in attempting to secure the prisoners' release through writs of habeas corpus. The kidnapping of the Hatfields, he claimed, "was a violation of the rights secured by the Constitution to West Virginia," and thus that state had a duty to appeal the Supreme Court for the "restoration of those citizens taken from her territory in violation of the supreme law of the land."[31] Despite the opinion of two dissenting justices, however, West Virginia and the Hatfields had lost their case in the nation's highest court. It was an era in which minority groups and the poorest classes of people did not fare well in the Supreme Court; just eight years later, in *Plessy* v. *Ferguson*, the court legalized segregation in the South.

The court's decision had some immediate consequences in feud country. Perry Cline acted as though he were convinced that, with no prospects for the legal release of his followers, Devil Anse would attempt to storm Pikeville and free them himself. That Cline actually believed this seems a remote possibility; he had been making such predictions since the previous December when the first "Hatfield," Selkirk McCoy, had been imprisoned in the Pikeville jail. But on the strength of his warnings that the Supreme Court's decision would prompt Devil Anse to invade Pike County, the county court authorized the hiring of two extra deputies to guard the jail.[32] The threat from Devil Anse never materialized; he was busy protecting himself from the second consequence of the court decision.

The court's ruling had the effect of a declaration of open warfare on all the feudists, whether on the McCoy or Hatfield side. If there were no legal reprisals for kidnapping of individuals wanted for crimes in other states, then the way was cleared for wholesale manhunts on both sides of the Tug. Kentucky had already offered rewards for Devil Anse and many more of the Hatfield group, and West Virginia had done the same for members of the Phillips posse who had been indicted for the murders of Jim Vance and Bill Dempsey. Private detectives from such agencies as Pinkerton, Eureka, and Baldwin-Felts had been involved sporadically in trying to capture the Hatfields since the Kentucky governor's proclamation nine months before, but now their efforts were intensified.

The first capture occurred less than a month after the Supreme Court's ruling. On 1 June the head of the Eureka Agency, Alf Burnett, and two detectives set out from Charleston, West Virginia, for the Pond Creek district of Pike County—McCoy country. Eventually they succeeded in capturing Dave Stratton, a former resident of Logan County who had joined Phillips's posse and had a hand in the killing of Bill Dempsey. After the battle Stratton, believing he would be safer living in Kentucky than in West Virginia, moved across the Tug River. It was false security, however, and the detectives were able to claim the rewards offered by Governor Wilson for members of the Phillips posse.[33] By midsummer rumors were flying of ambushes, fights, and scuffles between the reward seekers and residents of the Tug Valley—some of whom had never been involved in the feud. The suspicion and fear of strangers that had begun in the liquor tax era rose to alarming proportions as mountaineers put aside their old squirrel-hunting muskets and purchased new Winchester rifles.[34] By the fall of 1888, the detectives had succeeded in capturing three more Hatfield feudists—Charlie Gillespie, Ellison Mounts, and Alex Messer.[35] (Mounts was the slightly retarded, illegitimate son of Ellison Hatfield who had been persuaded to go along on the 1888 New Year's Day raid on the McCoy home.) Next to Valentine Hatfield, Mounts was considered by Perry Cline and J. Lee Ferguson to be their most important prisoner. Once in jail, Mounts was persuaded to confess his crimes and implicate Devil Anse, an event to which Ferguson and Cline delightedly invited reporters.[36]

Most of the detectives, however, sought the elusive and formidable Devil Anse Hatfield himself. Capturing the feud leader would result in more than reward money—it would bolster the reputations of both the victorious individual and the agency to which he belonged. Dave Cunningham and Treve Gibson, two such detectives, arrived in Logan in December 1888 proclaiming their intentions of hauling in the Hatfields, especially Devil Anse. For several weeks they strutted about Logan Courthouse boasting of their plans to surprise and overpower the famous feudist. Annoyed, Devil Anse retaliated. On 12 January 1889, he and some of his "boys" followed the detectives into the woods and took them prisoner. Laughing, Anse marched the captives back to Logan Courthouse, where they were arrested and locked up for a time in the Logan jail. Apparently satisfied, Devil Anse took no more initiatives in the feud but concentrated on protecting himself and his family from capture.[37]

Many of the stories of feud violence in the mountains emerged from this period when there was an open hunting season on both the Hatfields and the McCoys. Newspapers in Charleston, Catlettsburg, and Louisville were insatiable when it came to feud tales—

and detectives who emerged from the mountains had many hair-raising stories to tell even though they had captured no feudists. Although these events and tales were not part of the feud at all, even the second phase of the feud, but resulted from the rewards offered by the states of Kentucky and West Virginia, they were long regarded as belonging to the feud, thereby exaggerating the extent of the violence. Ironically, these detectives and their agencies were a product of modern America, not Appalachian society. The violence caused by their invasion of the mountains belongs more appropriately to industrialized America than to Appalachia, yet their stories have been used to confirm opinions of mountaineer violence and lawlessness.

Most stories that appeared in areas outside the feud region and in national newspapers were copies of dispatches sent from Catlettsburg, Charleston, or Louisville, and most of those, as we have seen, reflected the views of Perry Cline and his Pikeville group. Only a few papers took the trouble to send their own reporters to the Tug Valley for firsthand interviews. The most influential of these were the *Pittsburg Times*, which dispatched Charles Howell immediately after the Grapevine Creek episode, and the *New York World*, which sent T. C. Crawford in the summer of 1888. These two men, because their firsthand outsiders' view of the feudists was widely reprinted all over the country, probably had more to do with the development of the hillbilly stereotype than any other individuals. Unfortunately, their opinions only tended to reinforce the earlier images of "white savages" portrayed by the *Louisville Courier-Journal* and the *New York Times*. They convicted the mountaineers in public opinion more surely than any court ever could.

Charles Howell arrived in Pikeville at the end of January 1888, just at the point when the feud was at its height in the press. His paper, the *Pittsburg Times*, had already made clear its bias in the feud by repeatedly castigating the West Virginia "barbarians"; it seems obvious that Howell was in Pikeville, not to uncover new information, but to reinforce the already widely accepted Cline interpretation of the feud. During his three days in Pikeville—Howell never attempted to get to Logan County or to interview Devil Anse—he visited Old Ranel McCoy and the Hatfields who were held captive in Pikeville jail. From his visit to Old Ranel and Aunt Sally, Howell drew a sympathetic portrait. He found them, he said, living in a house denuded of furniture, because all their belongings had been burned in the New Year's Day fire. "The intensity of their suffering," he emphasized, "was unmistakable." Contradicting most observers' impression of Randolph as "morose" and "cantankerous," Howell found him to be "a man who had been bent and almost broken by the weight of his afflictions and grief."[38]

By contrast, Howell described Valentine Hatfield and his sons-in-law as sinister and calculating. Valentine, he said, was "cool and self-possessed at all times," while the Mayhorn brothers were accomplished at "bravery and cunning." Although Howell never laid eyes on Devil Anse, he declared that the feud leader was an absolute dictator who had cold-bloodedly set out to "exterminate" the McCoys without any provocation whatsoever. Despite Howell's pains to differentiate the opposing sides in the feud, it was probably his conclusion that made a lasting impression on the public and tarred all Appalachians with the same brush. "The Hatfield-McCoy War," concluded Howell, "is simply a succession of cowardly murders by day and assassinations and houseburnings by night. All of the murders have been cruel, heartless and almost without the shadow of provocation. Given, on the one hand, a family with its contingents of the same blood, allied and cemented by a common desire to avenge an imaginary affront, and on the other another family, small in the matter of alliance and collateral sympathies, doomed to destruction by the larger one, and the case is stated."[39]

Eight months later, after the Supreme Court had reached its decision and detectives were roaming the mountains searching for feudists, T. C. Crawford of the *New York World* made a more daring foray into the very heart of Hatfield country. Crawford proposed to visit and interview the notorious Devil Anse himself. In order to accomplish this, Crawford contacted the Hatfields' staunchest supporter, Assistant Secretary of State John B. Floyd, and asked for his help. Floyd, apparently convinced that personal acquaintance with and observation of the Hatfields in their home setting would correct some of the public misconceptions about them, agreed to be the journalist's companion and escort. But Floyd miscalculated the power of preconceived opinion; the *World* reporter saw only the "white savages" of his expectations.[40]

Upon his arrival in Charleston, West Virginia, on the first leg of his journey, the journalist found mountaineers the "most suspicious people on the face of the earth"; he failed to point out—if he was aware—that just at that point in time mountaineers, whether feudists or not, had every reason to be fearful and suspicious. In addition to federal revenue agents, Logan Countians now had to be on guard against armed private detectives out to collect the rewards for Hatfield feudists. But Crawford was convinced that it was not just the feudists who were lawless and violent; he believed that Appalachian society and culture were the root of the problem. Crawford reported that in "talking with many numerous citizens of the State," he learned "that it was rare that murder was ever punished in the State, and that quarrels were much more commonly settled with the knife or the pistol than in any other way." Even outside the "wild" and "barbarous" region of the feud, he said, the taking of life was regarded lightly. Crawford was willing to admit that there were no more murders in the mountains than in "more civilized" states but, he declared authoritatively, "it is a fact that the murders committed are by men in a different rank in life"— presumably he meant that in the North murder was more frequently committed by members of the lower class, whereas in the mountains all classes resorted to it—and "the pretexts are more often trivial, inconsequential quarrels than elsewhere."[41] These "facts" were apparently evident to journalist Crawford before he ever arrived in Logan County.

From Charleston, Crawford traversed the fifty miles to Logan Courthouse, a journey that took "two days of the roughest riding that one would care to find." The roads, he said, were not worth the name and when creek waters were up, they were completely impassable. The isolation fascinated Crawford. "Days and weeks will pass without any more word coming from Logan Courthouse to the outer world than could be gotten out from Central Africa." For middle-class Americans like Crawford, the world of "savages" was populated by Indians, Africans, and Appalachians. Once in Logan Courthouse, the reporter contacted John Floyd and began making arrangements to visit Devil Anse, the "celebrated" leader of the Hatfields, whom he said was the "talk and terror of the country." But the very next sentence of Crawford's report exhibited a contradiction that becomes more and more obvious the further one reads into his book. It was the contradiction between the world's assessment of Devil Anse as a "desperado" and the evaluation of him by family and neighbors. Without a hint of awareness that the information he was about to offer might undermine his own portrayal of Devil Anse, Crawford stated that "Ance Hatfield is universally regarded in this community in a favorable light." This was because, explained Crawford, "he possesses the extraordinary virtue of paying his debts," in addition to being "an able, intrepid, energetic mountaineer." However, Crawford resolved his seeming contradiction by explaining that in the mountains, whether one murdered someone was much less important than being "financially honest." What Crawford did not explain, or even perceive as a problem in his analysis, was why these "savages" who inhabited an extremely isolated, "wild," and "barbarous" region were concerned with matters of money and debts, even to the point of considering them more crucial to an individual's social standing and character than murderous behavior.[42]

Crawford, like Howell, recounted an extremely garbled and exaggerated version of the feud events and was obviously more interested in the feudists as examples of a degraded and uncivilized culture than in the details of the feud itself. Unlike Howell, however, and despite his ubiquitous assertions about mountaineer savagery, Crawford's description of Devil Anse at home with his family was sympathetically drawn. By the time Crawford visited what he called the "lair" of the "outlaw king," Devil Anse had moved his family out of the Tug Valley. In the spring of 1888 the Hatfields were building their new home halfway up the side of a mountain, on a site chosen for its commanding view of all approaches. As the Supreme Court was hearing arguments in the Hatfield case, Anse supervised his "boys" in putting the finishing touches on a "fort"— a separate structure located about one quarter of a mile from the new living quarters. Built of sturdy logs, with gun ports but no windows, it was equipped with an open fireplace for cooking and a large feather mattress in case the family needed to barricade itself in against the detectives and bounty hunters roaming the area. Crawford said that "there is nothing in which Ance Hatfield takes more pride than his fort."[43]

As yet, however, there was no threat severe enough to have driven the family into their fort. Crawford was received, like all other visitors, in the main dwelling house. The house into which he was ushered was, in the reporter's judgment, nothing more than a "primitive" log hut. There were two rooms; the one in back of the main room was hidden from the journalist's scrutiny. The main room, Crawford noted, was bare except for a large stone fireplace with a brick hearth, numerous beds laden with Winchester rifles, a big table, and a "broken down old fashioned sewing machine." On the table rested a single book, a southern publication on the history of the Civil War which, according to Crawford, stated that the South had won the war. In this single main room of the log house were carried on all the activities necessary to domestic life—cooking, sleeping, eating, talking, and entertaining. Crawford noticed that here, as in the town of Logan, privacy was an unknown and undesired state. But despite the seeming potential for confusion and disorder, Anse's household was functional and well organized.[44]

The choice made by the feud leader and his family in building their new home is revealing. Although Anse was wealthier than most of his neighbors and obviously had the financial resources to construct any kind of home he desired, he had chosen to preserve the house style traditional to the mountaineers. A white-frame, rambling farmhouse with a separate parlor and numerous upstairs bedrooms, such as some of the new middle-class mountaineers, especially in the towns, had chosen, did not appeal to Devil Anse. The spatial arrangements and lack of privacy that both shaped and reflected the Hatfields' domestic life emphasized Devil Anse's strong attachment to rural mountaineer culture rather than to the middle-class life in towns like Logan Courthouse.[45]

As the visit began, Crawford was fascinated by the "family circle." Anse seated himself next to the fireplace, with Cap to his left and the other men seated in a semicircle. Anse's wife and several grown daughters and daughters-in-law stood at the back of the room near the door; Crawford described them as "the most modest and quiet members of the family." "The daughters," he said, "were tall and broad shouldered, with lithe, natural figures, not one of which had ever felt the unnatural pressure of stays." During his sojourn, Crawford reported, the women said nothing, but courteously served a hearty dinner of corn pone, fried pork, and beans. Despite the unobtrusiveness of the women, the journalist noted that Levicy Hatfield's small dark eyes shone with matronly pride when her son Cap talked of his escapades in the feud. This description of the Hatfield women contrasted sharply with Crawford's more general assessment of mountain women: he later described the women he encountered in Logan Courthouse as "the most revolting women I have ever seen in my life." These "dissolute" and "idle" women, declared Crawford, "are responsible for many of the quarrels and the murders which darken" mountain culture.[46] Apparently, despite the favorable impression made by Levicy Hatfield and her daughters, Crawford was determined to preserve his preconceptions of mountain women.

When Devil Anse began to talk, all his family, even the younger children, listened with deferential respect. Crawford was impressed by the admiration shown by even the youngest children toward their elders, but this did not prevent him from suspecting even the children of sinister intentions. One youngster, as he sat and listened, "eyed the rows of Winchesters lying in the background with a hungry look, as if," inferred Crawford, "he were eager for the time when he would grow up and become a useful member of the society for the extermination of people obnoxious to the Hatfield interests."[47]

Anse received the reporter with "boisterous hospitality," and Crawford was struck by Hatfield's resemblance to the "noted" Confederate general, Stonewall Jackson. "He has a powerful frame, and is broad-shouldered and deep chested, but with that curve to his shoulders that goes with all the mountain types that I have seen in this neighborhood . . . a man of fifty years of age, has not a gray line in the brown of his thick hair, mustache, and beard. He has a pair of gray eyes set under the deepest of bushy eyebrows. His nose is such an enormous hook as to suggest the lines of a Turkish scimetar [sic]." Weighted down with both a Colt revolver and a Winchester rifle, Anse looked "awkward," but the reporter concluded that he was, nevertheless, "intelligent and well-informed." Indeed, Devil Anse was described by Crawford as "a jovial old pirate," who was "bright, ready," and a good conversationalist.[48]

The feud leader denied any knowledge of any killings but said quite frankly to Crawford that even if he knew anything about the murders, he wouldn't admit it to a reporter. It was clear that the subject was closed. Crawford tried another tactic: "Now what would you do if any detective came here and tried to take you?" he asked. To this question Anse was ready with a vigorous response: "Well, now, I don't propose to be bothered any more. I have been out hiding in the brush. I have been kept away from my wife and babbies many and many a time. I do not like to be kept away from my babbies." Crawford was well aware that Anse's "babbies were very much to him"; they swarmed about him as he talked. Signaling the end of the conversation, Anse declared, "I want this row settled, it has gone on long enough." But his final word was, "I simply will not be taken."[49]

At the end of this visit Crawford allowed that Anse had "some apparent justification" for his "outlaw acts." The feudist was an "energetic, soldierly" man who learned from his experiences in the Civil War "his first disregard for the taking of life." According to Crawford's analysis, the war had destroyed law enforcement in the community, making personal vengeance the only possible response to murder. Crawford even conceded that the three McCoy boys had brutally murdered Anse's brother "without reason and spurred on by the rage of a petty quarrel over the most trivial of subjects." Further, the reporter understood that Ellison had been attempting to stop a fight, not start one. So, concluded Crawford, "it is not hard to understand how Ance Hatfield organized a band of executioners to punish the three men." But despite this brief and half-hearted attempt to put the feud in some context and present Hatfield's perspective, Crawford adhered to his preconceived ideas about the "savage" nature of mountaineer culture.[50]

Fundamentally, Crawford was more interested in Appalachian culture than in the specifics of the Hatfield-McCoy feud. "The feud between these two families," he concluded, "lends a picturesque and dramative interest," but "much more importance has been attached to this petty war than it really deserves." Feud crimes had been greatly exaggerated, he believed. Crawford was even willing to admit that "the people generally here are hospitable and civil; the stranger is welcomed to their doors; if he can eat corn pone, fried pork, and fried chicken he is welcome to their table." But the important aspects of mountain culture, Crawford believed, were the physical hardships and isolation, lack of privacy, dissolute women, and "excessive independence of thought." Crawford concluded that "there isn't any such place for missionary work in the whole world as in this region," primarily because the mountaineers did not realize how badly off they were. "In spite of their lack of the ordinary comforts of civilization and their isolation from the world," declared the reporter, "they all have the exaggerated egotism and comfortable opinion of their surroundings common to provincial communities." Crawford's climax to his analysis of mountain culture revealed his own preoccupations. "Here freedom is asserted to its uttermost," he said, but worse, "privacy is unknown." Crawford was singularly representative of middle-class Victorian Americans, who evaluated all other cultures within the framework of their own concerns: women, family, morality, privacy, self-control—and underlying it all, the terrible fear of the dark or "savage" side of their own natures that might gain the upper hand if allowed the freedom that mountaineers enjoyed.[51] The title of Crawford's book eloquently sums up his bias—*An American Vendetta: A Story of Barbarism in the United States.*

Press coverage of the feud reached its height in the spring and summer of 1888, climaxing with the Supreme Court decision and the tales of detectives who emerged from the hills with descriptions of their escapades in hunting feudists. In the fall of 1888 and in early 1889, newspaper articles on the feud were sporadic and confined to the back pages. Thus, it was almost an anticlimax when, in the late summer, the nine Hatfield supporters who had been the object of so much attention in the Supreme Court case were tried for murder in Pikeville. By that time, due to the efforts of reward-seeking detectives, there had been several additions to their ranks. Alex Messer, Charlie Gillespie, and Ellison Mounts had all been captured in the fall of 1888 and were lodged in the Pike County jail with Valentine and the others.

The trials finally began in the last week of August 1889. The people of Pike County, and indeed the entire surrounding region, could talk of nothing else. After interminable delays the trials were actually about to begin and people streamed in from distant and remote hollows to the north, south, east, and west. "Everybody was excited—asking questions and prophesying how things would go with the Hatfields," wrote Truda McCoy, who knew some of the jurors.[52] The first to be tried was Devil Anse's own brother, Valentine, who still appeared confident that once his case was presented, the court would find him not guilty. Perry Cline, who had apparently deserted Randolph McCoy and his family, defended Valentine and several others of the Hatfield group. It seems likely that Valentine's belief in his ultimate vindication was based on this action of Cline's. The Hatfields were well aware that the second phase of the feud would never have occurred without the intervention of Cline and they had, as late as the fall of 1887, believed that he alone could put a stop to it. Valentine thus remained confident that with Cline on his side, he would be acquitted in a Pike County court.

Perhaps he also assessed Cline's motivation realistically, in terms of monetary gain. Valentine must have known that Cline was still angry about the loss of his rich timber and coal lands along the banks of Grapevine Creek—that he would like to regain some of those lost profits. In order to pay Cline and his law firm for legal services, Valentine and the three Mayhorn brothers signed over some of their lands on Beech and Grapevine creeks to the lawyer. In a trust deed, they promised to pay the fees in cash by a certain date, or these lands would revert to Cline.[53] In this way, perhaps Valentine thought he secured the loyalty and best efforts of Cline in the trials. Which side the lawyer was actually on remains questionable to this day. Truda McCoy says that Cline repeatedly assured Randolph McCoy that he was actually helping the McCoys by offering to act as the Hatfields' lawyer.[54]

During his trial, Valentine related the story of his involvement in the events following the stabbing of his brother, Ellison, in a simple and straightforward manner. He admitted persuading the Pike County guards to surrender their charges and taking the boys across the Tug into Logan County. But, he claimed, he was not present when Anse and seven others shot the boys; in fact, he had tried to persuade his brother not to take such drastic action.[55] Although several witnesses testified to having seen Valentine some distance away when the shootings took place, however, Pike Countians were ready to convict Hatfields, and they found all nine guilty. The surprise came when Valentine and most of the others were sentenced, not to death by hanging, but to life in the penitentiary. Randolph McCoy, disappointed that the Hatfields were getting off with life sentences, attempted to raise a lynch mob. As with so many of Old Ranel's efforts in the past, this one could not rouse enough support to enable Ranel to carry out his plans.[56] For Valentine Hatfield, however, the life sentence *was* a death sentence. Six months later the old man died in the Kentucky penitentiary; confinement had killed him.

The final trial in the series, that of twenty-five-year-old Ellison Mounts, proved quite different from all the others. Mounts came from a very poor family and had no land with which to pay an attorney, so the court appointed one for him.[57] Cline appeared uninterested in defending any Hatfields who had no way to pay his fees. Despite this disadvantage, however, Mounts seemed hopeful. After observing the trials that had gone before, it seemed that the worst he would get would be life imprisonment. This may have been the reason Mounts decided to plead guilty. In Ellison's trial the only witness called was Aunt Sally McCoy, who related the story of the New Year's Day raid on her home and the shooting of her daughter Alifair.[58] By calling Aunt Sally, an old woman who had suffered the loss of four children, the prosecution apparently hoped to get the death penalty for Ellison; Perry Cline is reported to have said, "we have to hang *someone!*" Although the official summary of the trial does not reflect it, Truda McCoy claims that Aunt Sally's testimony was a shock to the spectators in the courtroom. When asked whether Mounts had killed Alifair, she answered firmly, "no," and explained that "Alifair called Cap's name just before she was shot."[59] But whether Aunt Sally actually made such a statement or not, the jurors apparently shared Perry Cline's belief that someone had to hang and Ellison Mounts would be their last chance. The jury found Mounts guilty and he was sentenced to death by hanging. Shocked by this unexpected turn of events, Mounts had his lawyer attempt to change his plea from guilty to not guilty and ask for a new trial. But the judicial system in Pikeville was in hostile hands. Having finally found a scapegoat for the Hatfield-McCoy feud, they were not inclined to let him escape. His request was denied.

On 18 February 1890 thousands of spectators gathered in Pikeville from all over eastern Kentucky for the hanging of Ellison Mounts. It was the first hanging in Pike County in forty years and no one wanted to miss it. Yet a good part of the excitement stemmed from the rumors spread among the crowd that Devil Anse Hatfield would ride into Pikeville to save Mounts at the last minute. The prisoner himself seemed to find hope in the rumors and boasted that Cap had promised to get him out. But the Hatfields never appeared, and the only battle the sheriff had to fight was with

Frank Phillips. At midday, before the hanging, Phillips stormed into Pikeville, roaring drunk and declaring his intention to "take over" Pikeville—he wanted to be the law. When the sheriff tried to quiet him, a scuffle ensued, which resulted in Phillips's being safely locked in the jail while the hanging proceeded.[60]

Kentucky law stated that such executions could not be public, so the sheriff had erected a stockade fence around the scaffold. The scaffolding and its fence, however, were located at the base of a hill, and the thousands of spectators gathered on the side of the hill could see everything that occurred. It was clear that Ellison Mounts was to be a public example of what should have happened to all the Hatfields. Mounts obliged his captors by his last statement to the crowd. "The Hatfields made me do it," he cried, "the Hatfields made me do it."[61]

A few months before Ellison Mounts was hanged, Devil Anse himself had given a final word concerning the famous feud to the press. In November 1889, Anse and several of his supporters appeared in Charleston, West Virginia, to answer charges in federal court of selling illegal whiskey. A Wheeling reporter who was in the city said that it was "one of the greatest sensations Charleston has experienced for many years." The reporter soon unraveled the mystery of why Anse would make himself vulnerable to arrest for the Kentucky warrants by appearing in Charleston. A federal marshal had assured Devil Anse that if he would voluntarily come in to face the charges, the federal government would protect him from any other outstanding arrest warrants. As part of the bargain, the marshal also allowed Anse and his men to appear in the city, and in court, armed. With this guarantee, Devil Anse strode into Charleston to face not only the court but curiosity seekers and reporters. "Everybody wanted to see old Devil Anse," declared the Wheeling reporter. "Some seemed to think he had hoofs and horns." But when he finally appeared, declared the journalist, he turned out to be a rather good-looking old citizen." The Wheeling reporter "secured" a two-hour interview with the notorious feud leader and set about finding out how much of the vendetta "is pure fabrication."

Devil Anse proceeded to give a detailed narrative of his version of the feud, an essentially accurate one except that, predictably, he denied any involvement in the killing of the three McCoy boys or the McCoy home burning. Part of Anse's defense was to point to the respected position of his family in the community. He described his parents and grandparents with pride, indicating that they had always been held in respect in the Tug Valley. He concluded by arguing that "every man in Logan County who knows me will tell you I am a peaceful, law-abiding man, and no man will say I ever told a falsehood. In this contest I have only defended myself, as any man would do under similar circumstances." The reporter—who represented the *Wheeling Intelligencer*, a paper that had tended to defend the Hatfields against Kentucky—was predisposed to believe Devil Anse's story, concluding: "No more hospitable, honest or peacefully disposed people live than the Hatfields. Their enemies were the aggressors, and the blows they have struck have been in revenge for the unprovoked butchery of their nearest and best loved relatives."[62]

This latter-day attempt to rescue the Hatfield image was a futile one. No one was interested any longer in investigating the facts of the feud to determine who was at fault. A general impression had been created of mountaineer culture as not only lawless and violent, but unsuited to the march of civilization and progress. Mountaineers were viewed as obstacles to capitalist investment and cultural enlightenment. In the same issue of the *Wheeling Intelligencer* that presented Devil Anse's side of the feud, there appeared an article lamenting the effect sensational feud tales were having on economic development. "Capitalists," argued the paper, "refuse to come and prospect because they say they are afraid of our outlaws. You cannot get them to go into the interior to inspect our timber and coal lands for fear they will be ambushed."[63] It was a refrain echoed repeatedly by the national press.

The problem was more than one of economic development—it was also one of culture. The mountaineers' way of life—their flexibility and relaxed schedules, their lack of ambition, and their excessive independence—was seen as an obstacle to cultural enlightenment as well as economic progress. Appalachians, like the Indians before them, would have to alter their entire way of life and culture to fit in, or they would simply have to be removed. The feud was a convenient way of emphasizing the point that mountaineers were savages in need of modernization, both economic and cultural.

Whether the feudists were Hatfields or McCoys was of no consequence; they were all guilty.

When the feud and trials were over, the Tug Valley was not yet industrialized. Although the railroad was already under construction, residents of the valley were still isolated economically and culturally from the rest of the country. Therefore, modernization, defined as the actual integration of the region into the national economy and adoption of bourgeois social and cultural patterns, did not cause either the first or the second phase of the feud. As we have seen, the first phase emerged from more subtle market influences in combination with the internal dynamics of the community. The second phase was more directly linked to capitalist transformation—or more precisely, to the preparation for that transformation. The central issue underlying the second phase was that of control over the process. In that struggle, the modernizers had the advantage because they knew what it was they were fighting for, while the defenders of local autonomy and independence had no clear sense of how or what they had to fight. They merely responded, personally and impulsively, to unwelcome intrusions upon their traditional (albeit changing) way of life. The scattered and nonpolitical nature of their response was fatal when they were confronted with the superior political and economic power of the modernizers.

That obvious inequality in economic and political power fostered the conviction that Appalachian culture was inferior to bourgeois culture and consigned the mountaineers to the unreal world of savagery, whether degraded or noble. Once that pattern of thinking was established, industrialization and the reshaping of cultural values could proceed much more smoothly, with the complicity of many Appalachians themselves. The irony here is that the feud—at least the form it took in its second phase—was virtually created by the modernizers and then used as an argument for drastic alterations in Appalachian culture. In short, in this case the mountaineers were not even on the offensive, violently defending their way of life. Devil Anse, in fact, desperately tried to join the development process, but with an implicit demand that he retain some control over it. He, like other mountaineers, were complicated human beings who hoped to adopt the favorable and avoid the unfavorable aspects of economic and social change. But the modernizers were more single-minded in their purpose, first aggravating, if not creating the feud, then stereotyping it as a simple contest between primitive and civilized society. By the 1890s many Appalachians themselves had been convinced of the inadequacy of their own culture, and industrialization proceeded with little opposition. The feud had been only one step in preparing the ground.

Epilogue: The Devil Transformed

• •

Responses of the mountaineers to the barrage of social and cultural coercion from both within and without varied widely.[1] We have already observed Devil Anse's withdrawal from the judicial system and county government when it was clear he would not be fairly heard there. This passive defense turned violent when Perry Cline revived the feud and brought in state authority. Confronted with the destruction of their local system of authority and decision making, a few of the Hatfields such as Johnse and Cap resorted to violence and terrorism in the attack on Ranel McCoy's home. This was personal violence, not focused on the political or legal institutions that were at the root of the problem, and because of this characteristic it seems "irrational" to the modern observer. Historian Gordon McKinney has emphasized that this personal type of mountain violence—sometimes in the form of feuds and sometimes in the form of political fights and assassinations—became almost epidemic in the final decades of the nineteenth century. The mountaineers, he points out, had a very clear sense of their own community standards and were accustomed to the autonomous operation of the local system of legal and social authority. With the sudden wresting away of control of those institutions by outsiders and their local representatives in the late nineteenth century, the anger and frustration of the mountaineers frequently erupted in violence.[2]

The second phase of the Hatfield-McCoy feud emerged from just this conflict of local versus outside control of the authority system. As economic development steadily progressed and local elites became more visible and powerful, their values became the accepted ones. Resistance became, not only futile, but a sign of abnormality and deviance. Some mountaineers found it wisest simply to withdraw into the comfort of their own kin group or of religion. Devil Anse Hatfield is a good example. His retreat to Main Island Creek was as much a response to social and cultural change as it was to the threat of vigilante violence. Although Devil Anse had been on the cutting edge of economic transformation, his cultural values remained rooted in the traditional world.

Fortunately his financial losses from the feud did not leave him and his family destitute, to become part of the impoverished class in Appalachia; he retained enough of his assets to insulate himself from a changing world. Devil Anse lived out his life on Main Island Creek much as he had always done—logging with his family, hunting deer and bears, and making whiskey.[3] Occasionally he strolled into Logan Courthouse to vote, visit with his brother Elias, or chat with the editor of the *Banner*. H. C. Ragland never failed to report when Anse was in town and what he might have to say about the supply of game in the region. The editor always spoke of the old feudist with respect as a kind of grand old man, but one who no longer exercised real influence or power.[4]

From the time he moved to Main Island Creek until he died, Devil Anse never did anything to controvert Ragland's portrayal of him. Periodically, whenever any violence even remotely connected to a Hatfield erupted, there were dire predictions from local alarmists that Devil Anse would gather his "gang" and start trouble. But this never occurred—even on the two occasions when it seemed most likely. One of these took place in 1898 when Johnse, having eluded detectives for ten years, was arrested and turned over to Kentucky officials in Pikeville. Tried and convicted for his part in the New Year's Day raid on the McCoy home, Johnse soon found himself serving a life sentence in the Kentucky penitentiary. When one member of Devil Anse's family, his son Elias, did set out to take revenge, local journalists predicted a rampage of vengeance. But they couldn't have been more wrong; the old feud leader remained quietly at home. Eventually, his patience was rewarded— after six years Johnse was released and came home to Logan County.[5]

The other occasion on which everyone thought Devil Anse would again take up his Winchester came in 1896, when the ever-troublesome Cap became involved in a shootout with several men in the town of Matewan on the Tug River. At first Cap eluded arrest and, while he was in hiding, the sheriff of Mingo County actually brought Devil Anse in for questioning. The old man came voluntarily and peacefully but claimed he knew nothing of Cap's whereabouts. Within a few days Cap, in an uncharacteristic gesture, gave himself up to the sheriff, was tried, and spent several months in the Mingo County jail. At no time did Devil Anse interfere in any way with the course of events leading to his son's imprisonment. Although some newspapers heralded this incident as the outbreak of the "second war," more than anything it confirmed Anse's resignation to and even acceptance of the new order.[6]

In 1911, at the age of seventy-three, Devil Anse took a step that signified both his increasing withdrawal from the world around him and his adjustment to it: he underwent a religious conversion. For his family and neighbors, this must have been a startling turn of events. For three quarters of a century, Anderson Hatfield had played a role in the community—a role centered around his irreverence and good-natured skepticism. His refusal to be intimidated by the somber power of a set of judgmental religious beliefs had been one of his strongest and most endearing characteristics. When Anse told reporter Crawford in the summer of 1888 that he belonged to no church except the "Devil's church"—the church of the world— his assembled family had roared with admiring laughter, as though, wrote Crawford, "it was the funniest thing they had ever heard."[7] But now, it seemed, the devil himself had surrendered—had admitted that the world and the world's church was not for him. He agreed to be baptised in Main Island Creek by one of Logan's oldest and most respected hardshell preachers, Uncle Dyke Garrett.[8] A startling transformation had been accomplished. If the devil could be taken as a metaphor for the world of market capitalism, then Anse had managed to exorcise its influence just at the time when that cloven-hoofed creature tightened its grip on the Tug Valley. For Anderson Hatfield, it was still possible to reject the devil, but for his community it was not. Not, that is, unless the devil could be translated into enlightenment and progress—a task that Ragland, the *Banner*, and the capitalist forces they represented embraced with energy and enthusiasm.

The old feudist lived another ten years after his immersion in Main Island Creek. During this time, when it was evident that he was less and less a feudist, the feud legend grew more and more. When Anse died in January 1921, it was a newsworthy event all over the country. The *New York Times* reported that the old feud leader "died quietly in his bed last night of pneumonia."[9] His family and friends demonstrated their grief and adulation by staging the biggest funeral in the history of Logan County. Four to five hundred people gathered on the steep hillside near his home; his children and grandchildren assembled from distant places to renew family bonds and settle old quarrels.[10] To most of them Anse already was a symbol of a more heroic world, where individual pride, courage, and loyalty counted in some grander scheme. They expressed their feelings by commissioning a life-size marble statue, carved in Italy, to be placed over his grave. It was a striking contrast to the rough, hand-hewn stones that marked the graves of his family and friends in the same cemetery.[11] Anderson Hatfield had never been a typical mountaineer, so it is ironic that in death, his image, like that massive statue, came to symbolize all mountaineers.

In Pikeville, Old Ranel McCoy retreated in quite another fashion from the world of railroads and coal. After the house burning, he and Aunt Sally never returned to Blackberry Creek in the Tug Valley. With the help of Perry Cline, Old Ranel obtained a commission to operate a ferry in the town of Pikeville. This position allowed the old man—he was near seventy when the feud ended in 1890—to earn an adequate living and to do what he liked best, which was to talk endlessly about his troubles. The feud, especially the gruesome early morning raid on his Blackberry Creek home, furnished the material for his repeated and increasingly anguished public laments.[12]

As the years went on, fewer and fewer people were willing to listen; even Aunt Sally, so long a force for moderation and restraint on Old Ranel, was gone; she died sometime in the 1890s. The person who most shared his hatred of the Hatfields, Perry Cline, was no longer around. Cline died in 1891, two years after the Hatfields were tried in Pikeville. He was only forty-two years old.[13] Thus, alone and bitter, Old Ranel survived. When he was eighty-four the railroad reached Pikeville, but the old feudist barely noticed; he was still attempting to persuade people that the Hatfields had never been sufficiently punished for their crimes. At age eighty-eight, as Old Ranel tended a cooking fire, his clothes caught fire.[14] He died two months later and was buried in Dils Cemetery in Pikeville. There was no large, respectful gathering of family and friends, no Italian marble statue—not even a modest headstone. The impersonal forces of industrial capitalism that Old Ranel had unwittingly spearheaded in the feud eschewed the kind of loyalty and gratitude that the family of Devil Anse, even in defeat, continued to demonstrate.

For the next generation of Hatfields and McCoys, however, retreat was not a realistic possibility. The children, nieces, and nephews of the feud leaders, who were young men and women at the time of the feud, were forced to function in a new kind of world. Their choices were escape, rebellion, or accommodation, and they tried all of them. Old Ranel's nephew, Squirrel Huntin' Sam McCoy, always a loner, chose escape. In the 1890s he left the Tug Valley for the West, living in a variety of states and trying a variety of jobs. In the 1930s, noticing that the feud was becoming popular in pulp magazine fiction, Sam sat down to write his memoirs. He was near seventy when he composed his reminiscences, which portray boisterous arguments and horseplay that seemed to turn brutal almost accidentally with the use of knives and guns. Sam could not recall any specific cause for the feud except the hog trial and the McCoys' "wicked" habit of talking too much and thereby aggravating the Hatfields. He does not divulge any information on his own life after the feud, his reasons for leaving the Tug Valley, or whether he was successful in whatever he hoped to find outside it.[15]

Others of the younger generation chose defiance and rebellion. French Ellis, a Hatfield supporter in the feud who had also married a niece of Devil Anse, is the most obvious example. Ellis had been born into a large but impoverished family in the town of Logan Courthouse; his father was a farm laborer all his life.[16] In the 1880s, when the young man was in his twenties, he formed a lifelong connection to Devil Anse's family, working on the timber crew and marrying a daughter of the feud leader's sister. He became one of Devil Anse's most loyal and aggressive supporters, one of the young men like Cap and Johnse that Devil Anse had difficulty restraining. Ellis was a participant in the ill-conceived and ill-executed raid on the McCoy home. When Devil Anse moved his family to Main Island Creek, Ellis became an important part of the family and, for the first time, a landowner.[17]

Although his loyalty to his benefactor knew no limits, the young feudist never accepted the new order. He seemed to delight in disturbing the middle-class propriety and decorousness that the local elite were trying so hard to establish. In the 1890s, Ellis was one of the rowdy types who most annoyed and frustrated H. C. Ragland. He and his friends repeatedly showed up in the village of Logan Courthouse drunk and ready for action. Starting fights directly in front of mercantile establishments, shouting profanities outside the church on Sunday, and insulting candidates on election day were all part of the repertoire of rebellion.[18] Ellis seemed to consider it a game to foment a disturbance in the village, then escape across the river before the constables could catch and arrest him. Sometimes, however, he was caught and had to appear before the court; in these cases he was invariably bailed out by Devil Anse or Anse's brother Elias. Ellis, unlike so many mountaineers, was fortunate in having the protection of Devil Anse and his family. Many without the benefit of such protection fell prey to the jail terms meted out by the "law and order" circuit judge whom elite Logan Countians felt so fortunate to have on the bench. French Ellis died in 1924 at the age of sixty-seven; he was buried near the marble statue of Devil Anse in the Hatfield cemetery, an unregenerate mountaineer in every sense of the term.[19]

Nancy McCoy Hatfield Phillips, too, chose the path of defiance and rebellion. Since the age of sixteen, when she married Johnse Hatfield, Nancy had demonstrated an independence and assertiveness that was in one way characteristic and in another an exaggeration of mountain women. Women who knew Nancy told Truda McCoy that she was admired for her strong will and her beauty. One neighbor reminisced that "Nancy was as pretty a woman as you ever laid eyes on, but she was a crackerjack. She was the best thing you ever saw if she liked you, but if she didn't like you—look out!"[20] Once Nancy discovered that Johnse could not be prevented from having affairs with other women, she decided rather quickly to abandon him. Two months after the battle of Grapevine Creek, when Johnse had disappeared into hiding, she took their two children and moved back to her mother's home on Peter Creek. Soon

Nancy met and was attracted to Frank Phillips, who was at that time enjoying his greatest popularity as the hero of Grapevine Creek. For Nancy, twenty-four years old and with two young children, it was quite a coup to be identified with Phillips and, no doubt, she felt that it served to repay Johnse for his treatment of her. They began living together in 1888 and by December 1889 Nancy had another child. Although Johnse divorced her in 1890 on grounds of adultery, she did not marry Frank until 1895.[21]

In some ways, Nancy and Frank were well matched. Although Frank, like Johnse, could not be prevented from liaisons with other women, like Nancy he was openly defiant of authority and convention. His drunken claim, on the day Ellison Mounts was hanged, that he intended to "run" Pikeville was not an isolated incident during the ten years following the end of the feud. Frank was often observed drinking, fighting, and gambling, not only in Pikeville but also in the new Logan County towns of Matewan and Williamson. Both Frank and Nancy partially supported their family by making and selling whisky, despite the stepped-up campaign by the federal government to stop the practice. On two occasions, Nancy was hauled into court in Pikeville for illegally selling "spiritous liquor."[22] Never submissive or obedient, Nancy was not prepared to accept the model of retiring and frail Victorian womanhood presented in newspapers like the *Logan Banner*, which frequently ran fiction and articles designed to promote that image. For Nancy's husband, Frank, the price of defiance was high; in 1898, at the age of thirty-six, he was shot to death in a fight. Three years later, also at the age of thirty-six, a still "feisty" Nancy succumbed to tuberculosis.[23]

Despite these cases of continued open defiance of the new cultural parameters, most of the children of Old Ranel and Devil Anse opted for accommodation—testimony to the power of the new middle-class social and cultural values. Both the Hatfields and the McCoys seemed to accept the new values and strove to conform, with varying degrees of success. Jim McCoy, for example, the oldest son of Old Ranel and Aunt Sally, lacked the economic resources to become aligned with the middle class, but he did the next best thing; he became an ally by protecting their interests. Jim served for a while as sheriff of Pike County and later on the police force. His brother Sam, another hero of Grapevine Creek, managed to acquire some land—a 225-acre farm—just outside Pikeville, where he survived his father by only two years. His wife Martha, however, lived there until her death in 1944. It was from Martha that Truda Williams McCoy learned much of what she incorporated into her book on the McCoy side of the feud, and thus it is from her perspective that much of our information comes.[24]

Most of Devil Anse's sons, like Ranel's, attempted to become part of the new middle class. Cap, often considered the most blood-thirsty of the Hatfields, made a remarkable transition. Apparently Cap was badly shaken by the violent climax to the feud—the killing of Uncle Jim Vance before his very eyes, the battle of Grapevine Creek, and the deadly hide-and-seek game with detectives throughout the summer and fall of 1888. In January 1889, Cap addressed a letter to the governor of Kentucky offering to surrender and be tried in Frankfort. "My life is no satisfaction," he told Buckner.[25] Although he never actually surrendered, two years later Cap was still searching for an end to the Hatfields' struggle with detectives. In a letter to the *Wayne County News* in February 1891, Cap appealed for peace. "We have undergone a fearful loss of noble lives and valuable property in the struggle," he declared, and "I do not wish to keep the old feud alive and I suppose that everybody, like myself, is tired of the names of Hatfield and McCoy."[26]

Even while the struggle was going on, Cap was preparing for the new world to come. After his marriage in 1882, and in the midst of the feud, Cap's wife taught him how to read and write. When the feud was over she persuaded him to "improve" himself by attending law school in Tennessee, where he also would be safe from detectives. Although he completed only six months of formal legal education, Cap, after returning to Logan, continued to study law on his own and was eventually admitted to the bar in Wyoming, Logan, and Mingo counties. Despite occasional relapses in which he settled disagreements by fighting or pulling his gun—as in the 1896 Williamson incident—Cap was learning how to adapt. He even served several terms as deputy sheriff of Logan County.[27] Cap's children grew up with middle-class values and a middle-class education. Two children, a son and a daughter, became lawyers and, with their father, established a law firm in the town of Logan. Cap's daughter was the first woman attorney in Logan County. Although Cap financed the firm and was officially a partner, he left the actual practice to his children. His son remembered him as a somewhat authoritarian figure, but one who possessed an intellectual side as well—he would recite passages from classical works of literature completely from memory and especially liked Robert Ingersoll's "Oration on the Death of His Brother." In 1930, at the age of sixty-six, Cap died from the complications of old bullet wounds.[28]

Johnse, too, had by the end of his life joined the middle class. Although he was sentenced to life imprisonment, a fortunate incident had freed him. In 1904 Johnse happened to be present when the warden of the prison was attacked by a another prisoner with a knife. Quick-acting Johnse saved the warden's life and was granted a pardon. Returning to Logan, Johnse found a job as an agent for United States Steel, Coal and Coke Company. Thus he, like Cap, became a part of the new order that they had been accused so frequently of undermining. The same also held true for most of Anse's children: three became merchants in Mingo and Logan counties, another a physician, another a personnel manager for a mining company, and another a detective for a railroad.[29]

The most successful, however, in making the transition proved to be Devil Anse's brother, Elias, and his children. After Grapevine Creek Elias did not move to Main Island Creek with Devil Anse and the other feudists but settled in the town of Logan. In the 1890s Elias, who had once been indicted for the murder of the three McCoy boys, was elected councilman, constable, and chief of police; he became one of Logan's most respected citizens.[30] Elias's oldest son, Greenway, followed his father in law enforcement and was three times elected sheriff of Mingo County. His other two sons attended college and medical school, and the second, Henry Drury Hatfield, went on to become one of West Virginia's most famous politicians. First elected to the state assembly and then the senate, in 1913 he was elected Republican governor of West Virginia. As governor his most memorable action was to bring to an end a coal miners' strike at Paint and Cabin creeks. Although he did not sympathize with the demands of the miners, Hatfield at least showed human concern for the plight of the miners by visiting them personally—a gesture no other governor had made. What is ironic in all this is the role the Hatfields played in spearheading the process through which Appalachians lost the autonomy and independence so important to them. A kind of high-water mark, or perhaps the ultimate symbol for this trend, came when a daughter of Governor Henry Drury Hatfield—a granddaughter of Elias—married the president of the United States Steel Corporation.[31]

In 1921—the year of Devil Anse's death—Logan County and the Tug Valley reached a second pinnacle of notoriety, one also rooted in violence: the coal mine wars. By 1920 the economy of the region was completely dominated by the coal mining industry. Coal companies owned most of the land and employed most of the population; they built company towns, paid workers in company scrip rather than money, and controlled almost every aspect of the miners' lives. Most local middle-class professionals, small businesspeople, and mine supervisors were dependent on the coal companies as well. During World War I the mines had prospered, people were employed, and the future seemed promising even for the working class. However, the end of the war brought economic depression in the Tug Valley coalfields. Jobs were scarce and companies cut wages. In 1919 the United Mine Workers of America (UMWA), successful in organizing miners in other parts of the country, began organizing the miners of he Tug Valley in order to bring their wages in line with other coalfields. Coal operators reacted drastically to this effort, firing miners who joined the union or simply were seen talking to union organizers. When miners were fired they were also evicted from their company housing and were often left with no place to go.

Resentment of such tactics ran high in the Tug Valley, and that resentment was focused on the individuals hired by the companies to carry out their policies—detectives hired from private agencies such as Baldwin-Felts, Pinkerton, or Eureka. It was strangely reminiscent of the feud days when detectives had haunted the hills doing the bidding of outsiders; miners, both mountaineers and immigrants, focused all their resentment and passionate hatred for their ill-treatment on the detectives. Strangely, it was a Hatfield who led the new "war" against the detectives and became a folk hero for it. His name was Sid Hatfield. He was not a descendant of Devil Anse; in fact, no one knew his real name, as he was an orphan raised in one of the numerous Hatfield families in the valley. Yet there it was—a Hatfield defending miners against exploitation by outsiders.

Sid acquired status as a folk hero in 1920, when he was chief of police in Matewan. A group of Baldwin-Felts agents had arrived in Matewan (Devil Anse's home territory) with eviction orders that would put hundreds of miners out of their homes. Sid Hatfield and the mayor of Matewan tried to stop them by claiming the eviction orders were illegal. They had confronted the detectives and were arguing in the street when someone fired a shot and everyone pulled guns. The result was the "Matewan Massacre," in which the mayor and several bystanders were killed by the detectives, but Sid Hatfield managed to kill seven of the Baldwin-Felts agents. Overnight, Sid Hatfield became a working-class hero. But retaliation was not long in coming. A year later, when Sid traveled to McDowell County to testify in a court hearing, he and his wife were shot down by Baldwin-Felts detectives as they walked up the steps to the courthouse. Industrialization had brought neither peace nor prosperity to the Tug Valley.[32]

The "Matewan Massacre" and the murder of Sid Hatfield were only two incidents in a long series of labor-management conflicts in the feud region that came to be known as the West Virginia coal mine wars. The violence and lawlessness that resulted from these "wars" made the old feud days appear peaceful and idyllic. Despite the presence of Sid Hatfield and numerous miners who were either Hatfields or McCoys, most of the direct descendants of Devil Anse and Old Ranel were on the other side, representing the interests of corporations. The most obvious examples were Jim McCoy, Cap Hatfield, and Greenway Hatfield, all sheriffs or deputy sheriffs in Pikeville or Logan. Also, Johnse Hatfield was at the time a detective employed by U.S. Coal and Coke. The most notorious local defender of the coal interests, Don Chafin of Logan, was also related to the Hatfields—he was a cousin of Devil Anse's wife, Levicy. A native of Marrowbone Creek, which was a part of Magnolia district until 1881, Chafin was born in 1887, the year that Perry Cline persuaded the governor of Kentucky to revive the feud. One of eleven children, Chafin forged his own future in the new order. When, at the age of twenty-three, he became sheriff of Logan County, Chafin saw his major responsibility in that capacity as preventing the United Mine Workers not only from organizing, but from entering the county at all. To do this as well as to preserve "order" in the coal camps, he hired hundreds of men as his deputies and paid their salaries with money received from the coal companies.[33] A visitor to Logan described Chafin's antiunion operation as "a perfectly-oiled machine with an abundance of funds, and a set of loyal adherents."[34]

Chafin's flagrant abuse of the law, especially in declaring a whole county off-limits to the United Mine Workers, finally prompted the miners in neighboring Kanawha and Boone counties to take drastic action. Plans were made, against the advice of union officials in Charleston, for an army of miners to march across formidable Blair Mountain into Logan and wrest the county away from Chafin. In September 1921 four to six thousand miners began a march over the ridge that separated Logan County from Kanawha County. While the governor hurriedly appealed to President Harding for federal troops, Don Chafin personally led a comparable force of state police, sheriff's deputies, and mine guards to defend "his" county. Skirmishing took place along a ten-mile front but ended quickly when two thousand federal troops under General Bandholtz arrived on the scene. Union officials later claimed that the miners retreated so quickly because they were not really intent on violence but only wanted to get the attention of the federal government; they believed that awareness of their plight would bring help, not repression. Unfortunately, they were wrong.[35]

In the wake of the "battle for Logan," most newspapers across the country were preoccupied with the question of blame, not for the gruesome conditions in the coal mines, but for the laxity of law enforcement which allowed the miners to march on Logan. The union and the miners were assumed to be the troublemakers, not the coal companies with their oppressive and illegal tactics. Don Chafin continued as sheriff even though he spent two months of a two-year term in the federal penitentiary for bootlegging. Logan County remained unorganized by the UMWA throughout the 1920s. Only in 1933, with the passage of the National Industrial Recovery Act guaranteeing labor's right to organize, did Logan's miners flood into the union ranks.

In the same year in which the battle for Logan occurred, Devil Anse Hatfield died. The juxtaposition of the two events serves to underscore the changes that had taken place in the region. Sid Hatfield and Don Chafin, both in some sense Hatfields, were on opposite sides in the war. Their loyalties were defined by an identification with economic and social class rather than family and kinship bonds. Protest and violence had become politicized, rooted in class antagonisms and aimed at institutions and ideologies rather than at individuals. But this modernization of economic and social organization had not led to peace and prosperity. On the contrary, the greater portion of the population of both Pike and Logan counties were impoverished, both financially and culturally, by industrialization. And the violence was much more intense and frightening both in frequency and in numbers of people involved. To a far greater degree than in the Hatfield-McCoy feud, the law was simply an extension of the dominant class—the coal companies—who used and abused it with impunity. It is ironic that the local elite in the 1880s had accused the feudists of lawless violence and had insisted that their behavior was creating obstacles to economic and social "progress." Once feuding, whiskey, and guns were eliminated, these people argued, an impartial judicial system would readily bring about order. Now coal companies enforced their wishes with guns, reinforced by a county government and judicial system they had bought and paid for.

Still, despite the exploitation of miners, many of Logan's and Mingo's ordinary citizens—miners, small farmers, merchants, and professionals—as well as people outside the region believed that the violence of the labor wars was simply an extension of the earlier habits of feuding. Indeed, they were convinced that it was somehow an outgrowth of Appalachian culture, not a consequence of exploitation and impoverishment. They interpreted this new scale and dimension of violence as one still based on the gap between those enlightened by modern, rational culture and "backward" mountaineers. Perspective, however, did play a role. The middle classes in Logan and Pikeville saw themselves as the "civilized" element struggling to enlighten the workers and mountaineers, whereas people outside the region attributed the high levels of industrial violence to the "primitive" culture of *both* sides. The coal company executives who profited from industrialization were, of course, insulated in their New York, Philadelphia and Boston offices, aloof from involvement in or blame for the violence.[36]

In Logan and Pike counties, the elite's achievement of cultural hegemony by the 1920s shaped historical perceptions of the feud. The middle classes, many of whom were Hatfields and McCoys, were very well aware that the outside world perceived them as gun totin', moonshinin' mountaineers—an image they desperately hoped to alter. Thus there developed in both Logan and Pike counties a conspiracy of silence whenever the subject of the feud came up. For some this meant complete silence, even among themselves; Ranel's son Jim, for example, forbade his children or any of his family ever to mention the feud, and several Mingo County residents, interviewed about the feud as elderly people, said they had nothing to tell because they themselves had been only children at the time and their families refused to discuss it. Others maintained silence about the feud in the presence of strangers—journalists interested in writing a story about the feud, for example—but sometimes reminisced in private. Implicit in their silence was embarrassment at being part of a culture that produced the feud. It was better to bury the memories and overcome the legacy.[37]

When the first Logan County history was published in 1927, its author, G. T. Swain, clearly revealed this attitude toward the "dark ages" of Logan's history. In a single chapter on the feud, Swain sought to prove that the Hatfields were not the "bloodthirsty desperadoes" portrayed by the newspapers, but more important, he argued that the feud had occurred in "pioneer" days, before civilization had penetrated the mountains. Swain did not blame Appalachian culture specifically, but a more widespread "frontier" culture—one more easily identifiable as belonging to a stage in national history rather than being peculiar to Appalachia. "First, the reader must bear in mind," wrote Swain, "that we had no organized police forces during those days such as we have now." "Then," he continued, "it must be remembered that mountain people rarely sought redress for wrongs at the hands of the law," but settled their differences with violence. After summarizing the events of the feud, Swain declared, "the hills and valleys that once rang with the report of pistols and rifles, and whose soil was bathed with human blood, is now stilled in peace." Ironically, Swain was writing only six years after the "Matewan Massacre" and the "battle for Logan"; he considered Don Chafin Logan's most admirable citizen. Declaring that everyone involved in the feud would like to "blot from memory's pages those dreadful dark days of strife," Swain noted that Cap Hatfield had become a law-abiding, peaceful citizen and was then serving as deputy sheriff. "Those days of lawlessness and strife are gone forever," concluded Swain, and the participants would like to have the feud days forgotten and their "good deeds registered on the credit side of life's ledger." The imagery invoked here of a life's worth being summed up on a business ledger is an appropriate reflection of the almost complete achievement of cultural hegemony by business interests in what was considered at the time the most backward region of America.[38]

Both Devil Anse the entrepreneur and Devil Anse the defender (if only reluctantly) of traditional culture from outside intervention had been forgotten. In the view of Swain as well as many other mountaineers, he had become either a bloodthirsty outlaw or a frontier cowboy whose time had passed. He and the other feudists belonged to an era consigned by local historians to the "prehistory" of their region; the feud seemed to have lost its relevance to "modern" Appalachian history, which began with industrialization in the 1890s. Ironically, as the historical reality of the feud was lost, the popular media—books (such as the famous one by Virgil Carrington Jones), magazines, radio, television, and popular song—created a myth that firmly entrenched itself in the realm of American legend and folklore. This transformation from history to folklore, in fact, was so complete that, even though the feud is usually not mentioned in history textbooks, almost every American today is aware of the Hatfield-McCoy legend.

Why this happened and what was so appealing to the American public about the feud legend are fascinating questions in their own right, but they are not the question addressed in this study, which has attempted to "recover" the feud's historical reality and assess its relevance for the broad sweep of American history. Far from providing an example of a static and unchanging culture, the feudists were struggling with the same historical forces of capitalist transformation that had been changing America since before the American Revolution. They were not so different, after all, from the hundreds of Americans whose communities, at different times throughout the nineteenth century, were beset by social and cultural tensions as they attempted to accommodate or to escape or to resist being drawn into first a national, then an international, economic system. But if the initial patterns of economic conflict and struggle for cultural hegemony were similar to those found in other places, the consequences have been very different. Unfortunately, for Appalachians more than for most Americans, the "progress" of capitalist transformation inexorably has been accompanied by economic, social, and cultural exploitation.

Appendixes

Appendixes

APPENDIX I
Hatfield Supporters in the Second Phase, 1887–1888

Name	Residence	Age	Family Property in the 1880s			
			Acres	Value	Personal	Total
Chafin, John	Magnolia	28	0	$ 0	$ 375	$ 375
Chafin, Moses	''	41	400	700	220	920
Chafin, Tom	''	34	170	600	150	750
Chambers, Tom	''	34	0	0	200	200
Christian, Dan	''	56	400	500	200	700
Christian, Mose	''	27	50	63	0	63
Dempsey, Bill	Logan	?	?	?	?	?
Elem, Frank	Magnolia	30	0	0	0	0
Ellis, French	''	29	0	0	0	0
Ferrell, William	''	?	?	?	?	?
Gillespie, Charlie	''	?	?	?	?	?
Hatfield, Anse	''	50	3,000	3,700	550	4,250
Hatfield, Cap	''	22	600	750	0	750
Hatfield, Elias	''	42	650	2,000	1,000	3,000
Hatfield, Elias, Jr.	''	?	?	?	?	?
Hatfield, Elliot	''	21	215	400	200	600
Hatfield, Floyd	''	38	168	335	0	335
Hatfield, Johnse	''	26	300	450	100	550
Hatfield, Bob	''	21	3,000	3,700	550	4,250
Hatfield, Valentine	''	56	400	400	175	575
Mayhorn, Dock	''	38	83	200	100	300
Mayhorn, Plyant	''	36	110	200	190	390
Mayhorn, Sam	''	32	100	125	0	125
McCoy, Albert	''	26	120	250	100	350
McCoy, L. D.	''	33	0	0	0	0
McCoy, Selkirk	''	57	120	550	200	750
Messer, Alex	''	25	?	?	?	?
Mounts, Ellison	''	24	58	100	75	175
Murphy, Joseph	''	63	100	600	175	775
Staton, John	''	30	75	225	0	225
Thompson, John R.	Logan	42	50	50	50	100
Vance, Jim	Magnolia	58	1,975	1,738	600	2,338
Varney, Andy	''	34	236	600	300	900

Appendixes

| | | Family Property in the 1880s | | | |
Name	Residence	Age	Acres	Value	Personal	Total
Varney, Lark	''	32	105	185	25	210
Wallace, Tom	''	34	225	500	400	900
Whitt, Dan	''	31	0	0	0	0
Whitt, Jeff	''	22	0	0	0	0
Total = 37						

Sources: U.S. census, population and agricultural schedules for Logan and Pike counties, 1850–80, NA; land tax books, 1870–92, LCC; Pike County tax books, 1870–92, UKL.

APPENDIX 2
McCoy Supporters in the Second Phase Residing in the Tug Valley

Name[a]	Residence[b]	Age[c]	Family Property in the 1880s			
			Acres	Value	Personal	Total
Hurley, Josiah	7	46	0	$ 0	$ 0	$ 0
McCoy, Bud	7	26	0	0	104	104
McCoy, Jacob	7	35	100	150	600	750
McCoy, Lark	7	31	150	150	100	250
McCoy, Big Sam	Magnolia	18	0	0	0	0
McCoy, Paris	Magnolia	25	0	0	0	0
McCoy, Ranel	12	58	300	500	200	700
McCoy, James	12	32	0	0	130	130
McCoy, Samuel	12	31	0	0	0	0
Norman, Jim	7	38	0	0	70	70
Smith, Curtis	7	33	200	200	50	250
Smith, David	7	30	100	100	50	150

Total = 12

Sources: U.S. census, population and agricultural schedules for Logan and Pike counties, 1880, NA; land tax books, 1880–90, LCC; Pike County tax books, 1880–90, UKL.

[a]Individuals were identified as feudists if they were indicted by the Logan County Court for the murder of Jim Vance or if they were mentioned as part of the Phillips posses by Truda McCoy (The McCoys, p. 73).

[b]Pike County districts: 7 = Peter Creek (Tug Valley); 12 = Blackberry Creek (Tug Valley).

[c]Ages were computed as of the time the individual first became involved in the feud.

APPENDIX 3

Cline Supporters New to the Feud's Second Phase, 1887–1888

| | | | Family Property in the 1880s | | | |
Name	Residence	Age	Acres	Value	Personal	Total
Cline, Perry	1	40	300	$5,000	$1,230	$6,230
Coleman, Bud	?	?	?	?	?	?
England, John	2	22	0	0	105	105
Ferguson, J. Lee	1	37	610	610	660	1,270
Goff, George	8	57	450	700	300	1,000
Hardin, Lindo	4	27	0	0	0	0
Jones, James	2	29	125	250	108	358
King, Andrew	8	19	0	0	180	180
King, Burbage	8	21	0	0	180	180
Maynard, Moses	8	41	465	850	500	1,350
Maynard, Ransom	8	37	75	250	75	325
McCoy, George	5	21	200	1,500	160	1,660
Miller, Samuel	1	45	0	0	200	200
Phillips, Frank	8	26	1,600	1,600	1,053	2,653
Plymale, David	8	32	100	300	150	450
Ramsey, Joe	1	38	0	0	8	8
Rutherford, Ben	?	44	?	?	?	?
Sowards, James	1	21	780	3,000	314	3,314
Sowards, John	1	?	?	?	?	?
Sowards, William	1	44	780	3,000	314	3,314
Sowards, Mims	1	37	1,200	2,000	500	2,500
Stevenson, Charlie	?	?	?	?	?	?
Stewart, Ed	1	25	30	100	0	100
Stratton, Dave	Logan	34	?	1,000	1,500	2,500
Thompson, Albert	8	22	75	350	12	362
Thompson, Will	8	20	0	0	166	166
Wagner, Tobias	1	53	60	2,500	250	2,750
Yates, John	4	24	50	50	70	120

Total = 28

Appendixes

Note: The Pike County districts inhabited by Cline's supporters were: Pikeville region, districts 1–5, 8–11, 13–15; Tug Valley, districts 6, 7, 12.
Sources: McCoy, *The McCoys*, p. 73; Logan County Court indictments, Mar. 1888, LCC; U.S. census, population and agricultural schedules for Pike and Logan counties, 1880, NA; Pike County tax books, 1880–90, UKL; land tax books, 1880–90, LCC.

APPENDIX 4

Political Affiliations of McCoy-Cline Supporters

Name	Affiliation	Source
McCoy supporters		
Hurley, Josiah	?	?
McCoy, Big Sam	?	?
McCoy, Bud	Republican	son of Union soldier
McCoy, Jacob	"	"
McCoy, James	Democrat	son of Confederate soldier
McCoy, Lark	Republican	son of Union soldier
McCoy, Paris	?	?
McCoy, Ranel	Democrat	served with Confederates
McCoy, Samuel	"	son of Confederate soldier
Norman, Jim	?	?
Smith, Curtis	?	?
Smith, David	?	?
Cline supporters		
Cline, Perry	Republican	associated with leading Republicans
Coleman, Bud	?	?
England, John	?	?
Ferguson, J. Lee	Republican	contemporary historian
Goff, George	?	?
Hardin, Lindo	?	?
Jones, James	?	?
King, Andrew	Republican	son of Union soldier
King, Burbage	"	"
McCoy, George	"	son of registered Republican
Maynard, Moses	"	"
Maynard, Ransom	"	"
Miller, Samuel	Democrat	registered Democrat
Phillips, Frank	Republican	son of Union soldier
Plymale, David	?	?
Ramsey, Joe	?	?
Rutherford, Ben	?	?
Sowards, James	Republican	son of Union soldier
Sowards, John	"	"

Name	Affiliation	Source
Sowards, Mims	''	''
Sowards, William	''	''
Stevenson, Charles	?	?
Stewart, Ed	?	?
Stratton, Dave	Democrat	contemporary historian
Thompson, Albert	Republican	son of registered Republican
Thompson, Will	''	''
Wagner, Tobias	''	contemporary historian
Yates, John	?	?
Total = 40	Republicans/Unionists = 18 (45%) Democrats/Confederates = 5 (12.5%) Unknown = 17 (42.5%)	

Sources: "Roll of Company E of the 39th Mounted Infantry Volunteers"; "Pike County Voting Report for 1868." William Ely notes that Cline, Ferguson, and Wagner were all Republicans (*Big Sandy Valley*).

Notes

CCCO   Circuit Court Clerk's Office, Logan, W.Va.
HUL   Baker Library, Harvard University, Cambridge, Mass.
KSA   State Archives, Frankfort, Ky.
KSC   Clerk of the Supreme Court, State Capitol, Frankfort, Ky.
LCBS   Basement Storeroom, County Courthouse, Logan, W.Va.
LCC   County Clerk's Office, County Courthouse, Logan, W.Va.
NA   National Archives, Washington, D.C.
PCC   County Clerk's Office, County Courthouse, Pikeville, Ky.
UKL   Special Collections, University of Kentucky Library, Lexington
WVSA State Archives and Records, Charleston, W.Va.
WVUL West Virginia Collection, West Virginia University Library,
       Morgantown

INTRODUCTION

1. My summary of events closely follows the most accurate account of the feud yet published, Otis Rice's *Hatfields and McCoys.*
2. Frost, "Our Contemporary Ancestors," p. 311.
3. For a fine analysis of the way Americans have perceived mountaineers, see Shapiro, *Appalachia on Our Mind.* For a survey of the various causes assigned to feuding, see Klotter, "Feuds in Appalachia," pp. 290–317.
4. Jones, *Hatfields and McCoys,* p. 10.
5. Hofstadter and Wallace, *American Violence,* p. 397.
6. Crawford, *An American Vendetta,* p. 10.
7. MacClintock, "The Kentucky Mountains and Their Feuds," pp. 17–21.
8. Rice, *Hatfields and McCoys,* pp. 6–7.
9. Ireland, *Little Kingdoms,* pp. 71–89.
10. McKinney, "Industrialization and Violence," pp. 131–44; Williams, *West Virginia,* pp. 95–129.
11. Some of the feuds reported in the national press include: Howard-Turner in Harlan County, 1884–89; French-Eversole in Perry County, 1887–94; Hargis-Marcum in Breathitt County, 1879–1912; Martin-Tolliver in

Rowan County, 1884–87; Hill-Evans in Garrard County, 1877; Baker-White in Clay County, 1899.

12. The best overview of the economic transformation of the mountains is Eller, *Miners, Millhands, and Mountaineers.*

13. McKinney, "Industrialization and Violence," p. 137.

14. Thompson, *Making of the English Working Class;* Hobsbawm, *Primitive Rebels;* idem, *Bandits.*

15. Ayers, *Vengeance and Justice;* Hindus, *Prison and Plantation;* Holmes, "Moonshining and Collective Violence."

16. Thelen, *Paths of Resistance.*

17. Cubby, "Transformation of the Tug and Guyandot Valleys," pp. 150–66.

18. Thelen, *Paths of Resistance,* pp. 70–77, 87–99.

19. Klotter, "Feuds in Appalachia," p. 306.

20. Fannie Simpkins Booth, interview in *Williamson Daily News,* 8 Aug. 1982.

CHAPTER 1

1. Harmon's story is told in the most detail by Truda McCoy, *The McCoys,* pp. 5–11. See also Rice, *Hatfields and McCoys,* pp. 13–14; Jones, *Hatfields and McCoys,* p. 16.

2. Rice, *Hatfields and McCoys,* p. 10.

3. Ibid., pp. 14–15.

4. In 1865 the Pike County judge ordered the sheriff to collect taxes for the years 1861–65. County Court Order Book D, 1861–72, pp. 100, 109, 117, PCC.

5. Rice, *Hatfields and McCoys,* pp. 11–13. See also *John D. Payne v. Anderson Hatfield,* County Court Order Book B, p. 173, LCC. For Pike County, see *Asa P. McCoy v. Henry Davis, Ellison Hatfield, et al.,* file no. 2589; *Thomas Hatfield v. Joseph Smith et al.,* file no. 2038; *James Lesley v. Pleasant McCoy,* file no. 2606; *Fleming Stafford v. James Vance et al.,* file no. 2907; all in Pike County circuit court records, UKL.

6. Crowe-Carraco, *Big Sandy,* p. 11; Scalf, *Kentucky's Last Frontier,* pp. 20–23; Rice, *Allegheny Frontier,* pp. 11–12.

7. For a debate on the national origins of mountaineers, see Tallmadge, Caudill, and Drake, "Anglo-Saxon vs. Scotch-Irish." See also Campbell, *Southern Highlander,* pp. 50–71; and McClure, "Settlement of the Kentucky Appalachian Highlands," pp. 122–25, 163.

8. Rice, *Allegheny Frontier,* pp. 15–16; Mitchell, "The Shenandoah Valley Frontier," pp. 151–52.

9. Ely, *Big Sandy Valley,* pp. 202–4; Scalf, *Kentucky's Last Frontier,* p. 401; Pike County Historical Society, *Papers,* 2:5–12.

10. Hatfield, *The Hatfields,* pp. 184–85; Ely, *Big Sandy Valley,* pp. 202–4. Pike County was created in 1821 from Floyd County. Three years later, just

across the river, Logan County was created by the state of Virginia. The section of Logan nearest to the river is now Mingo County, West Virginia.

11. Land tax books, 1835, 1846, WVSA.

12. Swain, *History of Logan County*, pp. 68–69; Sims, *Index to Land Grants*, p. 405; land tax books, 1835, 1846, WVSA.

13. Bare, "Peter Cline," pp. 60–61; Swain, *History of Logan County*, pp. 74–75.

14. Jillson, *Kentucky Land Grants*, p. 1600; "Phillips Cemetery," in Pike County Historical Society, *Papers*, 5:50–51.

15. Jillson, *Kentucky Land Grants*, p. 1325.

16. Family backgounds of the feudists were traced through the U.S. census schedules, 1820–80, tax lists, genealogies, and Pike County court records. Paludan found the same patterns of persistence and continuity for Shelton Laurel, North Carolina (*Victims*, p. 9).

17. Some Appalachian scholars question the reality of Appalachian isolation. See Wilhelm, "Appalachian Isolation: Fact or Fiction?" in Williamson, ed., *Appalachian Symposium*.

18. Rice, *Allegheny Frontier*, pp. 119–49; Cubby, "Transformation of the Tug and Guyandot Valleys," pp. 180–84.

19. The figures were compiled from the 1850 population and agricultural schedules for Logan and Pike counties. There were differences between the counties: Logan schedules showed only 30 percent of all households without land, while in Pike County the figure was 42 percent. This discrepancy might be explained by the length of time each area had been settled; Pike had settlers in 1800, whereas most of Logan's settlers did not arrive until 1830 or after. These figures are similar to those reported for upcountry Georgia by Steven Hahn (*Roots of Southern Populism*, pp. 22–23) and Paul Salstrom ("Agricultural Decline").

20. U.S. census, population and agricultural schedules for Logan County, 1850, NA.

21. U.S. census, agricultural schedules for Logan County, 1850, NA.

22. Ibid.

23. Hurst, "Social History of Logan County"; Eller, *Miners, Millhands, and Mountaineers*, pp. 21–22; Spence, *Land of the Guyandot*, pp. 99–101, 107–19, 126–30.

24. Eller, *Miners, Millhands, and Mountaineers*, pp. 23–28.

25. Ibid., pp. 33–38; Steven Hahn discusses the household economy where production and exchange are organized around kinship ("The 'Unmaking' of the Southern Yeomanry," in Hahn and Prude, *Countryside in the Age of Capitalist Transformation*, pp. 179–203).

26. The issue of community versus individualism has become an important one for historians. Most have assumed that the tightly knit nucleated villages and community spirit of colonial New England were not characteristic of other parts of the colonies or of frontier settlements of the nineteenth century. Most historians have agreed with Frederick Jackson Turner that, if the frontier settlements did not exactly foster democracy, these

scattered rural homesteads did produce fragmentation and individualism. Recently, in studies of nineteenth-century rural areas, historians such as Robert McMath and John Mack Faragher have shown the existence and strength of community activities and institutions even on the frontier. Ronald Eller has argued that the image of atomistic Appalachian families is largely erroneous; he points out the pervasiveness of informal and formal networks that provided "fellowship, association, and community life" (McMath, "Sandy Land and Hogs in the Timber," and Faragher, "Open-Country Community," in Hahn and Prude, *Countryside in the Age of Capitalist Transformation,* pp. 205–29, 233–58; Eller, *Miners, Millhands, and Mountaineers,* p. 33).

27. The political and cultural functions of the county court system are documented in Isaac, *Transformation of Virginia,* pp. 89–94, and Sydnor, *American Revolutionaries in the Making,* pp. 44–59; the nineteenth-century court system in Kentucky is described in Ireland, *Little Kingdoms.*

28. Ireland, *County Courts in Antebellum Kentucky,* pp. 12–13.

29. County Court Order Book D, 1861–72, p. 193, PCC.

30. Smith, *History of Logan and Mingo Counties,* p. 46; McCoy, *The McCoys,* p. 244; Spencer, *History of Kentucky Baptists,* 2:593–94; Swain, *History of Logan County,* p. 196.

31. Preacher Anse Hatfield was born in 1835, four years before Devil Anse. In 1853 he joined the Enon or Old Pond Baptist Church. In 1868 he was licensed to preach and in 1869 ordained by the church. He died in 1920, just one year before the death of Devil Anse (*Williamson Daily News,* 2 Aug. 1982).

32. Spencer, *History of Kentucky Baptists,* 1:676–77.

33. Ibid., 1:694; Wyatt-Brown, "Antimission Movement in the Jacksonian South."

34. Wyatt-Brown, "Antimission Movement in the Jacksonian South," p. 502.

35. The literature on the connection between evangelical Protestantism and the emergence of a market economy is enormous. Examples include: Johnson, *Shopkeeper's Millennium;* Waller, *Reverend Beecher and Mrs. Tilton;* Ryan, *Cradle of the Middle Class.*

36. Whether you see evangelicals as promoting the market economy, as Paul Johnson does, or as defending themselves from it, as David Thelen does, the linkage between the market economy and evangelical beliefs is undeniable. Appalachians had not yet experienced the linkage.

37. The self-consciousness of such isolated mountain communities, especially in regard to their religious beliefs and ceremonies, is described in Miles, *Spirit of the Mountains,* pp. 134–35, and in Paludan, *Victims,* pp. 8–10.

38. Callahan, *History of West Virginia,* 1:360, 370–73; Williams, *West Virginia,* pp. 75–94; *Logan Banner,* 22 May 1890.

39. Scalf, *Kentucky's Last Frontier,* p. 500; McKinney, *Southern Mountain Republicans,* pp. 28–29.

40. U.S. census, population schedules for Pike County, 1860, NA.

41. Paludan, *Victims*, pp. 56–59; Hahn, *Roots of Southern Populism*, pp. 114–15.

42. Rice, *Hatfields and McCoys*, pp. 10–12.

43. Ibid. Rice offers three possible explanations: (1) that Anse deserted rather than carry out an order to execute two of his friends, George Hatfield and Phillip Lambert, for taking unofficial leave; (2) that he lost interest in the Confederate cause after his friend, Brig. Gen. John B. Floyd, was removed from command after the Union capture of Fort Donelson; or (3) that when the Confederacy was obviously losing in the fall and winter of 1863, Anse was only one of many Confederate soldiers who deserted.

44. Crowe-Carraco, *Big Sandy*, pp. 33–49; Scalf, *Kentucky's Last Frontier*, pp. 284–310.

45. Siber justified the burning of the courthouse to his superior by saying that "the inhabitants of this town had acted with so much animosity and treachery, as besides the court-house of Logan and other public buildings of this place had been long ago converted into barracks, used as a principal point of refuge for the rebel cavalry, I thought it to be my duty to deprive the enemy of such position, only valuable to him and useless to us, and ordered to set fire to these buildings before my departure" (Siber to L. Thomas, 23 Jan. 1862, in *The War of the Rebellion*, ser. 1, vol. 5, pp. 501–3. This report is also quoted in Spence, *Land of the Guyandot*, 149–52.

46. Hatfield, "Tales of the Feuding Hatfields," pp. 9–14, WVUL.

47. Ambler and Summers, *West Virginia*, p. 234.

48. Callahan, *History of West Virginia*, 1:551.

49. Election return, 23 May 1867, old records file drawer, CCCO; Magnolia district election, 1870, county commissioners record book, 1866–74, p. 242, LCC.

50. "Pike County Voting Report for 1868."

CHAPTER 2

1. For the history of Logan County, see Callahan, *History of West Virginia*, vol. 1; Cubby, "Transformation of the Tug and Guyandot Valleys"; Harvey, "From Frontier to Mining Town"; Hurst, "Social History of Logan County"; Smith, *History of Logan and Mingo Counties*; Spence, *Land of the Guyandot*; Swain, *History of Logan County*. For Pike County, Kentucky, see Crowe-Carraco, *Big Sandy*; Ely, *Big Sandy Valley*; Scalf, *Kentucky's Last Frontier*.

2. Although most authors agree that Anderson Hatfield earned the sobriquet "Devil" before the feud, there are some exceptions. G. T. Swain, for example, states that it was only after the hanging of Ellison Mounts in 1890 that Tug Valley residents began to call him Devil Anse (*History of Logan County*, p. 194).

3. Ephraim's wife Nancy and her brother, Jim Vance, were the illegiti-

mate children of Elizabeth Vance and this may have played a role in Ephraim's decision to part from the rest of his family (ibid., p. 75).

4. The 1846 Logan County tax list shows that Ephraim held 215 acres of land on Mates Creek, thirty miles south of the courthouse near the headwaters. By 1850 Ephraim owned two more tracts of 45 and 24 acres on Double Camp Fork and Strait Fork, respectively, of Mates Creek. By 1865 he had obtained two more tracts, one, of 70 acres, on Murphy's Branch of Mates Creek and the other, of 84 acres, on Beech Creek, another tributary of the Tug a few miles to the east. The tax records show that Ephraim continued to live on the original 215-acre plot on Mates Creek; he was apparently accumulating land for his sons. See Logan County land tax books for 1846, 1850, and 1865, WVSA.

5. Swain, *History of Logan County*, pp. 68–69.

6. Memorandum of interview with Jean Thomas by Edwin Cubby, quoted in Cubby, "Transformation of the Tug and Guyandot Valleys," p. 14.

7. Hatfield, *The Hatfields*, p. x.

8. Ibid.

9. Rice, *Hatfields and McCoys*, pp. 10–11.

10. This is one of many bits of evidence demonstrating that the McCoys and Hatfields were not separate families but rather were intertwined by bonds of marriage, kinship, and friendship. Anse's Civil War comrade was William Johnson McCoy, a nephew of Aunt Sally McCoy. Born about 1837, Johnson McCoy and his family lived on the Virginia side of the Tug. About 1857 Johnson married Sarah Chafin, a sister of Devil Anse's wife Levicy Chafin. Their only child was named after Levicy Chafin Hatfield. The 1860 census shows Johnson and Sarah living in the town of Logan Courthouse (then called Aracoma), and in 1870 and 1880 they were recorded in the Hardee district. Hardee was a district created out of Magnolia. See U.S. census, population schedules for Logan County, 1860, 1870, 1880, NA.

11. Hatfield, *The Hatfields*, p. 192.

12. Ibid., pp. 191–92. Valentine was first elected justice of the peace for Magnolia district in 1870 (Logan County Commissioners record book, 1866–74, p. 242). He served continuously until 1888, when he was arrested and taken to jail in Pikeville. Hatfield served as president of the court for the October 1879 term (county court minute book, 1879–89, pp. 18–19, LCC). See also deed from Ephraim and Nancy Hatfield to Valentine Hatfield, 7 Nov. 1876, deed book G, 357, LCC. For other landholdings, see land tax books, 1870–90, LCC.

13. Deed from Ephraim and Nancy Hatfield to Ellison Hatfield, 3 Aug. 1866, deed book G, 144, LCC; for Elias's landholdings, see entries in land tax book, 1880, LCC.

14. McCoy, *The McCoys*, p. 74.

15. Crawford, *An American Vendetta*, p. 50; Hatfield, *The Hatfields*, pp. 172–73.

16. Deed from Ephraim and Nancy Hatfield to Smith and Patterson Hatfield, 19 Feb. 1878, deed book G, 15, LCC. This deed also served as an

agreement between Ephraim and his youngest sons. He deeded all his land to them in return for "maintenance" in his old age. Ephraim died three years later, in 1881, and was buried in the Newtown cemetery on Mates Creek.

17. Deed from George and Nancy Hatfield to Levicy Hatfield, 19 Oct. 1867, deed book E, 174, LCC; U.S. census, population schedules for Logan County, Magnolia district, 1870, NA.

18. *Elliot Rutherford v. Magnolia Board of Education,* county court minute book, 5 Dec. 1870, LCC. Ephraim Hatfield also donated land for a school. See deed from Ephraim and Nancy Hatfield to Magnolia district board of education, 10 June 1876, deed book F, 329, LCC.

19. Interview with Ella Hatfield McCoy, in Woods, "History of the Hatfield-McCoy Feud," pp. 29–30. Ella McCoy remembers that there were four schools in existence in the Tug Valley in the 1880s and 1890s.

20. Deed from Ephraim and Nancy Hatfield to Ellison Hatfield, 3 Aug. 1866, deed book G, 144, LCC. The wording of the deed, "including all the land I have on the strait fork of Mate Creek," makes it clear that Anse's home was being given to Ellison.

21. West Virginia, *Annual Report of the Fish Commissioners,* p. 3; Kentucky, "First Report of the Fish Commissioners," pp. 3–4; idem, "Sixth Report of the Fish Commissioners," pp. 10–17.

22. See cases against Mat Cere, John Daniels, General Smith, Hibbard Thacher, Nathaniel Blackburn, David Blackburn, and George England, all in Pike County circuit court records, August 1888, UKL.

23. Williams, *West Virginia,* pp. 104–5; Campbell, *Southern Highlander,* pp. 109–10. For a comparison, see Holmes, "Moonshining and Collective Violence."

24. Between 1868 and 1889, Anse was indicted on ten different occasions for "retailing" (see county court order book, 1868, 1869, 1873, 1883, 1886, 1889, LCC). Although Ayers and other historians attribute much Appalachian feuding to either the excessive use of whiskey or the federal government's interference in the traditional practices of making and selling whiskey, this was not the cause of the Hatfield-McCoy feud. Federal "revenuers" played only a peripheral role in the feud itself (Ayers, *Vengeance and Justice,* pp. 263–64). For comparison, see Holmes, "Moonshining and Collective Violence."

25. These figures were computed from the U.S. census population and agricultural schedules for Logan County for the years 1850, 1860, and 1870, NA.

26. Ephraim Hatfield reached the peak of his wealth in 1860 (at age forty-nine) when he owned property valued at $2,514 (U.S. census, population schedules for Logan County, p. 94, NA). Four of his sons never approached that sum: Valentine owned $700 worth in 1870 (ibid., Magnolia district, p. 17); Ellison owned $600 worth in 1880 (ibid., p. 12); Smith and Patterson each owned $400 worth of property in 1880 (land tax book, 1880, LCC). Elias owned $3,000 worth in 1880, surpassing by $500 his father's estate

(U.S. census, population schedules for Logan County, Magnolia district, p. 10, NA).

27. Petition of Sarah Hatfield in the case of *Hatfield et al.* v. *Varney*, 1889, chancery court case file no. 29, CCCO.

28. Eller, *Miners, Millhands, and Mountaineers*, pp. 87–93; Crowe-Carraco, *Big Sandy*, pp. 60–62; Scalf, *Kentucky's Last Frontier*, p. 213; Williams, *West Virginia*, pp. 105–6.

29. John Smith's account book, exhibit in *Hatfield* v. *Smith*, 1874, chancery court case file no. 27, CCCO.

30. Thomas, "Romeo and Juliet of the Mountains," p. 190. Quoted in Crowe-Carraco, *Big Sandy*, p. 62.

31. Deposition of Margaret McCoy in *McCoy* v. *McCoy*, 1868–72, chancery court case file no. 3, CCCO.

32. *Anderson Hatfield* v. *Alexander Mounts, Michael Mounts, G. W. Taylor, Perry Cline, Jacob Cline*, 1872, ibid., file no. 4.

33. Ibid.

34. Dun and Bradstreet records, 37:171, HUL.

35. Hatfield, *The Hatfields*, p. 192.

36. Will of Jacob Cline, 30 Mar. 1858, will book A, p. 63, PCC.

37. Deed from Alexander Mounts et al. to Jacob Cline, 26 July 1855, deed book C, 432, and deed from John Lawson to Jacob Cline, 25 Oct. 1839, deed book B, 249, LCC.

38. John Smith's account book, chancery court case file no. 27, CCCO.

39. U.S. census, population schedules for Logan County, Magnolia district, 1870, p. 5, NA.

40. By 1874 Cline was deputy sheriff of Pike County (county court order book G, 142, PCC).

41. Deed from P. A. and Martha Cline to Anderson Hatfield, 23 Mar. 1877, deed book G, 538, LCC.

42. Trust deed from Anderson Hatfield to J. A. Nighbert and S. S. Altizer, 15 Oct. 1874, deed book B, 635, LCC; deed of trust between Moses Mounts, Anderson Hatfield, and John Smith, 29 July 1872, chancery court case file no. 27, CCCO.

43. P. A. Cline to E. W. Wilson, governor of West Virginia, Pikeville, 5 Nov. 1887. Published in *Wheeling Intelligencer*, 24 Apr. 1888, and Jones, *Hatfields and McCoys*, pp. 86–87.

44. T. C. Crawford, the *New York World* reporter who was biased against Devil Anse, verified that everyone he talked to in the neighborhood agreed that the feud leader was financially honest (*An American Vendetta*, p. 55).

45. Deed of trust between Moses Mounts, Anderson Hatfield, and John Smith, 29 July 1872, exhibit in *Hatfield* v. *Smith*, 1874, chancery court case file no. 27, CCCO.

46. John Smith's account book, ibid.

47. *Moses Mounts* v. *Anderson Hatfield*, 1876, chancery court case file no. 35, CCCO.

48. John Smith's account book, ibid., file no. 27.

49. Bill of complaint, *Hatfield* v. *Smith*, 1874, ibid.

50. The case took three days—19–21 October 1874—and the jury took "some time" to reach a verdict. The jurors were John F. Aldredge, Scott McDonald, John Dijernette, George W. Nighbert, John Peck, Jr., James Buchanan, Bryant McDonald, Hugh Toney, Obadiah Workman, Thomas Conty, John Buchanan, and Jonah McDonald (*Hatfield* v. *Smith*, ibid.).

51. Ibid.; *Stollings and Watt* v. *Hatfield and Rutherford*, Apr. 1878, chancery court case file no. 33, CCCO; *George Lawson* v. *Anderson Hatfield*, Apr. 1878, circuit court file no. 14, ibid.

52. Trust deed from Anderson Hatfield to J. A. Nighbert and S. S. Altizer, 15 Oct. 1874, deed book B, 635; deed from Anderson and Levicy Hatfield to Polly Hatfield, 29 Dec. 1874, deed book F, 136, LCC.

53. Deed of P. A. and Martha Cline to Anderson Hatfield, 23 Mar. 1877, deed book G, 538, LCC.

54. The arbitrators were J. A. Nighbert, J. A. Peck, and W. H. Peck, all merchants from Logan Courthouse (report of the arbitrators in *Hatfield* v. *Smith*, 28 Jan. 1878, filed in chancery court case file no. 27, CCCO).

55. Testimonies of Anderson Hatfield and John Smith, *Hatfield* v. *Smith*, ibid.

56. On changes in the law of contract, see Friedman, *History of American Law*, pp. 244–47, 464–68; Gabel and Feinman, "Contract Law as Ideology"; Horwitz, *Transformation of American Law*, pp. 160–210.

57. Thelen, *Paths of Resistance*, pp. 77–85.

58. *Lawson* v. *Hatfield*, circuit court file no. 14, CCCO.

59. *Anderson Hatfield* v. *G. W. Taylor*, May 1881, chancery court case file no. 13, CCCO.

60. Deed from Anderson Hatfield to Floyd Hatfield, 2 July 1877, deed book F, 429, LCC.

61. Deed from Anderson Hatfield to James Vance, 24 Dec. 1877, deed book G, 6, LCC.

62. Buyers of the Grapevine lands included: Floyd Hatfield, 1877; James Vance, 1877; Robert Cox, 1880; Johnson Hatfield (*not* Anse's son), 1882; Daniel Christian, 1882; Pliant Mayhorn, 1882; Samuel Mayhorn, 1882; Harrison Steel, 1883; Moses Christian, 1884; Anderson Hatfield, Jr., 1885; E. S. Murphy, 1885; Johnse Hatfield, 1886; James Mounts, 1886; Charles R. Mounts, 1886.

63. Trust deed from Anderson Hatfield to George Lawson, 28 June 1878, trust deed book A, 55, LCC.

64. Crawford, *An American Vendetta*, p. 75.

65. Paul Boyer and Stephen Nissenbaum, in *Salem Possessed: The Social Origins of Witchcraft* (1974), have explored similar patterns of cultural conflict in seventeenth-century Salem. In that divided community, neighbors began accusing each other of witchcraft and dealings with the devil. What Boyer and Nissenbaum show is that the accused witches were those most involved with the beginnings of merchant capitalism. The accusers lived a more traditional agricultural life-style and were frightened by this

new impersonal and aggressive economic behavior. Although they were neither unaware of nor uninvolved in opportunities for profit, they were overwhelmed by the social disruption that seemed inherent in the new patterns. Their response emerged from the only worldview they knew— one in which only devils would attempt to disrupt a divinely ordained, harmonious social order. Paraphrasing Boyer and Nissenbaum, a new force was abroad in Salem; the villagers called it witchcraft, we would call it merchant capitalism.

In the Tug Valley, the epithet "Devil" did not have nearly the bloody consequences it had in Salem. After the seventeenth century, few people believed that witches and devils should be subject to prosecution by the state. In the eighteenth century, witches and devils were driven underground, where they became much more a part of rural folk culture than the rationalized legal culture of the elite. But despite the fact that people like Devil Anse could invoke sarcasm concerning his marginal status, the underlying perception that worldly profit seeking and ambition were signs of capitulation to evil forces still reflected traditional rather than modern values. But this community was not as articulate, as close-knit, or as self-righteous as seventeenth-century Salem. Anse's activities and success made his neighbors uneasy and suspicious, but not enough to generate a direct challenge to his place in their community.

66. Crawford, *An American Vendetta*, p. 75.

CHAPTER 3

1. McCoy, *The McCoys*, pp. 238–39.

2. Jillson, *Kentucky Land Grants*, pp. 656, 1534–35; Sims, *Index to Land Grants*, p. 410.

3. U.S. census, population schedules for Logan County, 1850, 1860, NA. The property of the McCoy brothers was as follows:

Name	1850	County	Page	1860	County	Page
Daniel	$1,500	Logan	147	$2,000	Logan	100
Randolph	2,000	Pike	928	500	Pike	162
John	700	Pike	958	5,000	Logan	99
Samuel	5,000	Pike	941	(died in 1855)		
Richard	50	Pike	946	"pauper"	Pike	144
Joseph	800	Pike	964	800	Pike	175

4. Answer of Daniel McCoy, Oct. 1868, *McCoy* v. *McCoy*, chancery court case file no. 3, CCCO.

5. Answer of Margaret McCoy, 24 Mar. 1871, ibid.

6. Ibid. The children of Daniel and Margaret, with their birthdates, are as follows: John, 1819; Harriet, 1820; William, 1822; Randolph, 1825; Asa Harmon, 1828; Samuel, 1831; Ruth, 1833; Mary Etta, 1834; Pharmer, 1840;

Nancy, 1841; James M., 1843; Louisa, 1845; Jane or Jennie, 1846 (McCoy, *The McCoys*, pp. 305–19).

7. Ibid.

8. Ibid.

9. Deposition of Margaret McCoy, 23 June 1870, *McCoy* v. *McCoy*, chancery court case file no. 3, CCCO.

10. On marriage in Appalachia, see Campbell, *Southern Highlander*, pp. 133–51; Miles, *Spirit of the Mountains*, pp. 36–70.

11. McCoy, *The McCoys*, pp. 305–19.

12. U.S. census, population schedules for Pike County, Peter Creek district, 1850, 1860, NA. In 1850 Harmon and Patty were listed as having no property, but they were living on land owned by Patty's father, Jacob Cline (p. 474). In 1858, upon the death of Cline, Patty inherited the farm (Jacob Cline's will, dated 30 Mar. 1858, will book A, p. 63, PCC). In 1860 Harmon and Patty are listed in the census with $1,500 worth of real property and $400 worth of personal property (p. 148, dwelling no. 785).

13. Will of Samuel McCoy, 6 July 1855, will book A, p. 42, PCC.

14. *James Lawson* v. *Daniel McCoy et al.*, 1867, chancery court case file no. 467, CCCO.

15. *Pleasant McCoy* v. *Randolph McCoy and Wife*, 22 Jan. 1861, Pike County circuit court records, KSA.

16. County court order book I, 27 Jan. 1880, p. 292, PCC. The case was continued in February, March, April, May, June, August, September, November, and December 1880 and January 1881.

17. U.S. census, population schedules for Pike County, Blackberry district, dwelling no. 154, NA.

18. McCoy, *The McCoys*, p. 129.

19. Rice, *Hatfields and McCoys*, p. 31.

20. The various sources for the feud give two different dates for the hog trial, 1873 and 1878. The closest contemporary source is Devil Anse's interview with a *Wheeling Intelligencer* reporter in 1889, in which he said the "trouble over a sow and pigs" occurred in the fall of 1872 or 1873. Jones uses this date in his book. But Truda McCoy asserts that the date was 1878, and the latter was adopted by Otis Rice in his book. I believe that Truda McCoy is right. Despite what Devil Anse remembered, the date was surely 1878, for it was in early 1880 that Paris McCoy was arrested for the murder of Bill Staton. It seems likely that the reporter made the error in Anse's orally delivered story, or that Anse himself remembered the date of 1872 as a crucial one, as that was the year he began the lawsuit against Perry Cline. By 1889 it would have become clear to Anse that the lawsuit had caused Perry Cline's involvement, and he may have confused it with the date of the hog dispute.

21. The story of the hog trial is related in McCoy, *The McCoys*, pp. 13–19; Rice, *Hatfields and McCoys*, pp. 9–16; Jones, *Hatfields and McCoys*, pp. 17–24. No one has attempted to answer the question of whether or not Floyd actually stole Ranel's hog. I am inclined to think not, because such

theft was very rare in the Tug Valley. But either way, the hog seemed to be more symbolic of the already existing conflict than it was important in and of itself.

22. Deed from Anderson Hatfield to Floyd Hatfield, 2 July 1877, land tax book F, 429, LCC. The names of Floyd's children are in the U.S. census, population schedules for Logan County, Magnolia district, 1880, dwelling no. 147, NA. The friendship between Ellison Hatfield and Floyd was apparent as early as 1871 when Ellison apparently named a son after Floyd (Hatfield, *The Hatfields*, p. 192).

23. McCoy, "Hatfield and McCoy Feud," pp. 34–35.

24. John Smith's account book, chancery court case file no. 27, CCCO.

25. U.S. census, population schedules for Pike County, district no. 6, 1870; for Logan County, Magnolia district, 1880; agricultural schedules for Logan County, 1880, NA.

26. U.S. census, population schedules for Logan County, 1860, p. 54, NA.

27. Ibid., Magnolia district, 1870, p. 2, 1880, p. 37.

28. McCoy, *The McCoys*, pp. 20–21.

29. This episode has several different versions. See McCoy, *The McCoys*, pp. 20–24; Rice, *Hatfields and McCoys*, pp. 16–17; Jones, *Hatfields and McCoys*, pp. 22–24.

30. McCoy, "Hatfield and McCoy Feud," p. 27.

31. Warrants for the arrest of Sam and Paris were issued on 13 July 1880 by Justice of the Peace Valentine Hatfield on a complaint made by Amos and Clementine Acord. The warrants gave the date of the killing as 18 June 1880. The warrant was also signed by Tolbert Hatfield, justice of the peace in Pike County. Paris was arrested the following summer by E. S. Ferrell. Sam was arrested on 23 February 1882 by Elias Hatfield. His bail was set at $2,500. The McCoys who appeared as witnesses against Paris were Josephine McCoy, Denas McCoy, Elliot McCoy, Eva McCoy, Uriah McCoy, Sarilda McCoy, Sylvester McCoy, and Jasper McCoy. These records are from the Logan County law order books, but there is no further evidence of the disposition of the case. It simply disappears from the record.

32. Accounts of the romance appear in McCoy, *The McCoys*, pp. 25–40; Jones, *Hatfields and McCoys*, pp. 32–38; Rice, *Hatfields and McCoys*, pp. 19–22.

33. Campbell, *Southern Highlander*, pp. 132–33.

34. The most extensive account of women in the feud is given by Truda McCoy in *The McCoys*. In the 1920s and 1930s she talked at length with Martha Jackson McCoy, the wife of Randolph's son Samuel. Martha had known Aunt Sally and Roseanna intimately, and she provided a unique perspective on the feud.

35. McCoy, *The McCoys*, pp. 60–68.

36. Ibid., pp. 157–65.

37. Ibid., p. 169.

38. Campbell, *Southern Highlander*, p. 132.

39. Rice, *Hatfields and McCoys*, p. 23.

40. U.S. census, population and agricultural schedules for Pike County, Blackberry district, 1880, NA. Tolbert McCoy is listed as a laborer in the household of John Maynard.

41. McCoy, *The McCoys*, pp. 308–11.

42. There are many different accounts of the reasons for the arrest of Johnse. Jones says that the indictment was on moonshining charges (*Hatfields and McCoys*, p. 7), whereas Rice says that Johnse was arrested for "many" indictments, from carrying a concealed weapon to moonshining (*Hatfields and McCoys*, p. 22); Truda McCoy thinks that the warrant was issued on charges of "seduction" and that it was served by Randolph himself (*The McCoys*, p. 47). However, the court records mention only one indictment—for carrying a concealed weapon—served by the two McCoy brothers. See *Commonwealth of Kentucky* v. *Andrew Hatfield, Elias Hatfield, Sr., Thomas Chafens, John Chafens, Moses Chafens, John Staton, Elias Hatfield, Jr., Floyd Hatfield, Cap Hatfield, and Frank Ealem*, 26 Nov. 1880, Pike County circuit court records, KSA.

43. Statement of Tolbert McCoy, *Commonwealth of Kentucky* v. *Andrew Hatfield et al.*, 26 Nov. 1880, Pike County circuit court records, KSA.

44. Elias and Floyd were arrested on 8 January 1881 and were bailed out by a brother of Preacher Anse Hatfield. After the McCoy witnesses testified on 28 April 1881, no further action was taken against the Hatfields.

45. McCoy, *The McCoys*, pp. 72–73.

46. McCoy, "Hatfield and McCoy Feud," p. 13.

47. Ibid.

48. Versions of the fight mainly differ over who was the aggressor, Tolbert or Ellison, but everyone concurs that the McCoys had knives and guns while Ellison had only a rock. Despite Ellison's power and size, this would have been regarded as an extremely unfair fight by mountain standards. McCoy, "Hatfield and McCoy Feud," pp. 13–14; McCoy, *The McCoys*, pp. 72–75; Jones, *Hatfields and McCoys*, pp. 39–42; Rice, *Hatfields and McCoys*, pp. 24–25.

49. Testimony of Rev. Anderson Hatfield, *Commonwealth of Kentucky* v. *Valentine Hatfield*, Aug. 1889, KSC.

50. Testimony of Valentine Hatfield, ibid.

51. Testimony of John New, ibid.

52. Testimonies of Jacob Puckett, Valentine Hatfield, Randolph McCoy, James M. McCoy, James McCoy, and John New, ibid.

53. Testimony of Sally McCoy, ibid.

54. Testimonies of Valentine Hatfield, John W. France, and David J. Wolford, ibid.

55. Testimonies of Valentine Hatfield and Joseph Davis, ibid.

56. Testimonies of James McCoy, James M. McCoy, and Daniel Whitt, ibid. Coleman Hatfield believes that it was Charlie Carpenter who instigated the killings in the first place and then produced a written oath of

secrecy for everyone to sign ("Tales of the Feuding Hatfields," WVUL). For accounts of the execution of the McCoy boys, see McCoy, *The McCoys*, pp. 79–87; Jones, *Hatfields and McCoys*, pp. 39–53; Rice, *Hatfields and McCoys*, pp. 27–29; McCoy, "Hatfield and McCoy Feud," pp. 15–16.

57. Indictment, 14 Sept. 1882, Pike County circuit court records, KSA.

58. McCoy, *The McCoys*, p. 59.

CHAPTER 4

1. *Louisville Courier-Journal*, 25 Jan. 1888.

2. "The Howard-Turner Assassins," *Louisville Courier-Journal*, 23 Sept. 1889.

3. Montell, *Killings*, p. xiii. See also Billings, Blee, and Swanson, "Culture, Family, and Community in Preindustrial Appalachia," pp. 155–57. These three sociologists argue that what ethnographers "frequently saw as *antiquated* behavior were traces of a social logic and a set of values distinct from those of more advanced capitalist societies but nonetheless shaped by economic rationality."

4. On the family relationships of Selkirk McCoy, see Virgil Carrington Jones, who claims that Selkirk had married a Hatfield (*Hatfields and McCoys*, p. 20); Otis Rice says that Selkirk was a cousin of Randolph who became identified with the Hatfields *after* the hog trial (*Hatfields and McCoys*, pp. 16–17); and Truda McCoy says that Selkirk had married a Hatfield and "was considered a Hatfield by the McCoys" (*The McCoys*, p. 16). This latter statement implies that Preacher Anse knew that Selkirk was really a Hatfield when he placed him on the jury on the McCoy side. At this point, according to Truda McCoy, "Ranel was beginning to have grave doubts about his [Preacher Anse's] fairness." Except for the fact that McCoy's informants gave misinformation about Selkirk's marital status, they probably remembered accurately that Selkirk was a Hatfield long before the hog trial.

5. Selkirk's father was Asa McCoy, a brother of Aunt Sally McCoy and a cousin of Randolph. Selkirk married Louisa Williamson, a daughter of John and Nancy (Maynard) Williamson, in 1850 (McCoy, *The McCoys*, pp. 247–48). See also U.S. census, population schedules for Logan and Pike counties, 1840–80, NA.

6. Bryant, *We're All Kin*, p. 53.

7. Ely, *Big Sandy Valley*, pp. 202–4.

8. On the family basis of political factionalism in the colonies, see Henretta, *Evolution of American Society*; on Virginia, see Sydnor, *American Revolutionaries in the Making*, and Isaac, *Transformation of Virginia*; on New York, see Bonomi, *A Factious People*.

9. The conventional phrase used in criminal-case preprinted forms was "against the peace and dignity" of the state.

10. Hindus, *Prison and Plantation*, p. 67.

11. Rice, *Hatfields and McCoys*, p. 17; Hatfield, *The Hatfields*, pp. 31–32.

12. John Smith's account book, chancery court case file no. 27, CCCO. Dan Cunningham, a detective who later pursued Devil Anse, claimed that Samson and Hatfield "entered Mose's house without any provocation and shot him dead on the floor." But Cunningham's most interesting claim was that the Negro, Mose, belonged to Jacob Cline, the father of Perry Cline (see Johnson, " 'Horrible Butcheries of West Virginia,' " p. 40).

13. Testimonies of Ellison Hatfield and Anderson Hatfield, *State* v. *Riley Samson*, old felonies file drawer, CCCO.

14. A series of such cases appear in county order book D, Aug. 1871–June 1872, pp. 402–11, PCC. These cases resulted in 1¢ fines for "breach of the peace."

15. *Island Creek Mineral Company* v. *Anderson Hatfield*, 1916, circuit court file no. 55, CCCO.

16. Why does the belief persist in scholarly and popular circles alike that southern mountaineers contemptuously ignored whatever semblance of a weak judicial system they may have had? "Hillbillies/feudists/mountaineers shoot first and ask questions later," seems to be the pervasive conventional wisdom. In a recent book on the late-nineteenth-century counties of Kentucky, Robert Ireland describes the courts as weak and law enforcement as nonexistent. The title of his book, *Little Kingdoms*, reflects his assessment that the counties were completely corrupt, dominated by local officials who were only interested in collecting fraudulent fees and increasing their own power. Such a situation, he concludes, was conducive to crime, lawlessness, vigilantism, and feuds. His conclusions, however, like most others, are based almost entirely on newspaper accounts and court cases relating to counties in the western part of Kentucky. An important fact to remember is that there were no newspapers of any significance in the mountain regions of Kentucky before the twentieth century; the newspapers Ireland refers to are based in Louisville, Lexington, and New York. If the articles on the Hatfield-McCoy feud are representative of the usual coverage, then that coverage is almost completely worthless, containing staggering and garbled errors of fact—especially when it comes to the frequency of violence and murder. Newspaper articles alone could certainly persuade anyone that mountain society was completely chaotic and violent. Ireland's second source, court records from the western part of the state, reflect not the traditional or premodern society still prevalent in the mountains, but regions grappling with the effects of economic modernization. Those counties were undoubtedly plagued by polarization of wealth, economic competition, and political breakdown. This profile, however, does not apply to the mountain counties until after 1900.

17. Fannie Simpkins Booth, *Williamson Daily News*, 2 Aug. 1982.

18. *Logan Banner*, 2, 9 Jan., 14 Aug. 1890; 30 Aug. 1891.

19. Tom C. Chafin, *Williamson Daily News*, 2 Aug. 1982.

20. Gorn, " 'Gouge and Bite,' " p. 33.

21. Randolph's sons in 1880 were: James H., age 32, married, four children, no land; Tolbert, age 26, living with family of John Maynard and working as a laborer; Floyd, age 27, married, two children, sharecropping; Samuel, age 25, married, no land; Calvin, age 18, not living at home, still had no land at age 25 in 1887—the year before his death; Pharmer, age 17, living at home; Randolph, Jr., or "Bud," age 16, living at home; Bill, age 14, living at home (McCoy, *The McCoys*, pp. 308–11; U.S. census, population and agricultural schedules for Pike County, 1880, NA).

22. Asa Harmon McCoy's sons in 1880 were: Jacob, age 27, married, 150 acres; Larkin, age 24, married, 2 children, 110 acres; Lewis, or "Jeff," age 21, living at home; Asa H., or "Bud," age 18, living at home (McCoy, *The McCoys*, pp. 313–14; U.S. census, population and agricultural schedules for Pike County, 1880, NA).

23. Gorn, " 'Gouge and Bite,' " p. 33.

24. U.S. census, agricultural schedules for Logan County, 1850, NA. In 1850, the grandparents or parents of feudists, with the values of their properties, included Nathan Chafin ($676), Anderson Ellis ($8), Ephraim Hatfield ($1,179), John Hatfield ($432), John Mayhorn ($0), Asa McCoy ($825), Joseph Murphy ($385), William Staton ($680), Elizabeth Vance ($165), John Henderson Varney ($225), and William Whitt ($200). Property values represent the total of real and personal property. Average real estate value was $304; average personal estate value was $143.

25. Other Hatfield supporters who bought Grapevine lands were Daniel Christian (1882), Pliant Mayhorn (1882), Samuel Mayhorn (1882), Moses Christian (1885), Cap Hatfield (1885), E. S. Murphy (1885), and Johnse Hatfield (1886). Four others who were not identified with the feud also bought land from Anse.

26. Average household size for Logan and Pike counties was as follows:

	Pike County	Logan County	Families of Hatfield Supporters
1850	6.0	6.4	8.1
1860	7.4	6.3	8.0
1870	6.0	5.2	7.0
1880	5.8	5.7	7.6

For an analysis of Pike County household composition in 1900, see Acury and Porter, "Household Composition in Appalachian Kentucky in 1900."

27. Testimonies of Jacob Puckett, Valentine Hatfield, Randolph McCoy, James H. McCoy, James McCoy, and John New, *Commonwealth of Kentucky* v. *Valentine Hatfield*, Aug. 1889, KSC.

28. Twenty-one families furnished all thirty-seven Hatfield feudists. These twenty-one households constituted 5.6 percent of all Magnolia dis-

trict households. Put another way, the thirty-seven Hatfield feudists made up 2.4 percent of the total population of Magnolia district.

29. Rice, *Hatfields and McCoys*, p. 42.

CHAPTER 5

1. Williams, *West Virginia and the Captains of Industry.*

2. Williams, *West Virginia*, pp. 88–89; Ambler and Summers, *West Virginia*, pp. 267–69.

3. Williams, *West Virginia*, pp. 75–91; Callahan, *History of West Virginia*, 1:370–72, 551.

4. Callahan, *History of West Virginia*, 1:370–72, 414–18.

5. West Virginia, *Acts and Constitution*, art. 8, nos. 23–36; Callahan, *History of West Virginia*, 1:418.

6. West Virginia, *Acts of the Legislature*, chap. 5, art. 1, pp. 21–24; Callahan, *History of West Virginia*, 1:420.

7. "Judge E. Ward One of County's Great Jurists," *Logan Banner*, 1 Nov. 1937.

8. West Virginia, *Acts of the Legislature*, chap. 5, nos. 9–10, pp. 22–23.

9. The first two judges were Ira McGinnis and Thomas H. Harvey (Swain, *History of Logan County*, pp. 113, 191).

10. *Logan Banner*, 18 July 1889, 30 July 1891, quoted in Cubby, "Transformation of the Tug and Guyandot Valleys," p. 31.

11. *Logan Banner*, 21 May 1891; Swain, *History of Logan County*, p. 131; Spence, *Land of the Guyandot*, pp. 232–33.

12. The justices in 1879–80 were Isaac Morgan, James R. Perry, Valentine Hatfield, J. R. Chapman, J. S. P. Stafford, Anthony W. Ferrell, James Evans, William Chafin, L. D. Chambers, William H. Peck, Jonathan T. Vance, and Stephen Lambert (county court minute book, June–Dec. 1879, LCC).

13. Ibid., Feb. 1881, p. 41; U.S. census, population and agricultural schedules for Logan County, 1880, NA.

14. Swain, *History of Logan County*, pp. 341–43.

15. Dun and Bradstreet records, 37:170, HUL.

16. Swain, *History of Logan County*, p. 343.

17. Dun and Bradstreet records, 23:175, HUL.

18. Swain, *History of Logan County*, pp. 341–43; Spence, *Land of the Guyandot*, p. 26; *Logan Banner*, 22 Dec. 1898.

19. County court minute book, Feb. 1886, p. 123, June 1886, p. 127, LCC.

20. Swain, *History of Logan County*, p. 119.

21. Ibid., p. 131.

22. Atkinson and Gibbens, *Prominent Men of West Virginia*, pp. 937–38; Cubby, "Transformation of the Tug and Guyandot Valleys," pp. 66–67, 121–22.

23. *Logan Banner*, 8 Aug. 1890.

24. Ibid., 6 June 1889. Resistance to railroad subsidization in Missouri has been documented in Thelen, *Paths of Resistance*, pp. 62–70.

25. *Logan Banner*, 21 Mar., 18 Apr. 1889; 1, 8 May 1890.

26. Ibid., 6 Aug. 1891.

27. Williams, *West Virginia*, p. 125.

28. In a historical feature story in 1937, the *Logan Banner* asserted that Harrison Blair was the "first Democratic sheriff of Logan County" (*Logan Banner*, 4 May 1937).

29. Swain, *History of Logan County*, p. 139; county court minute book, Dec. 1879, p. 19, LCC.

30. Dun and Bradstreet records, 23:102, HUL.

31. Law order book A, 1873–78, pp. 110, 155, CCCO. Taylor was first appointed deputy sheriff in 1873 and sheriff in April 1874.

32. Ibid., Dec. 1875, p. 416. In 1874, Taylor made his own contract with merchants Adkins and Adkins for timber cut from the Grapevine Creek lands; the contract was witnessed by Perry Cline. But at this point, Devil Anse was considered the owner of all land bordering on Grapevine Creek. It is not known whether he knew about this contract. See trust deed book E, p. 76, LCC.

33. *Anderson Hatfield* v. *G. W. Taylor*, 3 May 1881, chancery court case file no. 13, CCCO; *G. W. Taylor for the Singer Manufacturing Company* v. *Anderson Hatfield*, 1881–87, ibid., file no. 26. In 1899 Taylor became sheriff of Mingo County. When he died in 1903, his obituary referred to him as a merchant who was "capable, efficient, and prompt" and "a friend of the poor class." "He and Mrs. Taylor were among the largest landowners in the county," declared the obituary, "and many tenants will mourn the death of a generous landlord" (*Logan Banner*, 5 Feb. 1903).

34. Complaint of Anderson Hatfield, *Anderson Hatfield* v. *G. W. Taylor*, chancery court case file no. 13, CCCO.

35. Index to judgment lien docket book, LCBS.

36. Law order book B, Aug. 1880, p. 243, CCCO.

37. All resided in the Magnolia district of Logan County. Rutherford and Murphy were business partners; William Ferrell had Ellison Hatfield at his home after the stabbing on Grapevine Creek; Uriah McCoy loaned Anse money.

38. Law order book B, June 1882, p. 340, CCCO.

39. Cubby, "Transformation of the Tug and Guyandot Valleys," pp. 183–85.

40. *L. D. Chambers, School Lands Commissioner* v. *Valentine Hatfield*, 1882, chancery court file on school lands, CCCO.

41. Cubby, "Transformation of the Tug and Guyandot Valleys," pp. 184–86.

42. Although Nighbert himself was not a commissioner, he belonged to the same group of Logan elite who supplied the commission's membership, and he profited enormously from the school land laws (Spence, *Land of the*

Guyandot, pp. 261–63; six deeds from the Logan school land commissioner to J. A. Nighbert, deed book N, 323, 324, 334, 335, 413, 415, LCC).

43. *L. D. Chambers, S.L.C.* v. *Valentine Hatfield,* 1882, chancery court file on school lands, CCCO; there were three similar cases, involving varying amounts of land, against Elias Hatfield in 1883 (171 acres), 1884 (749 acres), 1884 (322 acres). See chancery court index, CCCO.

44. Although Anderson Hatfield's deed to the "Cline Land" was dated 23 March 1877, it was not recorded by the county clerk until 30 August 1882 (deed book G, p. 538, LCC).

45. *Anderson Hatfield* v. *Ralph Steele,* 1886, chancery court case file no. 29, CCCO.

46. Will of Ralph A. Steele, 1 July 1886, wills, vol. 1, LCC.

47. Williams, *West Virginia,* pp. 123–25.

48. John Spivak papers, WVUL.

49. Swain, *History of Logan County,* p. 342; McCoy, "Hatfield and Mc-Coy Feud," p. 16.

50. Cubby, "Transformation of the Tug and Guyandot Valleys," pp. 132–38.

51. Eller, *Miners, Millhands, and Mountaineers,* pp. 87–93.

52. Ibid., p. 132; F. J. Kimball to M. R. Irwin, 7 Nov. 1883, quoted in Lambie, *From Mine to Market,* p. 121.

53. J. D. Sergeant began buying Logan and McDowell lands for a group of Philadelphia capitalists in 1883. His indenture or contract with them, dated 28 December 1887, appears in trust deed book B, pp. 37–80, LCC. The investors were William A. and Hattie Lathrop; John Graham, Jr.; James and Mary O'Keefe; William Pepper, M.D., and Francis Pepper; S. Edward and Laura O. Norris. By the time Sergeant resigned in 1891 he had 12,352 acres of Magnolia district land in his name (land tax book, 1892, LCC). Stuart Wood, another active buying agent from 1887 to 1909, owned 27,956 acres by 1892.

54. Banks, "Land and Capital in Eastern Kentucky," p. 10.

55. Caudill, "Strange Career of John C. Mayo"; Eller, *Miners, Millhands, and Mountaineers,* pp. 60–63.

56. Swain, *History of Logan County,* p. 131.

57. Spence, *Land of the Guyandot,* p. 263.

58. *Logan Banner,* 22 Dec. 1898.

59. Ibid., 12 Jan. 1899.

60. *Sixth Annual Report of the Norfolk and Western Railroad Company, 1886,* quoted in Lambie, *From Mine to Market,* pp. 121–22.

61. The first issue of the *Banner* appeared on 7 March 1889. Ragland stated his purpose as follows: "The paper will be devoted to the best interests of the people of Logan County. To the improvement of the education and morals of its people, and to the development of its great material resources" (*Logan Banner,* 28 Mar. 1889, also quoted in Cubby, "Transformation of the Tug and Guyandot Valleys," p. 17).

62. F. J. Kimball to Vivian, Gray and Company, 29 Jan. 1889, 16 Feb. 1889, quoted in Lambie, *From Mine to Market*, pp. 123–24; also quoted in Cubby, "Transformation of the Tug and Guyandot Valleys," pp. 151–52. Vivian, Gray and Company were London bankers who provided capital for the building of the Ohio Extension.

63. *Logan Banner*, 21 Mar. 1889. By April Stuart Wood was purchasing Tug River land for $4.00 an acre (ibid., 18 Apr. 1889).

64. Ibid., 2 May 1889.

65. Ibid., 30 Oct. 1890. The *Banner* reported that Henry Mitchell, who was a close friend and ally of Devil Anse and who held lands adjacent to Anse's on Mates Creek, "has sold . . . to McNutt and Company for $15.00 per acre." By 1891 Ragland was bragging about the profits to be made in the Tug Valley. "Three years ago," he reported, three Wheeling capitalists "purchased about 2000 acres of coal and timber lands on the head of Rockhouse Fork of Pigeon [Creek] for less than $3,000. Recently they sold to the Little Kanawha Lumber Company 1568 poplar trees . . . for $5.00 per tree, aggregating $7,840." And, he continued, waxing lyrical, "coal is still in the ground—more profits expected" (ibid., 6 Aug. 1891). Ragland speculated further that Logan County lands, like some other more developed coal counties, would be worth $100 an acre "if the land titles could be settled" (ibid., 16 Oct. 1890).

66. The six cases and the judgments awarded in each were: *G. W. Taylor and Singer Manufacturing Company* v. *Anderson Hatfield*, $51.80; *Stollings and Watt* v. *Anderson Hatfield*, $513.32; *J. B. Wilkinson* v. *Anderson Hatfield*, $81.55; *J. S. Miller* v. *Anderson Hatfield*, $94.00; *Singer Manufacturing Company* v. *Anderson Hatfield*, $15.40; *M. B. Lawson et al.* v. *Anderson Hatfield*, $101.30. The total is $857.37. All these judgments were rendered against Anse between 18 June 1887 and 4 February 1888 (judgment lien docket book 1, p. 64, LCBS).

67. Trust deed from Anderson Hatfield to J. B. Wilkinson, 21 Dec. 1887, and from Anderson Hatfield to H. C. Ragland, 6 Feb. 1888, both in trust deed book B, pp. 24, 30–31, LCC.

68. McCoy, *The McCoys*, pp. 99–107.

69. Ibid., pp. 108–18.

70. Jones, *Hatfields and McCoys*, pp. 70–76.

71. McCoy, *The McCoys*, pp. 114–15; Hatfield, *The Hatfields*, p. 74.

72. Jones, *Hatfields and McCoys*, pp. 76–78; McCoy, *The McCoys*, pp. 119–27; *Louisville Courier-Journal*, 17 Feb. 1888; *Pittsburg Times*, 1 Feb. 1888.

73. Anderson Hatfield to P. A. Cline, 26 Dec. 1886, UKL.

CHAPTER 6

1. U.S. census, population schedules for Logan County, 1850, p. 145, dwelling no. 367, NA; land tax book, 1850, WVSA.

2. Will of Jacob Cline, will book A, p. 63, PCC.

3. "Upon motion of Perry A. Cline to have John Dils jr. appointed his Guardian said Cline being over fourteen years old said Dils being in Court and entered into Covenant with the Commonwealth of Kentucky with William Scott as his surety and took the oath according to law" (county court order book E, Aug. 1868, p. 126, PCC).

4. "Autobiography of Colonel John Dils, Jr.," published in Ely, *Big Sandy Valley*, pp. 45–55.

5. County court order books D–J, 1865–82, PCC. During these years, Dils was the purchaser of 115 land warrants.

6. Ibid., book E, p. 199.

7. Pike County index to marriages, listed under Cline, PCC.

8. U.S. census, population schedules for Logan County, Magnolia district, 1870, dwelling no. 43, NA.

9. Pikeville's natural advantages and history are described in Ely, *Big Sandy Valley*, pp. 11–20; Scalf, *Kentucky's Last Frontier*, p. 87.

10. On the efforts of John Dils and Orlando Bowles, see Crowe-Carraco, *The Big Sandy*, pp. 54–57.

11. Johnson, *Shopkeeper's Millennium*, pp. 32–36.

12. Barnes's tour of the mountains is described in Ely, *Big Sandy Valley*, pp. 412–13; Scalf, *Kentucky's Last Frontier*, p. 549; and Price, *Without Scrip or Purse*, p. 1. For a comparison to Henry Ward Beecher, see Mc-Loughlin, *The Meaning of Henry Ward Beecher*, and Waller, *Reverend Beecher and Mrs. Tilton*.

13. Price, *Without Scrip or Purse*, pp. 221–24.

14. County court order book G, pp. 142, 246, PCC.

15. Ireland, *Little Kingdoms*, p. 42.

16. County court order book H, p. 13, book I, p. 345, PCC.

17. Dun and Bradstreet records, 37:109, HUL.

18. County court order book K, p. 43, PCC.

19. Rice, *Hatfields and McCoys*, p. 52; Jones, *Hatfields and McCoys*, p. 81.

20. Jones, *Hatfields and McCoys*, p. 74; Rice, *Hatfields and McCoys*, p. 33; McCoy, *The McCoys*, pp. 119–20.

21. Price, *Without Scrip or Purse*, p. 173.

22. *Louisville Courier-Journal*, 3 Mar. 1888.

23. Eller, *Miners, Millhands, and Mountaineers*, pp. 53–54.

24. Kentucky, "Kentucky Geological Survey."

25. County court order book L, May–July 1888, pp. 132–89, PCC. Suits were filed against "those who refuse to grant a right of way" by the Charleston, Cincinnati, and Chicago Railroad. Evidence of local resentment of development was often hidden, especially after the fact. Because

the local histories on which we now rely for regional history—and indeed, even the early local newspapers—were written by the educated elite who were on the side of modernization, readers might easily get the impression that everyone welcomed the development process. The opposing view is often hidden in public documents at the local level.

26. Klotter, "Feuds in Appalachia," p. 291.

27. Stories on this feud appeared in the *New York Times* on 23 June, 29, 31 July, 6, 14 Aug. 1887.

28. Ibid., 29 July 1887. For the Rowan County feud and the legislature's reaction to ·it, see Kentucky, "Special Report on Rowan County Affairs"; idem, "Majority and Minority Reports."

29. Jones, *Hatfields and McCoys*, pp. 82–83; Rice, *Hatfields and McCoys*, p. 52.

30. S. B. Buckner to E. W. Wilson, 9 Jan. 1888, in Kentucky, "Correspondence of the Governors," pp. 2–3; *Louisville Courier-Journal*, 11 Feb. 1888; Rice, *Hatfields and McCoys*, p. 52; Jones, *Hatfields and McCoys*, pp. 82–83.

31. Proclamation of Governor Simon B. Buckner in Frankfort, Ky., 10 Sept. 1887, quoted in Jones, *Hatfields and McCoys*, p. 83.

32. Logan County Regulators to Perry A. Cline, 29 Aug. 1887, printed in the *Wheeling Intelligencer*, 2 Feb. 1888; Jones, *Hatfields and McCoys*, p. 84; Rice, *Hatfields and McCoys*, pp. 50–51.

33. Brown, "American Vigilante Tradition," pp. 154–61; Hofstadter and Wallace, *American Violence*, pp. 21–23.

34. In addition to "regulation" as part of the American Revolution (about which the literature is voluminous), examples include Kay, "North Carolina Regulation," and Szatmary, *Shays' Rebellion.*

35. Holmes, "Moonshining and Collective Violence," pp. 590–92; for an analysis of the antimodernism in Jesse James's gang and the Bald Knobber vigilantes of Missouri, see Thelen, *Paths of Resistance*, pp. 70–77, 86–92. For a different perspective, see White, "Outlaw Gangs of the Middle Border."

36. Logan County Regulators to Perry A. Cline.

37. County court order book L, Oct. 1887, p. 33, PCC.

38. McCoy, *The McCoys*, pp. 129–30.

39. U.S. census, population schedules for Pike County, 1860, dwelling no. 384, NA.

40. Ibid., 1870, p. 9.

41. County court order book E, July 1867, p. 9, PCC: Jesse Phillips is appointed guardian for Phillips children—Sarah Jane, Pricey, John, Franklin, and Mary. Ibid., August 1868, p. 137: Jesse Phillips resigns as guardian and John Dils, Jr., "asks" to be appointed guardian. The request is granted.

42. Ibid., July 1868, p. 109.

43. In 1878, at the age of sixteen, Frank had married his first cousin, Matilda Phillips (see Pike County marriage records, published in Pike County Historical Society, *Papers*, 6:74. According to Frank's son Jesse

Phillips, Frank's second wife was Mary F. Rowe, whom he married on 17 September 1883 (see notes in the "Phillips" file in the Pike County Historical Society, Pikeville, Ky.).

44. Louisville Courier-Journal, 7 Feb. 1888; Jones, Hatfields and McCoys, p. 83; Rice, Hatfields and McCoys, pp. 52–53.

45. McCoy, The McCoys, pp. 129–31.

46. Williams, West Virginia, pp. 124–25; Crawford, An American Vendetta, p. 25. For a short biography of Floyd, see Atkinson and Gibbens, Prominent Men of West Virginia, pp. 720–21.

47. For biographies of Wilson, see Encyclopedia of Contemporary Biography of West Virginia, pp. 78–82; Morgan, "Emmanuel Willis Wilson," pp. 42–45. See also West Virginia, State Papers and Public Addresses of E. Willis Wilson.

48. Williams, West Virginia, p. 122.

49. P. A. Cline to E. W. Wilson, 5 Nov. 1887, published in the Wheeling Intelligencer, 24 Apr. 1888, and quoted in Jones, Hatfields and McCoys, pp. 86–89.

50. Rice, Hatfields and McCoys, pp. 54–55; Jones, Hatfields and McCoys, p. 86.

51. Frank Phillips to E. W. Wilson, 13 Dec. 1888, in Kentucky, "Correspondence of the Governors," p. 8; also published in Jones, Hatfields and McCoys, pp. 86–87.

52. County court order book L, 24 Dec. 1887, PCC.

53. Spencer, History of Kentucky Baptists, 2:593–94. Basil Hatfield is identified as a minister of the Mates Creek Association since 1877.

54. County court order book L, 24 Dec. 1887, PCC.

55. E. W. Wilson to S. B. Buckner, 13 Feb. 1888, in Kentucky, "Correspondence of the Governors," pp. 20–23.

56. Johnson Hatfield [not Anderson's son] deposition, 3 Jan. 1887, pp. 5–6; A. J. Auxier deposition, ibid., p. 6.

57. Statement of Charlie Gillespie, Wheeling Intelligencer, 17 Oct. 1888; Cincinnati Enquirer, 14 Oct. 1888. Gillespie's statement was also published in Hofstadter and Wallace, American Violence, pp. 398–400.

58. Statement of Charlie Gillespie. In 1888 Valentine Hatfield told a reporter that he refused to go along on the raid (see Pittsburg Times, 1 Feb. 1888; Rice, Hatfields and McCoys, pp. 58–59; Jones, Hatfields and McCoys, pp. 90–92).

59. For descriptions of the raid, see the testimony of Sarah McCoy, Commonwealth of Kentucky v. Ellison Mounts, KSC; statement of Charlie Gillespie, Cincinnati Enquirer, 14 Oct. 1888; McCoy, The McCoys, pp. 141–46; Jones, Hatfields and McCoys, pp. 93–98; Rice, Hatfields and McCoys, pp. 60–63.

60. Statement of Charlie Gillespie, Cincinnati Enquirer, 14 Oct. 1888, and Wheeling Intelligencer, 17 Oct. 1888.

CHAPTER 7

1. McCoy, *The McCoys*, p. 147.

2. *Louisville Courier-Journal*, 8 Jan. 1888.

3. Ibid., 28 Jan. 1888; *Pittsburg Times*, 1 Feb. 1888. In January 1888 a *New York World* reporter visited the Tug Valley. Although he claimed to have talked to the feud "chiefs," it is apparent that most of his information came from Mary Vance, widow of the slain Jim Vance. The reporter described Mary Vance as the "bravest" woman he had ever met and quotes, verbatim, her account of the murder of her husband. See "A Fight to the Death," *New York World*, 8 Feb. 1888.

4. Testimonies of Valentine Hatfield, Frank Phillips, and James Sowards, *Commonwealth of Kentucky v. Valentine Hatfield*, KSC; Jones, *Hatfields and McCoys*, p. 106.

5. *Louisville Courier-Journal*, 17 Mar. 1888.

6. On 3 January 1888, Pike County judge Tobias Wagner announced that there were "reasonable grounds" to believe that the jailed Hatfields "were liable to be rescued by a mob of lawles despordoes [*sic*]." In order to prevent this, Wagner authorized Perry Cline to "summon eight good sober discreet men" to guard the jail (county court order book L, p. 84, PCC).

7. E. W. Wilson to S. B. Buckner, 21 Jan. 1888, in Kentucky, "Correspondence of the Governors," pp. 3–8.

8. Indictment of Frank Phillips et. al. for the murder of James Vance, old felonies file drawer, Apr. 1888, CCCO.

9. Frank Phillips had been authorized by the governor of Kentucky only to "receive" the Hatfield prisoners when and if they were extradited from West Virginia, not to pursue them into that state. However, Phillips and Cline undoubtedly told the posse members that their authority included the raids into West Virginia. Both sides, then, were essentially vigilantes. David Thelen found similar patterns in his study of the Bald Knobbers in Missouri in this same era. In both situations, neither side had any basis in law for its terrorism and violence (Thelen, *Paths of Resistance*, pp. 87–92).

10. E. W. Wilson to S. B. Buckner, Charleston, W.Va., 26 Jan. 1888, in Kentucky, "Correspondence of the Governors," pp. 9–10; S. B. Buckner to E. W. Wilson, Frankfort, Ky., 30 Jan. 1888, ibid., pp. 11–17; McCoy, "Hatfield and McCoy Feud," pp. 25–26; McCoy, *The McCoys*, pp. 172–79; *Cincinnati Enquirer*, 30 Jan. 1888; *New York World*, 8 Feb. 1888; *Louisville Courier-Journal*, 25 Jan. 1888; *Pittsburg Times*, 1 Feb. 1888; Rice, *Hatfields and McCoys*, pp. 69–70; Jones, *Hatfields and McCoys*, p. 104.

11. Of the four, one, Tom Wallace, joined Cap in whipping the Daniels women and was present at the shooting of Jeff McCoy. His participation may have been prompted by a disappointed romance rather than the original feud. He was killed shortly after the second incident by "dangerous" Bud McCoy, ending his brief role. Another new feudist was Charlie Gillespie, who took part in the raid on the McCoy home. He was later arrested

and gave a graphic description of the raid to newspaper reporters but is otherwise an elusive figure; he cannot be identified in community records such as census schedules, deeds, or court records, even though the Gillespie family was an old and established one in the Tug Valley. The final two, John R. Thompson, constable of Logan County, and deputy Bill Dempsey, were involved only because of the arrest warrants issued for the Phillips posse by Logan County.

12. These included Old Ranel himself; his brother James H.; his sons James, Sam, and Floyd; his nephews Sam and Paris as well as Jake, Jeff, Bud, and Lark; Albert Thompson, the husband of his daughter Twinnie; and Perry Cline.

13. These four—Daniel and Curtis Smith, Jim Norman, and Joseph Hurley—all resided in the Peter Creek district, near the McCoy brothers, but none had shown any interest in the first phase of the feud. It seems likely that they responded to the plight of the Peter Creek McCoys or simply to the excitement of joining Perry Cline's posse. Still, even adding in the doubtfuls, all the Cline-McCoy supporters who resided in the Tug Valley number only twelve, or 30 percent of the total.

14. *Charleston Daily Star*, 26 Jan. 1888, quoted in Rice, *Hatfields and McCoys*, p. 72, and Jones, *Hatfields and McCoys*, p. 108.

15. John Spivak Papers, WVUL; McCoy, "Hatfield and McCoy Feud," p. 16.

16. *Wheeling Intelligencer*, 27 Jan. 1888.

17. "Pike County Voting Report for 1868."

18. "Roll of Company E of the 39th Mounted Infantry Volunteers."

19. "Pike County Voting Report for 1868."

20. Ely, *Big Sandy Valley*, p. 208.

21. But neither progress nor "justice" was really the issue. Neither the governor nor the posse members had any evidence (other than Cline's word) of the facts of the original feud. In a letter to Governor Wilson of West Virginia, Governor Buckner states that his information was "obtained from the County Attorney of Pike County" (30 Jan. 1888, in Kentucky, "Correspondence of the Governors," p. 16). The county attorney at the time was J. Lee Ferguson, although occasionally Perry Cline acted in his stead. Ferguson and Cline were close friends and allies; the perspective on the feud held by the governor was clearly that of Perry Cline.

And, as we have seen, there is much evidence to suggest that the county courts of both Logan and Pike counties were functioning reasonably well; most incidents in the feud's first phase were handled by the legal system. The extralegal violence in the killings of the three McCoys had been caused by the existence of an arbitrary state boundary that chopped the Tug Valley in half. This created a confusion over jurisdiction which led to unusual frustrations and, ultimately, private retribution. But in most cases, Devil Anse was the first to take his grievances to court.

22. McCoy, *The McCoys*, p. 177.

23. Ibid., pp. 183–85.
24. Judgment lien docket book, 28 Jan. 1888, LCBS.
25. Deeds from Anderson and Levicy Hatfield to J. D. Sergeant, 30 Jan. 1888 (deed book L, 6), 14 Feb. 1888 (deed book L, 34), 9 May 1888 (deed book K, 156, 157), 10 May 1888, (deed book L, 50), 4 July 1888 (deed book L, 59), 10 Mar. 1889 (deed book L, 171), LCC.
26. Judgment lien docket book, 28 June 1888, LCBS.
27. *Louisville Courier-Journal*, 17 Feb. 1888.
28. *Logan Banner*, 30 Oct. 1890. This article reported that Henry Mitchell, who was a close friend and ally of Devil Anse and who held land adjacent to Anse's on Mates Creek, "has sold . . . to McNutt and Company for $15.00 per acre."
29. Deeds from Lewis S. Steel and Lottie Steel to Vice Hatfield, 1 Apr. 1888, and L. D. Steel and A. E. Steel [his wife] to Levicy Hatfield, 1 May 1888, deed book L, 52, 53, LCC.
30. Smith, *History of Logan and Mingo Counties*, p. 52. On 19 May 1888 Johnson Hatfield (presumably Anse's son, although this is not certain because there was another Johnson Hatfield in Logan County to whom Anse sold some of the Grapevine land) granted a right-of-way to the Ohio and Norfolk Railroad for $1.00 "in order to induce and promote the building of a railroad up the Tug Fork" (see deed book K, 469, LCC).
31. *Logan Banner*, 24 Mar. 1892.
32. Scalf, *Kentucky's Last Frontier*, p. 212; Cubby, "Transformation of the Tug and Guyandot Valleys," pp. 231–32.
33. *Logan Banner*, 5 Mar. 1891, 4 Apr. 1892.
34. On the founding of Williamson, see *Logan Banner*, 21 May 1891, and Cubby, "Transformation of the Tug and Guyandot Valleys," pp. 157–58.
35. *Logan Banner*, 18 July 1889.
36. Ibid., 30 July 1891.
37. Smith, *History of Logan and Mingo Counties*, p. 46.
38. F. J. Kimball to Vivian, Gray and Company, 1 July 1892, quoted in Lambie, *From Mine to Market*, p. 129.
39. *Logan Banner*, 30 July 1891; Cubby, "Transformation of the Tug and Guyandot Valleys," pp. 161–64.
40. *Logan Banner*, 23 Oct. 1890.
41. Cubby, "Transformation of the Tug and Guyandot Valleys," pp. 162–63.
42. *Logan Banner*, 2 May 1889.
43. Ibid., 24 July 1890.
44. For a concise discussion of alcohol as a symbolic conflict between the working class and the emerging middle class, see Johnson, *A Shopkeeper's Millennium*, pp. 55–61.
45. For a discussion of Appalachian social structure before industrialization, see Eller, *Miners, Millhands, and Mountaineers*, pp. 9–12.
46. For a comparison to other areas of the South, see Ayers, *Vengeance and Justice*, p. 263.

47. U.S. census, population and agricultural schedules for Logan and Pike counties, 1870–1900, NA.

CHAPTER 8

1. *Logan Banner*, 20 Aug. 1891.

2. *Louisville Courier-Journal*, 25 Jan. 1888; *New York Times*, 25 Jan. 1888.

3. E. W. Wilson to S. B. Buckner, 21 Jan. 1888, in Kentucky, "Correspondence of the Governors," pp. 3–4. The enclosed depositions were those of G. W. Pinson, clerk of the criminal court of Pike County, who attested to having copied the indictments against the Hatfields for Perry Cline; Johnson Hatfield, Sr. (not the son of Anse but a hotel keeper in Logan Courthouse), who attested to making an agreement with Cline wherein, for the sum of $225, the lawyer agreed to "use all his influence with the Governor of Kentucky . . . to take no further steps for the arrest" of the Hatfields; A. J. Auxier, a Pikeville attorney who witnessed the transaction; and John A. Sheppard, a resident of Logan County and friend of John B. Floyd, who wrote to Floyd describing atrocities committed by the McCoys.

4. Telegram from E. W. Wilson to S. B. Buckner, 25 Jan. 1888, in Kentucky, "Correspondence of the Governors," p. 8.

5. E. W. Wilson to S. B. Buckner, 26 Jan. 1888, ibid., pp. 9–10; telegram from E. W. Wilson to S. B. Buckner, 30 Jan. 1888, ibid., p. 10. The trip to Frankfort by Wagner and Ferguson was reported in the *Wheeling Intelligencer*, 25 Jan. 1888; *Cincinnati Enquirer*, 24 Jan. 1888; *Louisville Courier-Journal*, 25 Jan. 1888. Apparently Cline, in his capacity as deputy jailor, was too busy guarding the nine Hatfields to accompany them. In the absence of Ferguson, who was the county attorney, Cline was appointed to fill in that post (see county court order book L, 23 Jan. 1888, p. 85, PCC). During Wagner's absence, another close friend of Cline's, A. J. Casebolt, served as county judge.

6. Telegram from E. W. Wilson to S. B. Buckner, 30 Jan. 1888, in Kentucky, "Correspondence of the Governors," p. 10.

7. Report of Col. W. L. Mahon, *Louisville Courier-Journal*, 1 Feb. 1888.

8. Statement of John B. Floyd, *Wheeling Intelligencer*, 27 Jan. 1888.

9. Sam E. Hill to S. B. Buckner, 6 Feb. 1888, in Kentucky, "Correspondence of the Governors," pp. 25–31.

10. "Innocents at Home," *Louisville Courier-Journal*, 1 Feb. 1888; "West Virginia Barbarians" (26 Feb. 1888), "Crimes of the Hatfields" (2 Feb. 1888), "West Virginia's Bad Character" (11 Feb. 1888), all in the *Pittsburg Times*; "West Virginia's Vendetta," *New York World*, 8 Feb. 1888.

11. *Wheeling Intelligencer*, 27 Jan. 1888.

12. Ibid.

13. Henry S. Walker, secretary of state of West Virginia, to S. B. Buckner, 8 Feb. 1888, in Kentucky, "Correspondence of the Governors," p. 19.

14. *Louisville Courier-Journal*, 9, 10 Feb. 1888.

15. *Cincinnati Enquirer*, 11 Feb. 1888; *Huntington Advertiser* (West Virginia), 18 Feb. 1888.

16. *Louisville Courier-Journal*, 12 Feb. 1888; Rice, *Hatfields and McCoys*, p. 83; Jones, *Hatfields and McCoys*, p. 117.

17. *Louisville Courier-Journal*, 17 Feb. 1888.

18. Ibid.

19. Ibid.

20. *New York Times*, 18 Feb. 1888.

21. *Louisville Courier-Journal*, 28 Feb. 1888.

22. Ibid., 4 Mar. 1888.

23. Ibid., 7 Apr. 1888.

24. Ibid., 15, 17 Mar. 1888.

25. *Wheeling Intelligencer*, 18 Feb. 1888.

26. Ibid.

27. *Louisville Courier-Journal*, 4 Mar. 1888. Varney's remarks are transcribed here verbatim from the newspaper account of the proceedings.

28. Ibid., 16 Mar. 1888.

29. Ibid.

30. Ibid., 15 May 1888; *New York Times*, 15 May 1888.

31. *New York Times*, 15 May 1888.

32. County court order book L, 24 May 1888, p. 132, PCC.

33. *Wheeling Intelligencer*, 29 June 1888; Jones, *Hatfields and McCoys*, pp. 134–35. Stratton, however, did not go to jail. In May 1890 he was run over by a train, apparently while he was in a drunken stupor (Jones, *Hatfields and McCoys*, p. 182).

34. Coleman Hatfield, in "Tales of the Feuding Hatfields," claims that Devil Anse and his supporters began purchasing Winchesters by mail only *after* the battle of Grapevine Creek, and then only because Cline's posse had them. See also Jones, *Hatfields and McCoys*, pp. 133–34.

35. *Pittsburg Times*, 16 Oct. 1888; *Wheeling Intelligencer*, 17 Oct. 1888; *Wheeling Register*, 18 Nov. 1888. For a different version, see Johnson, " 'Horrible Butcheries of West Virginia,' " p. 25.

36. *Wheeling Intelligencer*, 21 Oct. 1889.

37. *West Virginia* v. *Cunningham and Gibson*, 12 Jan. 1889, old records file drawer, CCCO; Jones, *Hatfields and McCoys*, p. 152.

38. *Pittsburg Times*, 1 Feb. 1888.

39. Ibid.

40. Crawford, *An American Vendetta*, pp. 12–13.

41. Ibid., pp. 12, 15.

42. Ibid., pp. 54–55.

43. Ibid., p. 82.

44. Ibid., p. 69.

45. By the last years of his life (he died in 1921), Anse had built another house, this time one very much like the houses being built by the middle

and upper classes in both Pikeville and Logan. It was a two-storied, white clapboard frame house with porches on both stories.

46. Crawford, *An American Vendetta*, pp. 69, 109, 97.

47. Ibid., p. 61.

48. Ibid., pp. 58–59, 61–64.

49. Ibid., pp. 61–64.

50. Ibid., p. 87.

51. Ibid., pp. 96–97.

52. McCoy, *The McCoys*, p. 198.

53. Trust deed from Plyant, D. D., and Samuel Mahon to Auxier, Ferrell and Connelly, Walter S. Harkens, and P. A. Cline, 15 Aug. 1888; and trust deed from Valentine Hatfield to Auxier, Ferrell and Connelly, W. S. Harkens, P. A. Cline, and J. S. Cline, 15 Aug. 1888; both in trust deed book B, pp. 106–10, LCC.

54. McCoy, *The McCoys*, p. 199.

55. Testimony of Valentine Hatfield, *Commonwealth of Kentucky* v. *Valentine Hatfield*, KSC.

56. McCoy, *The McCoys*, p. 201.

57. Ibid., p. 200.

58. Testimony of Sarah McCoy, *Commonwealth of Kentucky* v. *Ellison Mounts*, KSC.

59. McCoy, *The McCoys*, pp. 201–2.

60. Ibid., pp. 208–9.

61. Ibid., pp. 207–10; *Cincinnati Enquirer*, 20 Feb. 1890; *Louisville Courier-Journal*, 19 Feb. 1890.

62. *Wheeling Intelligencer*, 23 Nov. 1889.

63. Ibid.

CHAPTER 9

1. In a story published in 1890, the *New York Times* assessed what effect "progress" was having on "new Kentucky." "The buying up of the mountain lands has," according to the article, "unsettled a large part of these strange people." The paper believed that the mountaineers had one of three choices: (1) leave the mountains for towns or for lands beyond the Mississippi; (2) become absorbed into the new order—keeping stores, speculating in land, developing small businesses; or (3) the most prevalent response, retire "at the approach of civilization to remoter regions, where they may live without criticism or observation their hereditary, squalid, unambitious, stationary life" (*New York Times*, 2 Sept. 1890).

2. McKinney, "Industrialization and Violence."

3. Anse did not by any means give up his economic and legal wheeling and dealing. For example, in 1891 he gave permission to the Little Kanawha Lumber Company to build a splash dam near his home on Island

Creek, but in return he insisted that he be allowed to build a grist mill in the splash dam (see deed book Q, 557, LCC). In 1894 Anse, apparently convinced he had been unfairly coerced into selling his land so soon after the "battle of Grapevine," hired a lawyer to "recover" three thousand acres of the land. If successful, the lawyer was to get a one-third interest in the land (see deed book R, 319, LCC). Anse and his family also continued to log, although now on Island Creek rather than Grapevine Creek. In fact, in 1916 the Island Creek Coal Company sued Anse for damages, claiming he had illegally cut timber on company lands (see *Island Creek Coal Company v. Anderson Hatfield*, chancery count case file no. 55, 1916, CCCO).

4. *Logan Banner*, 30, 31 July 1890.

5. Jones, *Hatfields and McCoys*, p. 209.

6. Ibid., pp. 199–207; Rice, *Hatfields and McCoys* pp. 118–20.

7. Crawford, *An American Vendetta*, p. 75.

8. *Huntington Advertiser* (W.Va.), 16, 18 Oct. 1911.

9. *New York Times*, 8 Jan. 1921; see also *Logan Banner*, 14 Jan. 1921.

10. Hatfield, *The Hatfields*, pp. 173–74. According to the *Logan Banner*, "Capt. Hatfield of Stirrat and Dr. E. R. Rutherford Hatfield of Charleston, who had been on the outs for some time, again became friendly over the dead body of their father" (14 Jan. 1921).

11. Jones, *Hatfields and McCoys*, p. 239; also, my own observations on visits to the cemetery in 1982–84.

12. Jones, *Hatfields and McCoys*, p. 216.

13. Perry Cline's will, 6 Apr. 1891, will book B, p. 209, PCC.

14. McCoy, *The McCoys*, p. 215.

15. McCoy, "Hatfield and McCoy Feud."

16. U.S. census, population and agricultural schedules for Logan County, 1850–80, NA. The household of French Ellis is listed in 1850 as dwelling no. 49; in 1860 as dwelling no. 200, p. 34; in 1870, Logan district, p. 26; in 1880, Logan district, p. 2.

17. Land tax book, Logan district, 1892, LCC.

18. *Logan Banner*, 11 July 1889.

19. The stone in the Hatfield cemetery in Sara Ann, W.Va., reads: "French M. Ellis / Dec. 21, 1857–Apr. 13, 1924." His wife's gravestone reads: "Eska L. Ellis / Dau of L. P. Smith and wife of French Ellis / Born Oct. 22, 1865 / Died July 16, 1896." Both stones are near those of Devil Anse's children and grandchildren.

20. McCoy, *The McCoys*, p. 229.

21. Ibid., pp. 157–65; *Johnson Hatfield v. Nancy Hatfield*, circuit court records, Oct. 1890, CCCO.

22. Pike County circuit court records, Aug. 1888, KSA.

23. McCoy, *The McCoys*, p. 214.

24. Ibid., pp. 215–17.

25. Cap Hatfield to S. B. Buckner, 21 Jan. 1889, published in Klotter, "A Hatfield-McCoy Feudist Pleads for Mercy."

26. *Wayne County News*, 24 Feb. 1891, quoted in Jones, *Hatfields and McCoys*, p. 185; Rice, *Hatfields and McCoys*, p. 115.

27. Hatfield, *The Hatfields*, pp. 171–72; Swain, *History of Logan County*, p. 194.

28. Hatfield, "Tales of the Feuding Hatfields," WVUL; Hatfield, *The Hatfields*, pp. 171–72; Jones, *Hatfields and McCoys*, pp. 240–41; Rice, *Hatfields and McCoys*, p. 124.

29. Hatfield, *The Hatfields*, pp. 171–72.

30. Ibid., p. 173; *Logan Banner*, 11 Mar. 1889 (councilman), 5 Mar. 1891 (county constable); Lawson, *Autobiography and Reminiscences*, p. 41.

31. Hatfield, *The Hatfields*, pp. 172–73; Williams, *West Virginia*, pp. 127–48; Corbin, *Life, Work, and Rebellion*, pp. 87–101.

32. Williams, *West Virginia*, pp. 146–48; Lee, *Bloodletting in Appalachia*; Corbin, *Life, Work, and Rebellion*, pp. 195–224.

33. Swain, *History of Logan County*, pp. 77, 268; Corbin, *Life, Work, and Rebellion*, pp. 114–16; Lee, *Bloodletting in Appalachia*, pp. 87–93.

34. Gleason, "Private Ownership of Public Officials," *The Nation*, 29 May 1920, quoted in Cubby, "Transformation of the Tug and Guyandot Valleys," p. 322.

35. Cubby, "Transformation of the Tug and Guyandot Valleys," pp. 325–26.

36. For an exploration of the problems Appalachian miners have in finding and confronting the companies who control their lives, see Gaventa, *Power and Powerlessness*.

37. Interviews in the *Williamson Daily News*, 2 Aug. 1982: Nellie Alley Condit, Estelle McCoy Little, and Fannie Simpkins Booth.

38. Swain, *History of Logan County*, pp. 183, 194, 268–72.

Bibliography

MANUSCRIPTS

Baker Library, Harvard University, Cambridge, Mass.
    Dun and Bradstreet Records for Logan and Pike Counties
Basement Storeroom, County Courthouse, Logan, W.Va.
    Circuit Court Fee Book, 1815–92, 1885–94
    Execution Book, 1873–81
    Judgment Lien Docket Book (indexed)
    Jurors Fee Book, 1883–1900
Circuit Court Clerk's Office, Logan, W.Va.
    Chancery Court Index and Case Files
    County Court Index and Law Order Books, vols. A–C, 1868–90
    Old Felonies File Drawer, 1860–1904
    Old Records File Drawer, Misc. Judicial and Court Records
Clerk of the Supreme Court, State Capitol, Frankfort, Ky.
    Commonwealth of Kentucky v. *Valentine Hatfield*, Case No. 19594
    Commonwealth of Kentucky v. *Ellison Mounts*, Case No. 19602
County Clerk's Office, County Courthouse, Logan, W.Va.
    County Commissioners Record Books, vols. 1–5, 1866–1908
    County Court Order Book, 1895–1916
    County Court Minute Book, 1868–89
    Deed Books, 1835–1910
    Land Tax Books, 1865–1902
    Surveyor Records, vols. A–C, 1824–85
    Trust Deed Books
    Vital Records, Births, Marriages, and Deaths, 1872–92
    Wills, 1873–1900
County Clerk's Office, County Courthouse, Pikeville, Ky.
    County Court Order Books, vols. A–Z, 1822–1938 (indexed)
    Deeds, 1820–1909 (indexed)
    Marriage Bonds and Records, 1822–1940 (indexed)
    Vital Records, Births, Marriages, and Deaths
    Wills, 1839–1912
National Archives, Washington, D.C.
    U.S. Census, Agricultural Schedules, Logan County, W.Va., and Pike
        County, Ky., 1850–80 (microfilm)

U.S. Census, Population Schedules, Logan County, W.Va., and Pike
County, Ky., 1820–1900 (microfilm)
Special Collections, University of Kentucky Library, Lexington
Letter from Anderson Hatfield to P[erry] A. Cline, 26 December 1886
Pike County Circuit Court Records (microfilm)
Pike County Tax Books, 1870–92 (microfilm)
State Archives, Frankfort, Ky.
Pike County Circuit Court Case Files, 1860–67 (microfilm)
Pike County Circuit Court Records, 1879–90
Pike County Quarterly Docket Book, 1866–78
State Archives and Records, Charleston, W.Va.
Logan County Land Tax Books, 1824–1908
Emanuel Willis Wilson, West Virginia Governors, Letters and Papers
Box 65
West Virginia Collection, West Virginia University Library, Morgantown
Coleman Hatfield, "Tales of the Feuding Hatfields" (typescript)
John Spivak Papers

NEWSPAPERS

Big Sandy News (Louisa, Ky.), 1888
Cincinnati Enquirer, 1888–92
Logan Banner, 1889–1938
Louisville Courier-Journal, 1885–92
New York Times, 1882–95
New York World, 1888
Pittsburg Times, 1888–92
Wheeling Intelligencer, 1888–92
Wheeling Register, 1888–92

PUBLISHED GOVERNMENT DOCUMENTS

Kentucky. General Assembly. "Correspondence of the Governors." *Kentucky Documents 1888*, vol. 1, legislative document no. 2.
———. "Eighth Report of the Railroad Commissioners . . . for 1887." *Kentucky Documents 1887–88*, vol. 1, legislative document no. 27.
———. "First Report of the Fish Commissioners of Kentucky for the Year Ending Nov. 1, 1877." *Kentucky Documents 1877*, vol. 3, legislative document no. 17.
———. "Kentucky: Its Resources and Present Condition: The First Annual Report, 1878." *Kentucky Documents 1877*, vol. 1, legislative document no. 1.

Bibliography

———. "Kentucky Geological Survey." *Kentucky Documents 1887*, vol. 3, legislative document no. 19, pp. 2–28.

———. "Kentucky State Railroad Commission." *Kentucky Documents 1883*, vol. 2, legislative document no. 12, pp. 147–70.

———. "Majority and Minority Reports and Testimony Taken by the Rowan County Investigating Committee . . . March 16, 1888." *Kentucky Documents 1888*, vol. 1, legislative document no. 3.

———. "Ninth Report of the Railroad Commissioners." *Kentucky Documents 1888*, vol. 5, legislative document no. 17.

———. "Proceedings of the State Board of Equalization of Kentucky: Session 1888." *Kentucky Documents 1888*, vol. 2, legislative document no. 10.

———. "Report of the Commissioner of Agriculture, Nov. 30, 1889." *Kentucky Documents 1889*, vol. 1, legislative document no. 20.

———. "Report of the Inspector of Mines." *Kentucky Documents 1885*, vol. 2, legislative document no. 14.

———. "Report of the State Geologist." *Kentucky Documents 1889–90*, vol. 5, legislative document no. 3.

———. "Report of the Superintendent of Public Instruction." *Kentucky Documents 1889*, vol. 3, legislative document no. 1.

———. "Report of the Superintendent of Public Instruction, 1881–1886." *Kentucky Documents 1887–88*, vol. 1, legislative document no. 7.

———. "Seventh Annual Report of the Inspector of Mines, Oct. 10, 1890." *Kentucky Documents 1888–90, 1891*, vol. 1, legislative document no. 8.

———. "Seventh Annual Report of the Railroad Commissioners." *Kentucky Documents 1886–87*, legislative document no. 9.

———. "Sixth Annual Report of the Railroad Commissioners of Kentucky to November 30, 1885." *Kentucky Documents 1885*, vol. 3, legislative document no. 17, pp. 1–11.

———. "Sixth Report of the Fish Commissioners of Kentucky for the Year 1879." *Kentucky Documents 1879*, vol. 9, legislative document no. 3.

———. "Special Report on Rowan County Affairs." *Kentucky Documents 1887*, vol. 3, legislative document no. 23, pp. 1–23.

The War of the Rebellion: A Compilation of the Official Records of the Union and Confederate Armies. 128 vols. Washington, D.C.: Government Printing Office, 1880–1901.

West Virginia. *Acts and Constitution of the State of West Virginia*, 1872.

———. *Acts of the Legislature of West Virginia*, 1881.

———. *Annual Reports of the State Inspector of Mines*, 1883–86, 1890–91.

———. *State Papers and Public Addresses of E. Willis Wilson*, 1885–90.

———. Department of Natural Resources. *Annual Report of the Fish Commissioners*, 1877–78, 1889–90, 1891–92.

Bibliography

PUBLISHED PRIMARY SOURCES

Barnes, George Owen. *God's Love Story; or, The Gospel According to St. Ruth, Together with an Exposition of the Lord's Prayer and Other Sermons.* Edited by George W. Greenswood. New York: C. T. Dillingham, 1883.

———. "Journal." In *Without Scrip or Purse, or the Mountain Evangelist, George O. Barnes,* edited by W. T. Price. Louisville, Ky.: n.p., 1883.

Crawford, T. C. *An American Vendetta: A Story of Barbarism in the United States.* New York: Bedford, Clarke and Company, 1889.

Dyer, M. H. *Index to Land Grants In West Virginia.* Charleston, W.Va.: Moses E. Donnally, 1896.

Ely, William. *The Big Sandy Valley: A History of the People and County from the Earliest Settlement to the Present Time.* Catlettsburg, Ky.: Central Methodist Publishing Company, 1887.

Frost, William Goodell. "Our Contemporary Ancestors in the Southern Mountains." *Atlantic Monthly* 83 (March 1899): 311–19.

Johnson, Ludwell, ed. " 'Horrible Butcheries of West Virginia': Dan Cunningham on the Hatfield-McCoy Feud." *West Virginia History* 46 (1985/86): 25–43.

Lawson, Sidney B. *Autobiography and Reminiscences of Sidney B. Lawson, M.D.: Fifty Years a Mountain Doctor.* Logan, W.Va.: n.p., 1941.

MacClintock, S. S. "The Kentucky Mountains and Their Feuds." *American Journal of Sociology* 7 (July, September 1901): 1–28, 171–87.

"Pike County Voting Report for 1868." In *Pike County Historical Papers,* 5:34–44. Pikeville, Ky.: Pike County Historical Society.

"Roll of Company E of the 39th Mounted Infantry Volunteers of the Union Army in the War between the States." In *Pike County Historical Papers,* 5:31–33. Pikeville, Ky.: Pike County Historical Society.

Spears, John R. "The Story of a Mountain Feud." *Munsey's Magazine* 24 (June 1901): 494–509.

SECONDARY SOURCES

Acury, Thomas A., and Julia D. Porter. "Household Composition in Appalachian Kentucky in 1900." *Journal of Family History* 10, no. 20 (Summer 1985): 183–95.

Ambler, Charles H., and Festus Summers. *West Virginia: The Mountain State.* Englewood Cliffs, N.J.: n.p., 1940.

Atkinson, George W., and Alvaro F. Gibbens. *Prominent Men of West Virginia.* Wheeling, W.Va.: W. L. Callin, 1890.

Ayers, Edward L. *Vengeance and Justice: Crime and Punishment in the Nineteenth Century American South.* New York: Oxford University Press, 1984.

Bibliography

Banks, Alan J. "The Emergence of a Capitalistic Labor Market in Eastern Kentucky." *Appalachian Journal* 7, no. 3 (1980): 188–98.
_____. "Land and Capital in Eastern Kentucky, 1890–1915." *Appalachian Journal* 8, no. 1 (1980): 8–18.
Bare, Virginia M. "Peter Cline, Sr., Pioneer Settler." In *Pike County Historical Papers*, 2:60–61. Pikeville, Ky.: Pike County Historical Society.
Batteau, Alan. *Appalachia and America: Autonomy and Regional Dependence.* Lexington: University Press of Kentucky, 1983.
Beachley, Charles E., comp. *History of the Consolidation Coal Company 1864–1934.* New York: Consolidation Coal Company, 1934.
Bender, Thomas. *Community and Social Change in America.* Baltimore, Md.: Johns Hopkins University Press, 1978.
Billings, Dwight, Kathleen Blee, and Louis Swanson. "Culture, Family, and Community in Preindustrial Appalachia." *Appalachian Journal* 13, no. 2 (Winter 1986): 154–70.
Bonomi, Patricia. *A Factious People: Politics and Society in Colonial New York.* New York: Columbia University Press, 1971.
Bowen, Don R. "Guerrilla War in Western Missouri, 1862–1865: Historical Dimensions of the Relative Deprivation Hypothesis." *Comparative Studies in History and Society* 19 (January 1977): 30–51.
Boyer, Paul S., and Stephen Nissenbaum. *Salem Possessed: The Social Origins of Witchcraft.* Cambridge, Mass.: Harvard University Press, 1974.
Brown, Richard D. *Modernization: The Transformation of American Life, 1600–1865.* New York: Hill and Wang, 1976.
Brown, Richard M. "The American Vigilante Tradition." In *Violence in America: Historical and Comparative Perspectives*, edited by Hugh D. Graham and Ted R. Gurr, pp. 154–217. New York: Bantam Books, 1969.
_____. "Historical Patterns of Violence in America." In *Violence in America: Historical and Comparative Perspectives*, edited by Hugh D. Graham and Ted R. Gurr. New York: Bantam Books, 1969.
_____. *Strain of Violence: Historical Studies of American Violence and Vigilantism.* New York: Oxford University Press, 1975.
Bryant, F. Carlene. *We're All Kin: A Cultural Study of a Mountain Neighborhood.* Knoxville: University of Tennessee Press, 1981.
Burton, Orville Vernon. *In My Father's House Are Many Mansions: Family and Community in Edgefield, South Carolina.* Chapel Hill: University of North Carolina Press, 1985.
Callahan, James Morton. *History of West Virginia.* 2 vols. Chicago: American Historical Society, 1923.
Campbell, John C. *The Southern Highlander and His Home.* 1921. Reprint. Lexington: University Press of Kentucky, 1969.
Cassity, Michael J. "Modernization and Social Crisis: The Knights of Labor and a Midwest Community, 1885–1886." *Journal of American History* 66, no. 1 (June 1979): 41–61.
Caudill, Harry M. "The Strange Career of John C. Mayo." *Filson Club Historical Quarterly* 56, no. 3 (1982): 258–89.

Bibliography

Clarkson, Roy B. *Tumult on the Mountain: Lumbering in West Virginia, 1770–1920*. Parsons, W.Va.: McClain Printing Company, 1964.

Corbin, David Alan. *Life, Work, and Rebellion in the Coal Fields: The Southern West Virginia Miners, 1880–1922*. Urbana: University of Illinois Press, 1981.

Crowe-Carraco, Carol. *The Big Sandy*. Lexington: University Press of Kentucky, 1979.

Cubby, Edwin Albert. "The Transformation of the Tug and Guyandot Valleys: Economic Development and Social Changes in West Virginia, 1888–1921." Ph.D. dissertation, Syracuse University, 1962.

Dickson, Bruce. *Violence and Culture in the Antebellum South*. Austin: University of Texas Press, 1979.

Donnelly, Clarence Shirley. *The Hatfield-McCoy Reader*. Parsons, W.Va.: McClain Printing Company, 1971.

Durrill, Wayne. "Producing Poverty: Local Government and Economic Development in a New South County, 1874–1884." *Journal Of American History* 71, no. 4 (March 1985): 764–81.

Dykstra, Robert. *The Cattle Towns*. New York: Knopf, 1968.

Eller, Ronald D. *Miners, Millhands, and Mountaineers: Industrialization of the Appalachian South, 1880–1930*. Knoxville: University of Tennessee Press, 1982.

Encyclopedia of Contemporary Biography of West Virginia. New York: Atlantic Publishing Company, 1894.

Faragher, John Mack. "Open Country Community: Sugar Creek, Illinois, 1820–1850." In *The Countryside in the Age of Capitalist Transformation*, edited by Steven Hahn and Jonathan Prude, pp. 233–58. Chapel Hill: University of North Carolina Press, 1985.

Ford, Lacy K. "Rednecks and Merchants: Economic Development and Social Tensions in the South Carolina Upcountry, 1865–1900." *Journal of American History* 71 (September 1984): 294–318.

Friedman, Lawrence. *A History of American Law*. New York: Touchstone Books, 1973.

Gabel, Peter, and Jay M. Feinman. "Contract Law as Ideology." In *The Politics of Law: A Progressive Critique*, edited by David Kairys, pp. 172–84. New York: Pantheon, 1982.

Gaventa, John. *Power and Powerlessness: Quiescence and Rebellion in an Appalachian Valley*. Chicago: University of Illinois Press, 1980.

Gorn, Elliot J. " 'Gouge and Bite, Pull Hair and Scratch': The Social Significance of Fighting in the Southern Backcountry." *American Historical Review* 90, no. 1 (February 1985): 18–43.

Hackney, Sheldon. "Southern Violence." In *The History of Violence in America: Historical and Comparative Perspectives*, edited by Hugh D. Graham and Ted R. Gurr. New York: Bantam Books, 1969.

Hahn, Steven. "Hunting, Fishing, and Foraging: Common Rights and Class Relations in the Postbellum South." *Radical History Review* 26 (1982): 37–64.

Bibliography

_____. *The Roots of Southern Populism: Yeoman Farmers and the Transformation of the Georgia Upcountry, 1850–1890.* New York: Oxford University Press, 1983.

Hahn, Steven, and Jonathan Prude, eds. *The Countryside in the Age of Capitalist Transformation: Essays in the Social History of Rural America.* Chapel Hill: University of North Carolina Press, 1985.

Haney, William H. *The Mountain People of Kentucky: By a Kentucky Mountain Man.* Cincinnati, Ohio: Robert Clarke Company, 1906.

Harvey, Helen B. "From Frontier to Mining Town of Logan County." M.A. thesis, University of Kentucky, 1942.

Hatfield, G. Elliot. *The Hatfields.* Revised and edited by Leonard Roberts and Henry P. Scalf. Stanville, Ky.: Big Sandy Valley Historical Society, 1974.

Hays, Samuel P. "Modernizing Values in the History of the United States." *Peasant Studies* 6 (April 1977): 68–79.

Henretta, James. *The Evolution of American Society, 1700–1815.* Lexington, Mass.: D. C. Heath, 1973.

Hicks, George. *Appalachian Valley.* New York: Holt, Rinehart and Winston, 1976.

Hindus, Michael S. *Prison and Plantation: Crime, Justice, and Authority in Massachusetts and South Carolina, 1767–1878.* Chapel Hill: University of North Carolina Press, 1980.

Hobsbawm, E. J. *Bandits.* New York: Pantheon, 1969.

_____. *Primitive Rebels: Studies in Archaic Forms of Social Movements in the 19th and 20th Centuries.* New York: Norton, 1965.

Hofstadter, Richard, and Michael Wallace. *American Violence: A Documentary History*, pp. 397–400. New York: Knopf, 1971.

Holmes, William F. "Moonshining and Collective Violence: Georgia, 1889–1895." *Journal of American History* 67, no. 1 (June 1980): 589–611.

Horwitz, Morton J. *The Transformation of American Law, 1780–1860.* Cambridge, Mass.: Harvard University Press, 1977.

Hurst, Mary B. "A Social History of Logan County, West Virginia, 1765–1923." M.A. thesis, Columbia University, 1933.

Ireland, Robert M. *The County Courts in Antebellum Kentucky.* Lexington: University Press of Kentucky, 1972.

_____. *Little Kingdoms: The Counties of Kentucky, 1850–1891.* Lexington: University Press of Kentucky, 1977.

Isaac, Rhys. *The Transformation of Virginia, 1740–1790.* Chapel Hill: University of North Carolina Press, 1982.

Jacobs, James Henry. "The West Virginia Gubernatorial Election Contest, 1888–1890." Parts 1, 2. *West Virginia History* 7, nos. 3, 4 (April, July 1946): 159–220, 263–311.

Jillson, Willard Rouse. *The Big Sandy Valley: A Regional History Prior to the Year 1850.* Kentucky Historical Society. Louisville, Ky.: John P. Morton and Company, 1923.

Bibliography

————. *The Kentucky Land Grants. A Systematic Index to All of the Land Grants Recorded in the State Land Office at Frankfort, Kentucky, 1782–1924.* Filson Club Publication no. 33. Louisville, Ky.: Filson Club, 1925.

Johnson, Paul E. *A Shopkeeper's Millennium: Society and Revivals in Rochester, New York, 1815–1837.* New York: Hill and Wang, 1978.

Jones, Virgil Carrington. *The Hatfields and the McCoys.* New York: Ballantine Books, 1948.

Kay, Marvin L. Michael. "The North Carolina Regulation, 1766–1776: A Class Conflict." In *The American Revolution: Explorations in the History of American Radicalism,* edited by Alfred F. Young, pp. 71–123. DeKalb: Northern Illinois University Press, 1976.

Kephart, Horace. *Our Southern Highlanders.* New York: Outing Publishing Company, 1913.

Klotter, James C. "Feuds in Appalachia: An Overview." *Filson Club Historical Quarterly* 56 (1982): 290–317.

————. "A Hatfield-McCoy Feudist Pleads for Mercy in 1889." *West Virginia History* 43, no. 4 (1982): 322–28.

Klotter, James C., and Hambleton Tapp. *Kentucky: Decades of Discord, 1865–1900.* Frankfort: Kentucky Historical Society, 1977.

Lambie, Joseph. *From Mine to Market: The History of Coal Transportation on the Norfolk and Western Railroad.* New York: New York University Press, 1954.

Lee, Howard B. *Bloodletting in Appalachia.* Morgantown: West Virginia University Library, 1969.

Lewis, Helen M., Linda Johnson, and Donald Atkins, eds. *Colonialism in Modern America: The Appalachian Case.* Boone, N.C.: Appalachian Consortium Press, 1978.

McClure, Virginia Clay. "The Settlement of the Kentucky Appalachian Highlands." Ph.D. dissertation, University of Kentucky, 1933.

McCoy, Homer C. "The Rise of Education and the Decline of Feudal Tendencies in the Tug River Valley of West Virginia and Kentucky in Relation to the Hatfield-McCoy Feud." M.A. thesis, Marshall College, 1950.

McCoy, Samuel. "The Hatfield and McCoy Feud." In *Squirrel Huntin' Sam McCoy: His Memoir and Family Tree.* Compiled by Hobert and Orville McCoy, edited and annotated by Leonard Roberts. Pikeville, Ky.: Pikeville College Press, 1979.

McCoy, Truda Williams. *The McCoys: Their Story As Told to the Author by Eyewitnesses and Descendents.* Edited by Leonard Roberts. Pikeville, Ky.: Pikeville College Press, 1976.

McKinney, Gordon B. "Industrialization and Violence in Appalachia in the 1890's." In *An Appalachian Symposium,* edited by Joel W. Williamson, pp. 131–44. Boone, N.C.: Appalachian Consortium Press, 1977.

————. *Southern Mountain Republicans, 1865–1900: Politics and the Appalachian Community.* Chapel Hill: University of North Carolina Press, 1978.

Bibliography

McLoughlin, William G. *The Meaning of Henry Ward Beecher: An Essay in the Shifting Values of Mid-Victorian America*. New York: Knopf, 1970.

McMath, Robert C. "Community, Region, and Hegemony in the Nineteenth Century South." In *Toward a New South? Studies in Post-Civil War Southern Communities*, edited by Orville Vernon Burton and Robert C. McMath, pp. 281–300. Westport, Conn.: Greenwood Press, 1982.

Masters, Frank M. *A History of Baptists in Kentucky*. N.p.: Kentucky Baptist Historical Society, 1953.

Miles, Emma Bell. *The Spirit of the Mountains*. 1905. Reprint in facsimile edition. Knoxville: University of Tennessee Press, 1975.

Mitchell, Robert D. "The Shenandoah Valley Frontier." In *Geographic Perspectives on America's Past: Readings in the Historical Geography of the United States*, edited by David Ward, pp. 148–66. New York: Oxford University Press, 1979.

Montell, William Lynwood. *Killings: Folk Justice in the Upper South*. Lexington: University Press of Kentucky, 1986.

Morgan, John G. "Emmanuel Willis Wilson." In *West Virginia Governors, 1863–1980*, pp. 43–50. Charleston, W.Va.: Charleston Newspapers, 1980.

Mutzenberg, Charles G. *Kentucky's Famous Feuds and Tragedies: Authentic History of the World Renowned Vendettas of the Dark and Bloody Ground*. New York: R. F. Fenno and Company, 1917.

Otto, John Solomon. "The Decline of Forest Farming in Southern Appalachia." *Journal of Forest History* (January 1983): 18–27.

Paludan, Phillip Shaw. *Victims: A True Story of the Civil War*. Knoxville: University of Tennessee Press, 1981.

Pike County Historical Society. *Pike County Historical Papers*. Vols. 1–6. Pikeville, Ky.: The Society, 1976–86.

Price, W. T., ed. *Without Scrip or Purse, or the Mountain Evangelist, George O. Barnes*. Louisville: n.p., 1883.

Rice, Otis K. *The Allegheny Frontier: West Virginia Beginnings, 1730–1830*. Lexington: University Press of Kentucky, 1970.

———. *The Hatfields and the McCoys*. Lexington: University Press of Kentucky, 1978.

Ryan, Mary P. *Cradle of the Middle Class: The Family in Oneida County, New York, 1790–1865*. Cambridge, Eng.: Cambridge University Press, 1981.

Salstrom, Paul. "Agricultural Decline and the Origins of Southern Appalachia's Dependency, 1840–1860." Paper presented at the Conference on the Appalachian Frontier, Staunton, Va., May 1984.

Scalf, Henry P. *Kentucky's Last Frontier*. Pikeville, Ky.: Pikeville College Press, 1972.

Shackelford, Laurel, and Bill Weinberg, eds. *Our Appalachia*. New York: Hill and Wang, 1977.

Shapiro, Henry D. *Appalachia on Our Mind: The Southern Mountains and Mountaineers in the American Consciousness*. Chapel Hill: University of North Carolina Press, 1978.

Sims, Edgar B. *Sims Index to Land Grants in West Virginia.* Charleston, W.Va.: Rose City Press, 1952.

Smith, Nancy Sue. *A History of Logan and Mingo Counties Beginning in 1617.* Morgantown: West Virginia University Library, n.d.

Spence, Robert Y. *The Land of the Guyandot: A History of Logan County.* Detroit: Harlo Press, 1976.

Spencer, John H. *A History of Kentucky Baptists from 1769–1885, Including More Than 800 Biographical Sketches.* 2 vols. Cincinnati: n.p., 1885.

Sprague, Stuart S. "Appalachian Stereotypes: A History." *Mountain Review* 2 (December 1975): 1–3.

Stickles, Arndt M. *Simon Bolivar Buckner: Borderland Knight.* Chapel Hill: University of North Carolina Press, 1940.

Striplin, E. F. *The Norfolk and Western: A History.* Roanoke, Va.: Norfolk and Western Railway, 1981.

Swain, George Thomas. *History of Logan County, West Virginia.* Kingsport, Tenn.: Kingsport Press, 1927.

Sydnor, Charles. *American Revolutionaries in the Making: Political Practices in Washington's Virginia.* New York: Free Press, 1952.

Szatmary, David. *Shays' Rebellion: The Making of an Agrarian Insurrection.* Amherst: University of Massachusetts Press, 1980.

Tallmadge, William H., Harry M. Caudill, and Richard B. Drake. "Anglo-Saxon vs. Scotch-Irish." *Mountain Life and Work* 45 (February, March, April, June 1969).

Thelen, David. *Paths of Resistance: Tradition and Dignity in Industrializing Missouri.* New York: Oxford University Press, 1986.

Thomas, Jean. *Big Sandy.* New York: Henry Holt and Company, 1940.

———. "Romeo and Juliet of the Mountains." *West Virginia Heritage* 1 (1967): 190.

Thompson, E. P. *The Making of the English Working Class.* New York: Vintage Books, 1963.

———. "The Moral Economy of the English Crowd in the Eighteenth Century." *Past and Present*, no. 50 (February 1971): 76–136.

Turner, Carolyn Clay, and Carolyn Hay Traum. *John C. Mayo: Cumberland Capitalist.* Pikeville, Ky.: Pikeville College Press, 1983.

Vincent, George E. "A Retarded Frontier." *American Journal of Sociology* 4 (July 1898): 1–20.

Waller, Altina L. *Reverend Beecher and Mrs. Tilton: Sex and Class in Victorian America.* Amherst: University of Massachusetts Press, 1982.

Weller, Jack E. *Yesterday's People: Life in Contemporary Appalachia.* Lexington: University Press of Kentucky, 1965.

Werner, Randolph Dennis. "Hegemony and Conflict: The Political Economy of a Southern Region, Augusta, Georgia, 1865–1895." Ph.D. dissertation, University of Virginia, 1977.

White, Richard. "Outlaw Gangs of the Middle Border: American Social

Bibliography

Bandits." *Western Historical Quarterly* 12, no. 4 (October 1981): 387–408.

Wilhelm, Gene, Jr. "Appalachian Isolation: Fact or Fiction?" In *An Appalachian Symposium*, edited by Joel W. Williamson, pp. 77–91. Boone, N.C.: Appalachian Consortium Press, 1977.

Williams, Cratis D. "The Southern Mountaineer in Fact and Fiction." Ph.D. dissertation, New York University, 1961.

Williams, John Alexander. *West Virginia: A History*. New York: Norton, 1976.

———. *West Virginia and the Captains of Industry*. Morgantown: West Virginia University Library, 1976.

Williamson, Joel W., ed. *An Appalachian Symposium*. Boone, N.C.: Appalachian Consortium Press, 1977.

Woods, Roy C. "History of the Hatfield-McCoy Feud with Special Attention to the Effects of Education on It." *West Virginia History* 22, no. 1 (October 1960): 27–33.

Wright, William T. *Devil John Wright of the Cumberlands*. Pound, Va.: William T. Wright, 1932.

Wyatt-Brown, Bertram. "The Antimission Movement in the Jacksonian South: A Study of Regional Folk Culture." *Journal of Southern History* 36 (November 1970): 501–29.

———. "Community, Class, and Snopesian Crime: Local Justice in the Old South." In *Class, Conflict, and Consensus: Antebellum Southern Community Studies*, edited by Orville Vernon Burton and Robert C. McMath, pp. 173–207. Westport, Conn.: Greenwood Press, 1982.

Index

Index

Index

Index